NASCAR's *Wild Years*
Stock-Car Technology in the 1960s

Alex Gabbard

© 2005 by Alex Gabbard

All rights reserved. No part of this publication may be reproduced or utilized in any form or by any means, electronic or mechanical, including photocopying, recording, or by any information storage and retrieval system, without prior written permission from the author. All photos and artwork are the property of the owners as credited.

The information in this work is true and complete to the best of our knowledge. However, all information is presented without any guarantee on the part of the author or publisher, who also disclaim any liability incurred in connection with the use of the information.

The author and publisher recognize that some words, model names, and designations, for example, mentioned herein are the property of the trademark holder. We use them for identification purposes only. This is not an official publication of any of the firms mentioned.

Edited by Travis Thompson
Designed by Katie Sonmor

ISBN-13 978-1-932494-09-9
ISBN-10 1-932494-09-X

Item No. CT409

Printed in China

CarTech®, Inc.
39966 Grand Avenue
North Branch, MN 55056
Telephone: (651) 277-1200 or (800) 551-4754
Fax: (651) 277-1203
www.cartechbooks.com

Library of Congress Cataloging-in-Publication Data

Gabbard, Alex.
　NASCAR's wild years / Alex Gabbard.
　　p. cm.
　Includes bibliographical references and index.
　ISBN 1-932494-09-X (alk. paper)
1. Stock car racing--United States--History. 2. NASCAR (Association)--History. I. Title.
　GV1029.9.S74G33 2005
　796.72'0973--dc22
　　　　　　　　　　　　　　2005009716

Front Cover:

Top: USAC star Mario Andretti, in this Holman Moody 427 Fairlane, drove a dominating 112 laps in the lead to win the Daytona 500, his first Grand National win in seven starts. He then went on to win the Yankee 300. (Ford photo)

Lower Left: On a blustery day, November 24, 1970, Bobby Isaac wheeled the K&K Insurance Dodge Daytona onto Talladega's high banks and set a new closed-course speed record of 201.104 mph, breaking Buddy Baker's record set earlier in the year. When Chrysler cut the K&K team for 1971, little effort was made to repeat the team's 1970 NASCAR championship. Late in '71, Isaac was on the salt flats of Utah setting 28 new world speed records, 216.946 mph in the flying mile and 217.368 mph in the flying kilometer among them. (DaimlerChrysler Historical Collection photo)

Right: During 1961, the "big-3" made optional high-performance engines available primarily for advertising purposes gained from racing. Chevrolet's 409, rated at 360 hp, was simply the 348 casting with 4-5/16" bores rather than 4-1/8", and with the sides of main bearing webs machined to clear the thicker, heavier counterweights of the new 1/4" longer stroke crankshaft. Heads were also machined from 348 castings. While the 1960 348 was the powerplant of the Grand National champion, the 409 succeeded in winning only one race in 1961. (Chevrolet photo)

Back Cover:

Upper Right: Chrysler's 426 Hemi raised the bar in automotive high performance everywhere it raced. Factory rated at 425 hp in showroom models, the Hemi was capable of 600 hp in racing tune. (DaimlerChrysler Historical Collection photo)

Lower Left: Curtis "Pops" Turner won the debut race at Rockingham, the American 500. He held off hotshoe Cale Yarborough in the closing laps to show that he could still whip the youngsters. (Ford photo)

Lower Right: Ford's Boss 429 Mustang of 1969 had one purpose – to homologate the Boss 429 engine for stock-car racing. When the engines were not ready as the Ford Talladega and Mercury Cyclone Spoiler II were geared up for production in Ford's Atlanta assembly plant, plans were laid for stuffing the new Blue Crescent 429 hemi into Mustangs.

Title Page: LeeRoy Yarbrough in a Dodge (#12) won the first 100-mile qualifier at Daytona at 163.934 mph, then blew his engine on lap 71 of the Daytona 500. Tiny Lund, winner of the 1963 Daytona 500, drove a Petty Plymouth to fourth, the highest Plymouth finish. A. J. Foyt (#27) blew his engine on lap 46. (Ford photo)

Dust Jacket Front Upper: Dodge Charger 500 and Ford Talladega were the best efforts of their respective factory engineers, but with high-speed instability, the Charger 500 proved to be less than hoped for against the faster and more stable Fords and Mercurys. (Ford photo)

Dust Jacket Rear: Because of his winning the Daytona 500 in 1967, Smokey Yunick contracted Mario Andretti to drive his updated 427 Chevelle in 1968, the car that Curtis Turner put on the pole the year before. During practice, Andretti wrecked the car, and it never turned another race lap afterward. (Smokey Yunick photo)

OVERSEAS DISTRIBUTION BY:

Brooklands Books Ltd.
P.O. Box 146, Cobham, Surrey, KT11 1LG, England
Telephone 01932 865051 • Fax 01932 868803
www.brooklands-books.com

Brooklands Books Aus.
3/37-39 Green Street, Banksmeadow, NSW 2109, Australia
Telephone 2 9695 7055 • Fax 2 9695 7355

CONTENTS

INTRODUCTION	.5
CHAPTER 1: THE FABULOUS 1950s	.9
STOCKERS AND THE AMA BAN	.15
ZORA ARKUS-DUNTOV	.23
CHAPTER 2: 1960: RACING AND THE KIDS	.33
CHAPTER 3: 1961: AN EXPLOSION OF SPEED	.45
CHAPTER 4: 1962: THE BIG-INCH RUMBLE	.53
CHAPTER 5: 1963: THE SHOWDOWN	.69
REX WHITE	.81
CHAPTER 6: 1964: WEDGE VERSUS HEMI	.87
RAY FOX	.97
CHAPTER 7: 1965: SHAKING THE RULES TREE	.107
ENGINE EVOLUTION	.118
CHAPTER 8: 1966: FRANTIC FANATICS	.121
SMOKEY'S CHEVELLE	.126
THE HEMI	.128
CHAPTER 9: 1967: NEW BEGINNINGS	.137
CHAPTER 10: 1968: POWER AND AERODYNAMICS	.151
CHAPTER 11: 1969 AND BEYOND: THE AERO-WAR	.165
FACTORY PULLOUT	.182
INDEX	.190

INTRODUCTION

Drivers Ray Ward (#50), Gary Doodeman (#38), Paulie Ambrose (#71), Harvey Sheeler (#5), Pete Peterson (#7), and Hal Ruyle (Ford in front) get to know each other a little better at Raceway Park in Chicago, Illinois. This photo was taken April 30th, 1950. (Photo courtesy International Motorsports Hall of Fame)

Introduction

Stock-car racing is as old as the automobile itself. In every era since drivers first got behind the wheel, that itch to go as fast as possible has never been satiated. Racers evolved from workshop tinkerers to tuners and engineers, but they've never been able to pacify the demand for more power. Driving skill with the technology of speed became the racer's edge. The combination of more power and more speed grew into the world's favorite sport. Auto racing in all its forms has become a worldwide favorite in spectator appeal, and stock-car racing has emerged in the last half-century as the all-time favorite.

What was once an obscure Sunday afternoon pastime broadcast on a few Southern radio stations, attentively listened to in service stations by hot-blooded young men with greasy fingernails, has grown into a weekend favorite for millions of television viewers around the world. Along the way from grease pits to corporate boardrooms, those hot-blooded young men become the greats of the sport. What once could be financed by local businesses became the arena of corporate financiers who vied for the top drivers and best teams to showcase their logos. Today's great thunder domes of high-banked oval tracks are weekend destinations for spectators to spend an afternoon

Modifying the 1930s and '40s flathead V-8 Ford made it the hot setup in Southern stock-car racing until the arrival of mass-produced overhead-valve engines in the 1950s.

Southern California hotshoes handled a team of stock cars backed by Ford's Lincoln-Mercury Division. They took victory in the stock class of the 1953 Carrera Panamericana, held in Mexico as re-created in this Capri.

watching fast cars and daring drivers. Others gather around high-definition televisions and watch the machines roar by on the precarious edge of sanity. Race fans are captivated for hundreds of miles and many hours of racing as drivers push their machinery to the limit. The roar of open exhausts from 40 cars running at 8,000 rpm is like no other sport-man and machine in concert. Afterwards, corporate bean counters assess their "race on Sunday, sell on Monday" investments.

This book examines the origins of the fiercely competitive sport of stock-car racing, focusing primarily on the 1960s. This decade witnessed extraordinary entanglements among America's Big Three, when stock cars actually began as assembly-line cars, and General Motors, Ford, and Chrysler each hoped to attract customers away from their competitors. As the 1950s automobile evolved into the very different 1960s version, styling was influenced

INTRODUCTION

Carl Kiekhaefer, Mercury outboard motor tycoon, fielded the most professional team of stock cars yet seen in stock-car racing and won NASCAR's championship in 1955 (27 wins of 45 races) and 1956 (22 wins of 56 races). The 1955 season equaled the best winning season of the 1950s, Hudson's 27 wins in 1952.

Darel Dieringer's #26 Mercury Marauder receives a little attention in the shop. This is quite a bit different from the way race teams do things now. (Photo courtesy International Motorsports Hall of Fame)

A modern, unrestricted NASCAR V-8 of 358 ci cranks about 720 hp, 123 hp/liter.

by technical innovations and improved aerodynamics grown from the need for more speed.

During the mid-1950s, General Motors led the way using competition successes in national advertising, and both Ford and Chrysler had to respond in kind. Chevrolet bragged about "The Hot One" in 1955 when drivers had any sort of racing success, however small the achievement. From that beginning, the factory wars matured in the 1960s, leading to larger, more powerful engines, faster cars, and advanced technology on Southern high banks and showroom floors.

Although modern stock cars share little resemblance to assembly-line cars, drivers have always put their lives on the line. Over the years, the hardware has greatly improved driver safety, but the itch to go faster always pushed the envelope. Stock-car racing still enthralls hot-shoe spectators who envision themselves out there with the big boys.

This book is a walk down memory lane to a time when intense factory battles gave birth to America's Muscle car era. It was a time when showrooms were filled with the hardware that continually upped the ante at the track and thundering big-inch engines echoed in the air.

INTRODUCTION

Chrysler's winged warriors of 1970 closed the era of factory-dominated stock-car racing by winning the NASCAR championship with oval-track versions of the wildest showroom models ever seen in dealerships. The Dodge Daytona and Plymouth Superbird were radical sales busts, but the fastest, most stable stock cars ever seen, and the first over 200 mph.

Unlike the plain exteriors of 1960s racing cars that were products of closely controlled factory teams, modern stock cars are colorful, eye-catching, rolling billboards of corporate advertising. While '60s racing cars were modified showroom models, modern cars are built to NASCAR specifications and bear only silhouette resemblance to showroom models.

Factory involvement by the mid-1960s financed teams whose logos became legends in the sport. Holman Moody was Ford's base of operations in Charlotte, North Carolina, and "Competition Proven" became the most feared logo on the side of a NASCAR machine on any track. Fords won 48 of 55 races in 1965, the highest-percentage win record in the book.

NASCAR'S WILD YEARS 7

CHAPTER ONE

Edsel Ford (left) and his father, Henry Ford, admire the new V-8 engine introduced in 1932 model cars and built by the millions through the 1953 model. (Ford photo)

The Fabulous 1950s

The close of the World War II in August 1945 brought a wave of GIs returning home. They arrived with a new spirit seasoned in combat, nerves honed to an edge, and a thirst for adventure that moved them into the workforce and college during the week, and then out looking for adventure on the weekend. Many went to work in garages and machine shops where they developed speed equipment to be proven at the racetrack. Tracks from straight lines to road courses to dirt ovals popped up in town after town, drawing droves of paying spectators. Postwar auto racing flourished and enjoyed its second golden age (the first being the mid-teens through the 1920s).

Returning GIs married and went to work building America into the greatest industrial power the world had ever known. Their children were to become the baby boomers, who began reaching driving age in 1961. These two generations brought their influence to automobile design, production, marketing, and racing as never seen before or since. The era from about 1955 to 1971 remains America's great age of speed. It produced the most exciting year-to-year developments in new-car showrooms, and out the factories' back doors. It was America's most intense and most creative era of engineering excellence proven in competition.

By the late 1940s, promoters saw the financial opportunity of providing the hotshoes a place to go as fast as they could where paying spectators could watch. The Indianapolis 500 and its enormous numbers of spectators proved the concept of a thunder dome year after year. Even if the boys didn't have the sophisticated equipment seen at Indy, their modified stockers could put on quite a show. People were willing to pay to watch regular Friday-night stock-car racing during summer months, and local speed demons took to the ovals throughout the South. They formed a new style of auto racing that flourished into today's arena of corporate showmanship.

The returning GIs were not happy with the selection of new cars available to them. They had seen the spirited European cars, the small and exciting machines from England, France, and Italy, and many servicemen brought their favorite examples back home with them. This was the beginning of a revolution in the way

Stock car racing reached national attention with the Elign Raod Races held in Elign, Illinois. In 1933, during the depths of the Great Depression, the Ford factory team swept the top 7 positions in the stock car category. (Ford photo)

automobiles were manufactured and marketed in America. It took time, and at first, change was slow in coming. Several years of retooling were required to switch from wartime to peacetime production, and the first few postwar years offered opportunities for enterprising sorts to respond to the clamor created by this new force in the automobile market. Names such as Tucker, Kaiser-Frazer, King Midget, and Muntz were among many new marques that sprang up alongside Studebaker, Ford, Chrysler, and General Motors. Their cars didn't look like warmed-over 1941-like models from the major manufacturers, and the public liked what it saw.

CHAPTER ONE

Gober Sosbee and his hotted-up Ford earned winner's laurels in 200 races that include three Daytona Beach victories in the Modified class. Sosbee ranks among stock-car racing's all-time winners and is one of the best owner/builder/driver combinations the sport has ever seen. (Sosbee collection photo)

Major redesigns began with the 1947 Studebaker. The Virgil Exner design was so advanced that viewers had to look closely to determine which way the car was going. It was smooth with integrated fenders, not even a hint of running boards, and featured curved glass. Its aeronautic look was so different from prewar designs that it had to be all-new. The next year, Hudson launched its equally radical design of smooth sides flush with fenders from front to rear. Automotive design took a leap forward, lower and lower, with hood lines melding into fender lines, and occupants sat lower. The trend was toward roomier cars with larger trunks with bodies built lower around frames rather than on them.

Things got serious in 1949 when both General Motors and Ford Motor Company introduced entirely new models that left prewar styling in the dust. Fully integrated designs from bumper to bumper graced showrooms all across America, and buyers lined up to buy them by the millions. Ford invested over $118,000,000 to design and retool for its new-for-'49 model that sold a total of 841,170 units, over 300,000 more than the year before. Even though Ford's flathead V-8 engine was by far the fastest in the low-price field, buyers flocked into Chevrolet showrooms to set a new sales record, buying 1,031,466 cars. The sleek '49 Chevys were handsome cars with a more rakish styling than Ford's rather boxy design.

To give passengers more room, cars grew larger and heavier, and new engines were needed. Buick, Oldsmobile, and Cadillac had their own high-compression, overhead-valve V-8 engines in 1949, but Chevrolet Division boss Thomas H. Keating did not recognize the rising youth market and opted to keep the ultra-conservative "stove bolt" inline 6-cylinder in production. Its ancient forebear debuted in 1928 with standardized 1/4-20 bolts common to stoves of the era. The name "stove bolt stuck," and 20 years later it was synonymous with staunch reliability. Chevrolet marketers championed their smoother-running engine as "a six for the price of a four." For 1949, Chevy's stove-bolt 6 outsold Ford's well-proven flathead V-8 by 23 percent, a remarkable testimony to the public's respect for the Chevrolet.

After a few years, Chevrolet Chief Engineer Ed Cole set his team of designers on the course toward a new overhead-valve V-8 very different from the big, heavy Cadillac-inspired engine in GM's other lines. The new Chevy was lighter and more compact, and quickly became a tremendous force in the future of American automobiles. The small-block is still in production, and more than 60 million have been produced since its introduction in September 1954.

Over in Dearborn, Ford's engineers produced their own new V-8 for 1954 models. While the Oldsmobile Rocket 88 proved to be the fastest production car, the much larger production quantities of Chevrolet's engine brought about the Chevy-versus-Ford battles that

Ford Motor Company's huge success with the flathead V-8 introduced in 1932 was displaced in late 1953 with the introduction of the Y-block, so named because of the cross-sectional shape of the block. In overhead-valve form displacing 239 ci, the same as the flathead, the new engine arose because of management's mandate to produce a single engine design for all product lines. While the previous year's flathead produced 110 hp, the new Y-block cranked out 130 hp in base form. It soon went to 292 ci, then 312, and by 1957, it had a 4-bbl carburetor and a supercharger and was rated at 300 hp (58.7 hp/liter). The heated factory wars of the time saw this Ford V-8 topping Chevrolet's best of 283 hp from 283 ci as the fuel-injected small-block (61 hp/liter). (Ford photo)

10 — NASCAR'S WILD YEARS

escalated year-to-year across America into all-out war. The cubic-inch war was just one facet of the HP war, that took over advertising and captured the imaginations of buyers everywhere.

Each make sought an edge over competitors and hawked their edge with advertising as never seen before. Battle lines for new-car sales became more entrenched than ever, and although automobiles had been a major part of the American economy for four decades, the influence of the car-hungry postwar buying boom was at a fever pitch, producing a time fertile for innovation. Designers and engineers eyed something new from their competitors and rushed back to their drawing boards to invent something newer. Buick offered buyers the first torque-converter-type automatic transmission, the DynaFlow, in its 1948 models, and then released the rakish convertible-like hardtop for 1949. Both Buick and Cadillac shared this styling advance with Oldsmobile, and all three introduced overhead-valve V-8 engines that year. The high-compression Rocket88 set buyers ablaze with performance never seen before in a car styled so handsomely. Compared to Fords and Chevrolets, the Rocket88 was a higher-priced car that shared some styling influence with Chevrolet. Chrysler trumped them all with a simple method of starting their car's engine with an ignition key instead of a key and a push button. GM returned in 1950 with Buicks featuring tinted glass. The next year, B.F. Goodrich stepped into the market with "puncture-sealing" tubeless tires for top-of-the-line cars. Chevrolet introduced its 2-speed Powerglide automatic with a reliable, if rather stodgy, 105-hp, 235-ci 6-cylinder.

With so many all-new cars, Americans everywhere were caught up in the buzz. Manufacturing methods advanced to produce more and better products. Advertising shifted into high gear to attract more and more buyers who were spending increasing amounts of money on themselves, especially on cars. Americans took to the highways like never before. "See the USA" became a theme of Chevrolet marketing, and the nation was making it happen with an extensive interstate highway system resulting from the Federal Aid Highway Act of 1944. For the young movers and shakers of the emerging car culture, cars were no longer simple utility vehicles, they were freedom machines of status and class. Buyers were willing to spend far more on their cars than in previous years, and along with the blossoming hot-rod and street-machine movement came a burgeoning aftermarket industry. Cars allowed Americans to move to the suburbs and commute to work. More and more homes were built with integral garages and paved driveways. Car-care products beyond gas, oil, and grease were a growing part of the multitudes of service stations that sprang up across the horizon. Growing prosperity fostered optimism that spread confidence and fueled a flamboyant era of two-tone paint, fins, and chrome. America's growing love affair with the automobile and the "let's go" spirit of a time led to the decade being known as the "fabulous '50s."

Chevrolet marketeers heralded the new-for-1955 Chevrolet as "The Hot One" after Herb Thomas won the Southern 500 that year in Smokey Yunick's "Best Damn Garage in Town" Chevrolet, although at a lower average speed than his 1954 Hudson win (93.28 mph versus his previous record of 94.93 mph). The victory was half of Chevy's NASCAR Grand National wins, but an advertising boon. (Silhouetted in the background is Chevrolet's first overhead-valve V-8 powered car, built in 1917 with the 288-ci Series D engine.) (Chevrolet photo)

Although the 1950s weren't as good as we sometimes nostalgically recall, the mid-1950s were a time when cars became the expression of America's predominately youth-oriented dream. Convertibles and high-style two-seaters, a new theme from Detroit and Dearborn, were the rage among the masses. Cars brought America's youth together for roadside gatherings at drive-in restaurants, an outgrowth of the 1930s-era diners that were usually made from surplus railway dining cars. Daytime shopping strips with angled parking slots in front catered to customers who drove from the suburbs to shop. In time, shopping centers moved to the suburbs where the cars

CHAPTER ONE

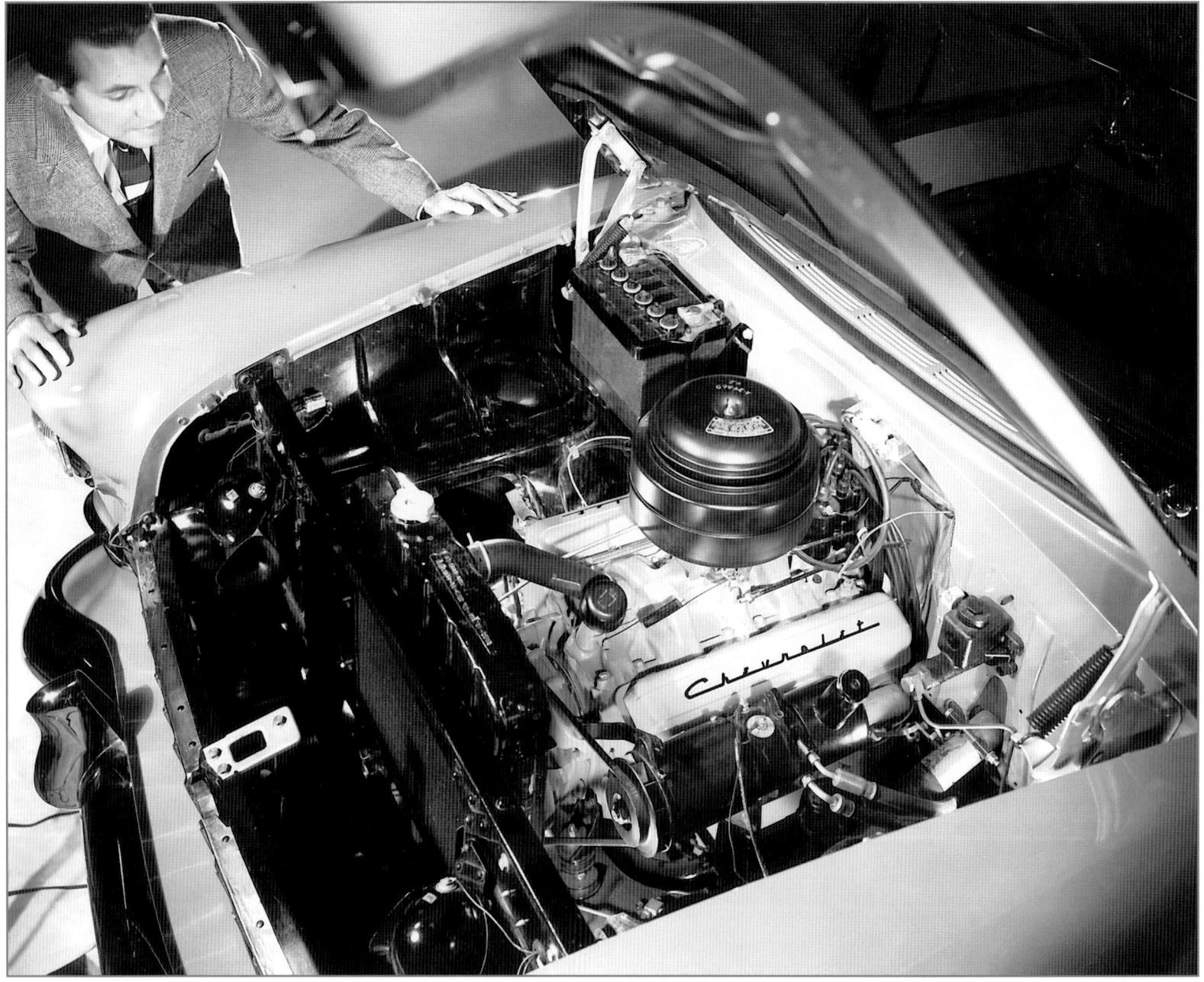

The Turbo-Fire V-8 was campaigned widely and ignited stock-car racing nationwide. All sorts of aftermarket speed equipment soon displaced Ford's flathead as the hot-rodder's choice. Rated at 180 hp in 4-bbl showroom form, the quick-revving, dual-exhaust engine was a spirited performer in new models that turned Chevrolet's image from a dull-but-durable car for Dad to a youthful performer with pizzazz in a single model year. (Chevrolet photo)

were. Cars also became inextricably entwined with courtship and nighttime "cruisin'." They made great transportation to the drive-in movies for an inexpensive evening of fun at 50 cents a carload (including all the jokesters in the trunk). Drive-ins became passion pits for couples who could just as easily drive to a secluded lover's lane, but "goin' to the movies" was more acceptable for Mom and Dad.

Countless after-dark arguments about whose car was fastest were settled with races between stoplights and on lightly traveled public highways. Hot rodding flourished, and to make it both legal and safe, the first drag strips were built. Drag racing as a sport became formally organized in 1951 when Wally Parks established the National Hot Rod Association in California. Many other racing organizations across America

THE FABULOUS 1950s

Gober Sosbee's famous ride – the car he built, maintained, and raced to one of the best records in auto racing.

responded to the growing interest in competition from high-speed record attempts on Muroc Dry Lake, now Edwards Air Force Base, to Southern stock-car racing. Bill France gathered a group of promoters and established NASCAR (National Association for Stock Car Auto Racing) in Daytona Beach, Florida, in late 1947. Erwin G. "Cannonball" Baker, America's cross-country record holder (Los Angeles to New York in 7 days in 1916), was NASCAR's first commissioner. Robert "Red" Byron won NASCAR's first race, a 150-mile Modified event on Daytona's 4-mile beach/road course, driving a Ford coupe, on February 15, 1948, six days before the fledgling organization was incorporated. He went on that year to win NASCAR's first national championship, a Modified title. The next year he became the inaugural Grand National Champion while Dawsonville, Georgia's Gober Sosbee, by way of his Atlanta-based Cherokee Garage, raced his flathead-powered Ford coupe to win three Daytona Beach Modified races on his way to an astounding record of 200 victories. Gober and his Ford were king of the dirt tracks.

By 1950, big-time stock-car racing was under way when the first superspeedway opened, Darlington's 1.25-mile paved, egg-shaped oval. Johnny Mantz won the first Southern 500 in a Plymouth, followed by Herb Thomas' Hudson victory in 1951. The Oldsmobiles of Fonty Flock and Buck Baker took the next two Southern 500 wins. Then Herb Thomas repeated his trip to the winner's circle in 1954, again in a Hudson.

In Wilkes County, North Carolina, word reached Junior Johnson and his brothers that a new high-banked track down in South Carolina's flat cotton country was holding some races. Although youngest brother, Junior, had no experience racing on asphalt, only driving hopped-up Fords carrying cases of moonshine during nighttime deliveries, the Johnson boys gathered up a few friends, hitched up their stripped-down, beefed-up, high-powered whiskey hauler and headed for Darlington. Junior quickly learned his way around banked left turns and went back home the winner. The stock-car boys were left shaking their heads. Junior Johnson, "just some cucumber from up in the mountains," soon became one of the toughest competitors stock-car racing would ever see.

Junior Johnson's first car painted as a race car was a moonshine hauler belonging to Roscoe "Doc" Combs of Wilkes County, North Carolina. It was identified by Federal agents and no longer useful as a hauler. This re-creation illustrates the typical sportsman stocker of NASCAR's early years.

The manufacturers in Michigan were slow to recognize the potentially huge Southern market for high-performance cars and products, but in a few short years, they were deep into racing with factory sponsorship. The explosive growth of hot rods was too big a market to ignore. The yearning for more exciting cars and the desire to do it yourself pushed hot rodding in new directions. Southern California's dry climate and year-round sun was conducive to the stripped-down, hot-rod roadster at a time when the Ford flathead V-8 (introduced in 1932) was king. The SoCal movement soon spread throughout America.

By the late 1940s, the flathead was in every conceivable type of hot rod, and builders were spending millions of dollars on their cars. The man who would later become immortalized as "Mr. Corvette," Zora Arkus-Duntov, earned widespread acclaim for his cast-aluminum, hemispherical-combustion-chamber head conversions for the flathead. The Ardun equipment made the flathead the most powerful production-based engine of the time.

Hot rodding and racing stock iron was not a passing phase; it was here to stay. Early 1950s stock-car competition was an untapped market for the Big Three who noticed that hot rodders were highly brand-conscious, and mostly Ford addicts. A billion-dollar aftermarket industry had sprung up in support of Ford hot rodders and racers, and anyone who wanted to go fast for low bucks thought Ford. GM marketers had pegged the more affluent market with Buick, Olds, and Cadillac V-8s, but not Chevrolet. Keating held his division back a half-decade, but when Cole's all-new Chevrolet and its all-new V-8 were unveiled in 1954, a new force was placed in motion. Hot rodders didn't take to the big, heavy, upscale GM V-8s and were lukewarm to Ford's "Y-block" V-8 in the impressive Thunderbird. But they loved the small-block. Time put all of the first-generation V-8s onto the dusty shelves, but the small-block was here to stay.

STOCKERS AND THE AMA BAN

After two years of stock-car racing in 1955 and '56, Ford Division management became serious about the sales potential of winning stock-car races. Chevrolet's new fuel-injected 283-ci V-8 offered in 1957 models was a potent adversary, and the Ford men saw that they might be in deep trouble. To boost performance for racing, Ford engineers turned to the well-established technique of supercharging to surpass Chevrolet's celebrated 1-hp-per-ci powerplant and turned up the heat in the HP war. Millions in sales were on the line.

Carl Kiekhaefer's team of privately financed Chryslers consisted of the fastest and most powerful yet cars seen in stock-car racing. Twenty-seven victories in 1955 swept NASCAR's schedule and proved the advantage of a well-financed, professionally run team. Buck Baker's nine wins in 1956 led Chrysler's 22 victories that year to lock up the Championship for him.

CHAPTER ONE

Above, left and right: On the beach again in a re-created "Purple Hog." Interest in the "old days" of stock-car racing has emerged as veneration and acclaim for the Living Legends, who laid the foundation of today's most popular sport.

THE FABULOUS 1950s

Ford sales almost matched Chevrolet in 1954. During 1955, Ford sales soared by a huge margin, 51.3 percent over the previous year, but still fell short of Chevrolet by about 1 percent, and then fell precipitously during 1956. Suddenly down 12 percent from 1955 sales (over 390,000 vehicles) Ford managers had to scramble, and winning races was a gamble that paid off in 1957. Sales that year jumped by almost 209,000 units and came within just 141 units of matching Chevrolet sales. However, a strange turn of events occurred that curtailed Ford racing and similarly affected sales.

Early in 1955, Chevrolet's Ed Cole launched his division into stock-car racing. He saw the sales potential of the emerging youth market and hired Henry "Smokey" Yunick to head up racing in the field. Yunick's Daytona Beach garage became the center of everything Chevrolet racing, and Smokey became the principal developer of Chevrolet stockers. That fruitful arrangement was proven when Herb Thomas won NASCAR's feature race that year, the Southern 500, in Yunick's Chevrolet.

By 1957, Chevrolet engineer Zora Arkus-Duntov, a lifelong racing enthusiast, was installed both as director of high-performance hardware development and manager of racing. Arkus-Duntov designed the mass-flow fuel-injection system, discarding the speed-density concept that Chevrolet engineers were working on. The Rochester fuel-injection unit arrived for 1957 Chevys, along with a new 4-speed transmission. Arkus-Duntov cams, high-performance heads and manifolds, and thoroughly developed high-output engines were produced by his team of engineers. A complete heavy-duty parts inventory, along with a manual for selecting and preparing a Chevy for racing, showed that Chevrolet targeted racers and racing fans as a major market. Arkus-Duntov's Southern Engineering Development Company (SEDCO), set up by Chevrolet in Atlanta, was the Southern base of factory racing.

Ford was far behind. During the 1956 season, Ford recommended existing heavy-duty parts for racing, but only a Service Manager Bulletin (No. M-116a, issued August 26, 1955) gave recommendations for building a stock car. As Ford's lightest and cheapest car, the Mainline Tudor sedan was recommended. Ford's stock-car racing kit consisted of a close-ratio Thunderbird transmission (PN B5A-7003-L), a station-wagon rear axle (4.27:1 gear ratio for short tracks and 3.78:1 for longer tracks), heavy-duty springs, stabilizer bar, and shocks, and a heavy-duty radiator (PN B5A-8005-L), along with stronger Lincoln spindles, hubs, and brakes. Only a more powerful engine was needed, and Ford engineers answered with the 205-hp, 292-ci, high-output Interceptor engine. Fitted with hydraulic lifters, valve float occurred at 5,600 rpm. Thus, recommended axle ratios gave about 111- and 120-mph top speeds, respectively.

The Interceptor V-8 was a powerful engine that easily spun narrow racing tires of the time, then squealed them on shifts into second, and barked them again when speed-shifted into high gear (third). This was an awe-inspiring feat in 1956, especially for a 3,425-lb stock car. It could go 0-60 mph in an impressive 8.8 seconds.

The Interceptor engine received specially modified cylinder heads, heavy-duty gaskets, pistons, pushrods, valves and springs, a performance cam, an advanced-curve distributor, and a stronger flywheel. These parts listed in the bulletin really constituted little more than the top 292-ci Thunderbird engine with its 202 hp.

New for 1956 was the 312-ci engine, enlarged with slight bore and stroke increases. The 312 Interceptor was the top-performing Mainline Ford. Thunderbirds received 215-hp engines with manual transmissions and 225-hp mills with automatics. The Thunderbird powerplant was the prime engine for Ford stock-car racers.

CHAPTER ONE

This recreation of the Lincoln 430-powered Thunderbird illustrates the cars that Holman Moody built from reject parts in 1959. This was done to survive the doldrums brought on by a slack economy and Ford's withdrawal from racing in mid-1957. Ford offered the high-image 430 T-Bird as the ultimate street cruiser for the upscale man, while just happening to meet NASCAR's ruling that cars raced had to be sold to the public.

For 1957, the Thunderbird 312's rated output jumped to 245 hp with a single 4-bbl carburetor. Stockers got the same results, but they could also use a supercharger. Instead of using huffers, Mercury Division made the 368-ci Lincoln engine an option, an action that can be described as producing the first factory muscle car, in this case a factory-built high-performance car with a larger, more powerful engine from a line offered in the Mercury only as a special edition. The supercharged Ford 312 engine was advertised to produce 300 hp but actually developed 325. While Chevy's fuel-injected 283 developed 283 hp, achieving the widely celebrated 1-hp-per-ci figure, Ford got 1.04 hp per ci but received no fanfare as a result of the advertised rating.

As added teasers, early in 1957 Ford announced two engines called the Special High Performance and the Special Extra-High Performance as options in full-size cars. These engines used the same compression ratio as the Thunderbird 312, 9.7:1, but were equipped with dual 4-bbl carbs and higher-performance internals, giving ratings of 270 and 285 hp.

These engines were thoroughly tested during 20 days of flat-out record setting on Bonneville's salt flat in September 1956. In strict secrecy, the Ford team established 462 new records. One was 130.94 mph for 100 miles using the 285-hp powerplant. Another was a record of 108.16 mph for 50,000 miles with the standard V-8. The records Ford set with strictly stock 1957 models surpassed the Dodge records set in 1955 and clobbered everything that the Pontiac team did a few weeks earlier. The United States Auto Club (USAC) supervised timing and scoring, then certified Ford's records by inspecting the cars to confirm compliance with regulations.

THE FABULOUS 1950s

Henry "Smokey" Yunick, born in Maryville, Tennessee, became a legend in his own time. His "Best Damn Garage in Town" became the headquarters of his lifetime involvement in racing and was the focus of factory teams for Hudson, Chevrolet, Ford, Pontiac, and then Chevrolet again.

Another record was 51,430 miles at 107.13 mph for the specified 20-day period. Afterwards, the car's engine was torn down to reveal very little bearing, piston, or cylinder wear. Ford engineers had accomplished their objective of making durable high-performance parts. Another Bonneville objective was making pit stops as short as possible. The Ford team made 17-second stops for 17 gallons of fuel, a quart of oil, and a driver change.

Ford's Curtis Turner won NASCAR's most acclaimed race of 1956, the Southern 500, and Chevrolet was almost shut out that year with just three wins to Ford's 14. In the second half of that season, Ford's racing program picked up steam by scoring those 14 wins in the last 25 NASCAR Grand National races. The Southern racers had learned how to make Fords win, and with the Bonneville experience proving heavy-duty hardware, the stage was set for 1957.

By then, Ford's top stock-car racing team was the works of John Holman and Ralph Moody in Charlotte, North Carolina. Moody was a winning Ford team driver from the '56 season who knew how oval-track cars should be prepared. Holman was an effective manager who knew how to get things done. With the Holman and Moody organization located in the center of NASCAR country, Ford had a well-experienced professional team in the South, along with California-based Bill Stroppe's team, and SoCal tuners Jim Travers and Frank Coon, of later TraCo (Chevrolet) fame, developing advanced engines.

Ford racing was a thorn in Chevrolet's side. Yunick was hired away from Chevrolet, becoming Ford's man in Daytona Beach. His job was to get results with the supercharged engines.

NASCAR rules specified that a minimum number of supercharged cars had to be built and offered to the public, so Ford contracted with McCulloch, America's foremost blower manufacturer, to build the necessary number of superchargers for Thunderbirds and Mainline models. The package was offered both on showroom models and in parts catalogs. For stock-car racing, only the Grand National Division allowed supercharging or fuel injection. This exotic equipment was not permitted in the Convertible Division. Consequently, the Ford teams ran normally aspirated engines in Grand National cars as backups to the blown cars, thus utilizing the Bonneville experience in both divisions.

Unlike Chevrolet, with its fuel injection and speed equipment, other GM divisions responded to stock-car racing like Mercury – with bigger engines. Pontiac went to a larger-displacement engine, 347 ci and 325 hp. Oldsmobile showed up with 325-hp, 371-ci engines. With the withdrawal of Karl Kiekhaefer and his Chryslers after the 1956 season, stock-car racing took on a decidedly Ford-versus-General Motors air. Dodge and Plymouth, with their smaller, less-developed Hemi engines, made only token appearances in 1957.

The Ford teams boasted top drivers Marvin Panch and Glenn "Fireball" Roberts in Grand National cars, with Curtis Turner and Joe Weatherly in ragtops. Bill Amick and Jim Reed were the short-track specialists in both divisions. Moody was overall field general on race day and drove only when needed. Each driver had two cars of equal preparation, and Holman assigned a 10-man crew of mechanics to each division.

Bill Stroppe fielded a NASCAR team of Mercurys with two-time (1952 and 1955) NASCAR champion Tim Flock, and NASCAR veterans Billy Myers and Jim Paschal as drivers.

The 1957 NASCAR season opened with the Daytona Speed Week and grew to exciting proportions when the Ford armada moved in. Then an unexpected problem revealed itself; during Saturday's 160-mile Convertible Division warm-up for the Sunday feature, modifications to the steering linkage produced too much toe-in, and the cars handled poorly. However, the finish was

CHAPTER ONE

The Holman Moody "garage" at Darlington is preparing for the Convertible Division race prior to the Southern 500 of 1958. Joe Weatherly's No. 12 is in the foreground, with Curtis Turner's Ford in the background. (T. Taylor Warren photo)

"Strictly stock" didn't mean showroom perfect! With a broken windshield smacked by a piece of Darlington's flying debris, along with messages to the driver to use his head and stay in front, an afternoon in this office during South Carolina's heat was tough duty. (T. Taylor Warren photo)

Joe Weatherly, the second of Ford's top driving team with Turner, was fearsome opposition to anyone who wanted to race. (T. Taylor Warren photo)

Dialing in the suspension and wheel alignment. After the factories pulled out in mid-1957, stock-car teams had to scramble to finance their racing. Most of the cars were year-old models updated with new sheet metal, except for 1958 Chevrolet entries that incorporated Chevy's new coil-spring suspension all around and the 348-ci W engine, which was new that year. (T. Taylor Warren photo)

THE FABULOUS 1950s

Tire service has come a long way from 1958! (T. Taylor Warren)

Mercury-Ford-Mercury (Flock, Weatherly, Myers). For Sunday's featured 39 laps around the 4.1-mile highway and beach course, Cotton Owens won the race in a Pontiac followed by Johnny Beauchamp in a Chevrolet.

The Ford camp was stunned by the loss and stung when Pontiac advertisements promoted Owens' victory in a "Drive the Champ" national campaign that included giving away 100 cars.

Then the Ford machine started rolling. Through May 5, 1957, Ford enjoyed a near sweep of NASCAR races, winning 12 of 16 features. In the Convertible Division, Fords won every race except for Daytona, which was taken by Mercury, Ford's only loss in 17 ragtop races. On short tracks, Fords won 8 of the first 11 races. In an expanded schedule, NASCAR added the Rebel 300 to Darlington's schedule, and Fireball Roberts roared to victory in the early season's top race. Fords were on a roll, leading every race. Failures were few and due primarily to supercharger problems.

Although blowers were well known for their power-producing potential, they added mechanical complexity and increased fuel consumption. Drive belts were known to break or be thrown off, and supercharger internal parts tended to be delicate, with close tolerances required for properly balanced assembles. That made them temperamental and subject to failure in dust-laden 1957-era racing.

With few losses early in the season, Ford's mission of smashing Chevrolet was on track. To cap its program, only one more addition to the Ford team was needed to smother Chevrolet – Smokey Yunick.

Born in Maryville, Tennessee, Yunick received his nickname as a boy when racing a smoking motorcycle in Pennsylvania. He then built a reputation for winning automobile races once he relocated to Daytona Beach after being a World War II test pilot. By 1957, Yunick had prepared cars that won three straight AAA stock-car racing titles (1952, '53, '54) and three straight NASCAR Championships in the same years. He was, quite simply, the best in the business.

Ford negotiated with Yunick and signed him with an offer amounting to four times what Chevrolet had paid him in two years. The move created intense ill will among the Chevy men he worked with, but Yunick simply threw them out of his shop and gave away all the Chevrolet cars and equipment he had on hand. "I work for Ford now," he said.

In the bargain came Yunick's driver, Paul Goldsmith, who added five Ford wins that year. With Holman, Moody, and Yunick, Ford was unstoppable – almost.

In June 1957, the Ford steamroller ran out of steam due to decisions made in a Detroit boardroom. During the February meeting of the Automobile Manufacturer's Association (AMA), an assembly of CEOs from each of the manufacturers, Harlow "Red" Curtice of General Motors made what appeared to be an offhand, end-of-meeting comment that manufacturers really should not be competing against their customers. The result of that comment was an agreement that the manufacturers would end factory involvement in racing, eliminate all high-performance and competition equipment from catalogs, remove personnel from racing, and delete any mention of competition or engine output from advertisements. The agreement, later known as the AMA ban, cost Ford millions, tilted NASCAR racing toward Chevrolet, and didn't cost GM a dime.

These were sweeping changes that caught Ford boss Robert McNamara napping. He suspected that the cost of racing adversely affected his profit margin, although no correlation existed beyond dealer proclamations that racing actually produced sales. McNamara accepted the terms of the ban, a move that no doubt sent old Henry's ghost raging up and down Ford corporate corridors kicking ass for letting his company be controlled by outside influences, something he never allowed. As of June 6, 1957, Ford was no longer in racing. Money was cut off. Parts supplies dried up, and racers were left to race what they had on their own.

Yunick was paid off but chose to race his Fords for the duration of the season, then went to Pontiac and dominated NASCAR's major races through the early 1960s. Goldsmith won the last Daytona Beach race in 1958 in Yunick's Pontiac, and just before executives arrived to admire their victorious

NASCAR'S WILD YEARS   21

CHAPTER ONE

Fan-O-Matic was the latest technology in gaining a power edge. (T. Taylor Warren)

machine, Yunick sold it for $1 to avoid the media frenzy he knew would soon arrive.

Zora Arkus-Duntov ran Chevrolet racing under the guise of a marine engine development program. Before the ban, Ford won 15 of 21 Grand National races, and Chevrolet only won 5. In the 32 races after the ban, Ford won 12 and Chevy won 14. Buck Baker won the NASCAR Championship in Chevrolets. Oldsmobile won five races that year, and Pontiac won two. Out of 53 races, Ford Motor Company cars won a total of 27, while GM cars won 25, including the Southern 500, the biggest race of the year.

In the Convertible Division, Ford's normally aspirated 312 engine showed its superiority to Chevrolet's carbureted 283 by winning 26 races to Chevy's 12. Mercury and Oldsmobile had one win apiece. However, Bob Welborn's consistently high finishes and eight wins gave Chevrolet the Convertible Division championship. On the short tracks, Jim Reed carried Ford's banner, winning five races and emerging as champion.

In what began as a year promising overwhelming Ford superiority, Dearborn was sidetracked with a deft maneuver by Curtice. With McNamara's consent, he toppled Ford's well-honed racing machine in midseason, apparently without intention to honor the ban he had proposed. GM kept its high-performance parts in catalogs, and Ford did not. GM continued clandestine support of engine and heavy-duty equipment development, while Ford ended development completely. Curtice's accomplishment stands as a major corporate coup that left Ford racers and fans wondering what happened, and Chevrolet fans cheering the superiority of their cars, proven by win after win.

During the next three model years, 1958 to '60, America's huge number of baby boomers began reaching driving age and increasingly turned to GM for exciting cars while Ford promoted safety and lost its image as the young man's car. When the sharpest postwar recession began in late 1957, Ford's annual sales plummeted 31.8 percent while Chevrolet sales dropped only 17.5 percent in 1958. In 1959, a rare styling goof at Chevrolet dropped sales a further 13.8 percent while Ford sales surged 47.2 percent, surpassing Chevrolet for the first time in years. Topping 1.5 million vehicles sold that year, Ford planners thought they were on a roll, but Chevrolet bounced back the next year with more appealing styling to surpass 1.8 million sales, a gain of 31.1 percent. The Ford men went away pondering what it would take to get back into the good graces of youthful buyers who increasingly went to GM showrooms for excitement.

In 1957, Ford's new chief engineer of the Engine and Foundry Division, Robert Stevenson, recognized that the 312 was about as far as the Y-block could go, considering that bigger, heavier Fords, Edsels, and Mercurys were in the works. A new "Ford Engine" (FE) was put into production for the '58 models and remained in production for 11 years in many variants, winning multiple NASCAR Championships. Bore center spacing was selected for expansion up to 425 ci, though for 1958 the new engine ranged between the 332- and 352-ci versions in Fords. Edsels came optioned with 361-ci FE mills, while Mercury's new FE displaced 383 ci. The top Thunderbird FE was planned to be 390 ci, but that engine was shelved in favor of the 430-ci Lincoln, another Ford of the soon-to-emerge muscle car concept. The 390 sat on the shelf until 1961 when its potential began to be developed. The FE's near decade-long run saw it become stock-car racing's winningest engine, and a world endurance racing champion.

With the AMA ban of mid-1957, Ford Motor Company lost the momentum that, if continued, would likely have propelled the company into subsequent record-breaking sales years. The ban cost Ford billions in lost sales over the next five years that went to General Motors and Chrysler Corporation. When NASCAR outlawed superchargers and fuel injection at the end of April 1957, the huffer exercise came to naught, and without Ford backing, the remainder of the 1957 Grand National season tilted further toward Chevrolet, which continued its back-door support of stock-car teams. When the 390 was finally put into production, and when the FE was finally matched to a 4-speed transmission in 1962, Ford began to recover from the effects of the AMA ban. Ford started again with a new corporate image: "Total Performance."

ZORA ARKUS-DUNTOV

At the 1953 Motorama in Detroit, Zora Arkus-Duntov saw the new Corvette on display and was interested. With proper development, he thought the new car could become a challenger to the European sports-racing cars he knew well. Zora was not yet an employee of GM, but when he signed on a little later, he quickly rose to oversee the Corvette's rise as the flagship of Chevrolet's lineup.

The two, man and machine, made a striking contrast at the Motorama. Zora, once an immigrant seeking freedom, stood before the latest machine from the capitalist world's largest corporation. He was born in Belgium, and about a year later his family moved to Russia where he grew up. Of his youth, he said, "I was interested in anything that moved, any motorized propulsion ship. At home in Moscow when I was a boy, that meant rail cars, then motorcycles, anything." His own competitive urge materialized in a motorcycle he tinkered with and raced. Following objections from his parents, he traded the two-wheeler for a car, a racing car, and quickly learned the art of going fast.

He relocated to Germany as a student engineer with notable accomplishments in the principles of supercharging. His work took him to France, then to the U.S. as a consultant. He caught the eye of influential people, resulting in a special visa just as Nazism cast its shadow over Europe. His own bootlegging experience, trafficking gold out of Germany on high-speed nighttime flights in his hopped-up flathead V-8 Ford, taught him many tricks he put to use later. Settling in New York, he and his brother Yura teamed to design and manufacture speed equipment for the flathead, most notably the late 1940s Ardun head conversion that replaced Ford's inefficient head and combustion chamber combination with sophisticated hemispherical combustion chambers. From the original 85 hp,

Following its debut in 1949 stock-car racing, NASCAR soon expanded into sanctioning the Daytona Speed Weeks held in February. Officially timed high-speed runs were staged on the beach as NASCAR's official Performance Trials. (Chevrolet photo)

Zora Arkus-Duntov was the force behind development of the hardware that made the Corvette America's sports car. His name lives on with the Duntov cams and the first-generation Chevrolet speed equipment. He was instrumental in making the Rochester fuel-injection system work, for the introduction of Chevy's 4-speed transmission, and the development of the 348-409 Z11-series racing engines. He was also director of Chevrolet's behind-the-scenes stock-car racing into the 1960s, the era when GM officially claimed, "We don't race." (Chevrolet photo)

Lee Petty and his #42 Dodge make avoid Ralph Moody and his #12 Ford. Moody actually finished third, while Petty came in 12th. (Photo courtesy International Motorsports Hall of Fame)

the 239-ci flathead's output could easily be tripled or quadrupled with Ardun heads, a supercharger, and three Strombergs. The Ardun hemi-head-equipped flathead emerged as the top rung of hot rodding, catching the eye of engineers at Chrysler who recognized the value of the design. When Chrysler's own design appeared as a 1951 production engine, the two designs were remarkably similar.

Arkus-Duntov joined GM in May 1953, where his fertile mind and strong "can do" personality produced innovation after innovation, many of which sat on shelves collecting dust. What he saw in the Corvette was a dual-pronged attack on the world's two-seater market: production and racing. By the time V-8-powered Corvette perfor-mance hardware began appearing on the market between 1955 and 1958, another application had emerged: stock-car racing. Although Chevrolet's Ed Cole was looking into racing, GM was not in the race car-building business and had no racing department, unlike most European manufacturers that treated racing as both big business and a proving

THE FABULOUS 1950s

Lee Petty won this 1954 Daytona Beach race in his #42 Chrysler. The crowd (not to mention the racers) had much less protection in the old days. (Photo courtesy International Motorsports Hall of Fame)

A '55 Chevy (left), a '55 Chrysler (center), and a '55 Oldsmobile (right) square off. Unlike modern stock cars, these really started out as stock cars. (Photo courtesy International Motorsports Hall of Fame)

CHAPTER ONE

Ford's $2 million investment in stock-car racing paid off when Curtis Turner won the biggest race of the year, the 1956 Southern 500. (Ford photo)

Facing page: The interior of the Stroppe Mercury was strictly stock, a handsome showcase for going faster than anyone. (Ford photo)

Californian Bill Stroppe, longtime Ford racer and instrumental in the 1953 Lincoln team that won the stock class of the Carrera Panamericana in Mexico, built the fastest stock car in 1956 – this fuel-injected Mercury. (Ford photo)

THE FABULOUS 1950s

NASCAR'S WILD YEARS

CHAPTER ONE

California hotshoe Bill Amick poses with Stroppe's Mercury. The Stroppe team was too far from Southern stock-car racing, and even when Holman Moody and Stroppe combined their efforts at Ford's behest, Stroppe proved to have little impact while Holman Moody rose to greatness. (Ford photo)

ground for new ideas. About six months after joining Chevrolet, Zora sent a memo to his boss, Maurice Olley, titled *Thoughts Pertaining to Youth, Hot Rodders, and Chevrolet.* In this memo, he showed his awareness of markets Chevrolet management had never even thought about. This memo proved so far-reaching that if a single document can be cited as the beginning of Chevrolet's factory racing, this is it. He outlined the dominant position Ford held in both hot rodding and racing, and showed where GM could gain significantly. The idea of a new market caught on with management, and Zora influence grew so rapidly that he become the czar of Chevrolet's performance development.

Zora went on to note that it takes about three years for a new idea to catch on with hot rodders, and even though the new RPO (Regular Production Order) Chevrolet V-8 was due out in less than a year, it would be the latter part of the decade before hot rodders would catch on to its potential. With Ford's new overhead-valve Y-block V-8 already on the market, Zora proposed a plan to accelerate the learning curve and enhance the marketability of Chevrolets in the hot-rod market sector by introducing well-developed high-output parts such as camshafts and manifolds. He proposed the image of a true high-performance Chevrolet, namely the Corvette, receiving RPO parts sold on showroom models and over the counter. Hot-rodders were swapping out the Vette's stove-bolt 6 for overhead-valve Cadillac and

Speed Weeks 1957 brought a huge turnout from Ford, everything from NASCAR-type stockers to aerodynamic Thunderbirds. The Performance Trials were a warm-up for the racing season. (Ford photo)

Sand, sun, and speed during Speed Weeks broke the off-season doldrums with opportunities to test the latest equipment. (Ford photo)

Olds V-8s, and marketing a Cadvette, Corvilac, Oldsmovette, or Cormobile had no place in Chevrolet's structure. Cross-branding the Corvette was not in Cole's plan, and he led a team in designing a small, OHV Chevrolet-only engine, largely the work of Al Kolbe, which later became known worldwide as the small-block. It still ranks among the most influential engines of all time.

Zora proposed to help people racing Corvettes do a better job with all sorts of light alloys and heavy-duty parts from brakes to driveline hardware. These parts, developed through extensive research and development, would make any Corvette a complete racing package for those buyers who wanted to race. He was given the go-ahead, and he put together a group that produced more sales than any marketing strategy before or since – racing sold cars. In a few years, just as he had predicted, Chevrolet displaced Ford as the hot-rodder's store. Ad man Barney Clark told the world about the new and exciting V-8 Corvette and V-8 Chevrolet.

Clark was Chevrolet's outlet to the public. His ad campaigns introduced Chevrolet to the "win on Sunday, sell on Monday" market, and the new V-8 in the new-for-1955 Chevrolet instantly became a young man's car. When the new Bel Air was selected as the official Indianapolis 500 Pace Car, the racing public was treated to a thrilling new Chevrolet, and Ford went away licking its wounds. Dearborn's new line that year showed an equally extensive redesign with the Crown Victoria and Thunderbird as Ford Division's showcase, both with larger-displacement engines of higher output.

The most intense factory war every seen began unfolding. In one heated battle after another on racetracks throughout America, Chevrolet and Ford poured money into stock-car racing. It was mere crumbs by corporate standards, but enormous amounts of money for Southern round-track racers. When the factories arrived, competition ratcheted upward several notches, and NASCAR grew by leaps and bounds.

The beginning of Chevrolet's rise as a stock-car racing threat began when Jack Radtke entered his Chevy in the February 1955 NASCAR Grand National at Daytona Beach. The beach race had, on occasion, been called when the tide came in and covered the course. It was 4.1 miles around with parallel straights, one on the beach, the other along the adjoining highway, connected at each end by turns through sand. As a whole herd of stockers, usually around 100 cars, came roaring down the hard surface at the start, many didn't make it past the ditch just off the south turn. Radtke started from back in the pack and drove a more cautious race. When he came in tenth overall, a lot of people noticed.

"Fireball" Roberts set the pole at 117.99 mph in his Chevrolet, but only the Fords of Curtis Turner and Joe Weatherly were on the lead lap of the Rebel 300 at Darlington in 1958. Ford swept the field first through fourth. (Frank Wells photo)

Since the first beach race in 1938, with its more than 20,000 spectators, stock-car racing fans flocked to Daytona. Why Daytona drew such large numbers is still being debated. Perhaps it was simply that racing was the most exciting thing to come along during the Depression years. Whatever the reason, spectators saw a lot to talk about.

When the Chevy men, led by Ed Cole, wanted to go racing in the mid-1950s, they looked around for the best mechanic and chose Smokey Yunick. With Yunick's driver, Herb Thomas, they also got a two-time NASCAR champion. Smokey got the first factory Chevrolet. Yunick met with three-time Indianapolis 500 winner Mauri Rose, who was sent south by Cole to organize Chevrolet's entry into racing. Yunick's "Best Damn Garage in Town," located just off the inland waterway at Daytona, was Rose's choice as a Chevrolet base of operations.

NASCAR's strictly-stock rules were so restrictive that durability to win was all that was needed – almost. Powerful engines certainly helped, but while both Chevrolet and Ford factory men suspiciously eyed each other on race day, Kiekhaefer's Chryslers cleaned house in '55, and did almost as well the next year. However, the biggest race of the year, the Southern 500, was a Chevrolet-Ford slugfest in both 1955 and 1956, Chevrolet winning the first round, Ford the second.

What gave Chevrolet the edge in '55 was tires. Rose had located several sets of special Firestone tires in Dayton, Ohio leftover from Briggs Cunningham's sports-car racing days. The better-balanced Chevys with softer-compound rubber stuck better than the bigger cars, which simply wore out their tires. The Chevys went by the Oldsmobiles, Buicks, and Kiekhaefer's Chryslers during tire-change pit stops, and after Ford's suspensions collapsed, it was an all-Chevrolet show.

The crowd saw a great race, but few recognized what really happened. It was the first race of the new age, the age of corporate commitment to stock-car racing. True, Hudson had earlier been behind Marshall Teague, Yunick, and Thomas, but with both GM and Ford now out there doing battle (soon followed by the tire companies),

NASCAR would never be the same. Manufacturers saw stock-car racing as a marketing tool, and NASCAR's "Big Bill" France not only hooked Chevrolet, he snared Ford and got Firestone to boot.

A half-century of Chevrolet-versus-Ford wars has unfolded since then on NASCAR's tracks, beginning with Zora's memo. Four years after that memo, in mid-1957, the AMA ban caused factory withdrawal (Ford did; GM didn't, and Zora was Chevrolet's man behind the scenes). The ban changed things on the surface, but in fact, GM simply went underground. Zora was responsible for upgrading the performance and durability of the small-block and Chevy's truck engine, the 348-ci big-block, to turn them into racing engines using his clandestine marine engine development program.

Zora, recalling 1957: "We had fuel injection and Ford had supercharger. I wind up director of high-performance vehicles and chassis, and we had SEDCO (Southern Engineering Development Company), Atlanta outfit because of proximity to racing. Very accessible to stock-car racing. My responsibility included Atlanta. I intend to go visit my new acquisition, then – BAM! – we are no longer in racing.

"The AMA ban did not affect me at all because I continue development high performance, and I still retained director of high performance except I have responsibility of police car and export car.

"In '58, summer, I got telephone call from Rosenberger. He was assistant chief engineer for Chevrolet. I was on vacation. Ed Cole told him to contact me, and I should go to Trenton, meet Buck Baker. [Baker was NASCAR champion in 1956 and '57, the latter year being Chevrolet's first driver championship season.] Okay, I am in Trenton, go in grandstand, select a room upstairs, sitting alone. After while, racing uniformed man sat with me.

"'May I have a light?' I give him light.

"'You are Zora Duntov?'

"'Yes.'

"'I am going. You look where I am going and follow me.'

"I did so. Through the grandstand, get outside, car waiting, get in the back seat. Car maybe travel three hundred yards, and Buck Baker get in. We arrange following modus operandi: he continue racing stock car and I supply everything, and he will supply me back with failing engine.

"In 1958 I start to work with Buck Baker. In '59, two things happen: opening of speedway in Daytona, and two preliminary heat races, 125 miles each [actually, they were 100 miles each. Bob Welborn in a 1959 Chevrolet No. 59 won the second, Lloyd "Shorty" Rollins won the first in a 1958 Ford No. 99].

"Then I decide engine good enough to go, 348 cubic inches, but not supposed to be racing, right? Cole devised following plan: sales department to buy five cars. I get $25,000, enough to buy cars and additional money to buy heavy-duty equipment, suspension pieces to transform passenger car from showroom to race car. Sales department, engineering was not involved except myself.

"I meet with Jim Rathmann in Miami. He subsequently won Indy race in 1960, but he was employed in my SEDCO before. He buy all this heavy-duty parts for nominal sum, and I am sitting in his shop in Miami with sales department man, Bob Lund [subsequently General Manager of Chevrolet] and Fred Warner. Jim Rathmann contact drivers on telephone and I have another telephone. If driver seems to me enthusiastic, then Jim tell them what it is all about.

"Okay, I disburse this money. Five Chevrolet bought. Jack Smith, stock-car driver, he decided to buy a car, but he has no money. I arrange for him to buy at cost, a sixth car. That was the sixth car, 1-2-3, 1-2-3. At the time, we still not legally can race.

"Jim Rathmann ran 348-cubic-inch displacement engines, part of my development. Dick Keinath came to my group and was instrumental in 348 and 409 and 427, but not Mk II. That was just Dick [the legendary Mk IIS Mystery Engine]. The 427 exist only for drag racing, the Z11. Identical block like 409 but 427 cubic inches [with a unique dual 4-bbl intake improved over the 409].

"Other was Z-28. I think the 'Z' for 'Zora.' Starting '63, Z06 heavy-duty suspension and Z03… some dress items also carry Z because specification man ask, 'I am responsible?' Okay, put Z. Z11, actually, the car was Vince Piggins' idea. I was responsible for engine. Or like Z28, I did only engine. And ZL1 was Corvette Group work [the ZL1 was the ultimate Mk IV big-block in showroom Chevys]. You see, Corvette Group in my time was responsible for engines. Not any more.

"We had six cars that had no support throughout the season, improvement, failing parts – all required money. Cole and [Harry] Barr came up with idea – to establish Marine Division. The Marine Division was, at that time, subterfuge. Marine Division was organized under me and provide means and engineering budget to funnel money, material and work for the racers. At that time, we did not realize that Marine engines grow to be 60 percent of all engines built in U.S.

"348 Marine engine. I was director of high performance including Marine engine. But I will tell you, in 1960, 80 percent of the starters at Daytona were Chevrolets [10 of top 20 finishers, 23 of 67 entrants]. Mechanically, all cars were scot-free. That proved the 348; started out as a truck engine, was a very good racing engine also. In '60, Junior Johnson won Daytona 500 but Rex White was overall champion." [Rex White finished the 1960 season with 21,164 points to lead Richard Petty in second place with 17,228 points. White won six races with 25 top-five finishes, all in Chevrolets.]

So, "We Don't Race" was, in fact, back-door support through Zora and his deep factory connections, just as the Ford men suspected. The Corvette Group developed all sorts of exotic engines that never saw the light of day until the mid-1960s when Zora and his engines made a *Hot Rod Magazine* cover story. By then, Chevrolet had a single win (1964) in stock-car racing. When GM management finally backed up "We Don't Race" by putting jobs on the line after the 1963 Daytona 500, performance parts development went further underground.

CHAPTER TWO

The #5 Cotton Owens '60 Pontiac, driven by Bobby Johns, is seen here leading the #12 Holman Moody '60 Ford, driven by Joe Weatherly, at the Atlanta 500. Johns went on to win the race, while Weatherly finished eighth. (Photo courtesy International Motorsports Hall of Fame)

1960: Racing and the Kids

The automotive industry in 1960 was a muddled heap of confusion about what American buyers wanted versus the low-bucks fun desired by the rapidly emerging youth market. "Old" said big cars, statements of prosperity and status; "New" said excitement on a budget. Cars hadn't changed much in five years, just year-to-year styling changes, but now the factories were in the crossfire of market adjustments. Keeping a high market share meant holding on to old as the main effort while developing and introducing new performance cars. Performance was led by the "Red Hot and Rambunctious!" Chrysler 300F, a sleek, high-style 2-door hardtop with leather bucket seats and a 400-hp Ram Induction V-8 backed by a floor-shifted 4-speed gearbox. It was a 4,300-lb car that could, in grand fashion, gobble up anything on America's wide, smooth, open roads.

New also said inexpensive, and that meant small cars. AMC's tiny, 2-seat Metropolitan sold over 22,000 units in 1959. The new Studebaker Lark proved the point, upping Studebaker sales by 270 percent. By 1960, each of the Big Three nervously committed manufacturing resources to increasing production of compacts: Ford's Falcon with the anemic OHV inline-6; the Chevrolet Corvair with its flat-6 and that serpentine fan belt that was notorious for flipping off; the Buick-Oldsmobile-Pontiac look-alikes that turned so many people off – until they drove the Buick Skylark/Olds F-85 with the new cast-aluminum V-8 engine that pushed the lightweight cars to about 135 mph. Meanwhile, Pontiac went with half of its V-8 in the Tempest, a 197-ci slant-4-cylinder that was less than anemic.

The big three planners noticed that sales of small, nimble, low-cost imports steadily increased to over 600,000 units in 1959, roughly 10 percent of the U.S. market. The bean counters dutifully reported that they'd lost a billion dollars in new-car sales to the "new" market that bought among 60-odd makes and models. So, they turned grudging attention to cars even smaller than their new compacts. Ford's top man, Robert McNamara, pushed his company toward the Cardinal (an Americanized Taunus from its European branch), Dearborn's answer to the VW Beetle. The Lincoln-Mercury Division was said to have its compact in the

By 1960, stock-car racing teams were beginning to receive substantial support from the factories, but race-day preparations had not changed. Garages with uniformed team members and vans stuffed with parts and equipment were yet to come. (T. Taylor Warren photo)

works, the Comet version of the Falcon, but that badge became Mercury's upscale variant of the midsize Ford Fairlane, which was on the drawing boards for a 1962 release. It included the company's new compact thin-walled 221-ci OHV V-8, the engine that changed Ford's image among the kids. GM rushed its compact Corvair line into production, and Cadillac was rumored to have a variant slated for release. Chrysler had not yet designated which division was to market the Valiant – first it was Dodge but ultimately Plymouth, with Dodge pinning the Dart badge on its version.

Meanwhile over in Dearborn, a front-drive Cord 810 had been bought and restored. It was the beginning of Ford's future small car with front-wheel drive matched to the German built Taunus V-4 that evolved into the GT-40. The industry was

CHAPTER TWO

Chrysler engineers borrowed the principle of ram induction from pipe organs, and the new 383-ci SonoRamic Commando V-8 introduced in 1960 models was the first engine of this type offered to the public. The long resonator tubes forced fuel-air mixtures into the combustion chambers at a much higher velocity than normal carburetor placement, and Plymouth-DeSoto Chief Engineer Jack Charipar said, "We feel that ram induction is one of the greatest single engine developments since the invention of the supercharger." (DaimlerChrysler Historical Collection photo)

Although a strong performer delivering at least 10 percent more midrange power, about 1 hp per 10 ci, the Cross-Ram induction made working on the engine time-consuming and difficult. The 383-ci Plymouth engine was factory-rated at 330 hp, while the 413 Chrysler engine was rated at 400 hp. (DaimlerChrysler Historical Collection photo)

moving from the 1950s norm of one multipurpose car per family into multiple cars for different purposes.

Chrysler's 413-ci F-series in the 300F engine cranked out a whopping 495 ft-lbs of torque at just 2,800 rpm, and was backed up by its European Pont-a-Mousson 4-speed stick. Only GM had 4-speed transmissions in mass production. Its Borg-Warner T-10 family proved a good match to V-8 power. Manual shifting was just more fun, even though 80 percent of new cars were sold with automatics. Corvettes, Corvairs, Chevrolets – all of them offered buyers proven performance with floor shifts and driving pleasure well below the price of a 300F. Meanwhile, Ford's 360-hp, 352-ci V-8 for its Thunderbird and sedans delivered performance surpassing the 300F at much lower costs, although still beyond the budgets of the kids.

1960: RACING AND THE KIDS

Joe Weatherly roars by the flagman at Darlington in one of the last convertible races featuring premier drivers. (Tom Kirkland photo)

From plowing with a mule to hauling moonshine, Junior Johnson had come a long way from Wilkes County, North Carolina, dirt tracks to win the Daytona 500.

With the driver easier to see, convertible racing was fun to watch, but the cars were slower than their hardtop counterparts. "Fireball" Roberts (22) takes the high line with Joe Weatherly (12) at Darlington. (Tom Kirkland photo)

Marketers noticed that the "new" influence on Dad to buy a more exciting car was shifting toward higher-image, higher-performance cars, though not necessarily a compact. That kept the "old" market going. Dad just wasn't interested in compacts.

Driving, going, and doing were the watchwords of the new culture, and even though the new compacts didn't demonstrate the fuel efficiency expected of smaller cars – miles-per-gallon numbers were generally in the high teens – they did offer high tinker factors. Lots of add-on aftermarket equipment increased compact performance toward sedan level, except for the top end. However well the small cars negotiated curves and accelerated out of turns, HP was still king.

What did it all mean, anyway? The kids paid attention to figures like BHP, DIN, SAE, and CUNA. More and more advertising from around the world expressed engine output in BHP (brake horsepower), but what it meant wasn't so clear. Still, the bigger the HP rating, the bigger the smile it put on young faces. Detroit set about to exploit this relationship and tested engines

NASCAR'S WILD YEARS

CHAPTER TWO

A smiling Rex White, 1960 NASCAR Grand National Champion, turns wrenches with chief mechanic Louie Clements. With a 50-50 partnership, the two ran their Chevrolets out of the White & Clements Garage, Spartanburg, South Carolina. They split $57,525 in earnings that year. (Rex White photo)

per SAE (Society of Automotive Engineers) methods, in stripped-down form without a generator, water pump, or cooling fan. The test methods also permitted optimizing performance by adjusting carburetor jets and air/fuel mixtures, ignition timing and distributor setup, and other performance-enhancing techniques to get the highest peak power independent of torque. The best possible performance was then advertised as engine HP. For the kids, the concept of torque was not so clear, but they knew that reciprocating motion in the engine became twisting motion in the transmission, drive shaft, axles, and ultimately the smoking tires, and the bigger the twist number the better. The SAE methods allowed optimizing torque, as well, and adjusting ignition timing and air/fuel mixture to get highest torque values independent of output power. Germany's DIN ratings and CUNA figures from Italy were widely known to be more accurate, but their numbers were not as big as those describing American engines, and big numbers held bragging rights. DIN and CUNA data were gathered from engines in stock configuration for road use with all accessories as sold installed on cars, with generators, water pumps, fans, and belts attached, and with stock carburetor

1960: RACING AND THE KIDS

In 1960, Pontiac offered buyers the broadest selection of performance options in the world. Heavily dialed in to the marketing potential of winning races, and with option levels including the Bonneville denoting speed and Catalina for sport, Pontiac stock cars and drag cars set the tone for coming years of factory-built big-ci Super Stocks.

jetting. The HP war of the mid-1950s was on, and American numbers were bigger.

"Bigger is better" ran contrary to the emerging compact-car market, except for engines, and whatever the BHP rating, cubic inches were the real measure of an engine. Stuffing a big American V-8 into a small, lightweight European car had already become the Southern California answer to anemic performance, and Carroll Shelby immortalized the idea when he described his 1965 427 Cobra: "Too much is just right!"

"Too much" never applied to stock-car racing, though. The European method of putting factory-built stock cars through grueling performance trials was a great way to prove a car's worth, but stock-car racing was fast becoming a showcase of speed with large proportions of entertainment and spectacle. Speed took HP, and "the only answer to cubic inches is cubic dollars." With the giant ovals at Daytona, Charlotte, and Atlanta, along with the already legendary "Too Tough to Tame" Darlington International Raceway, stock-car racing moved into

CHAPTER TWO

the big time of increasing media attention and corporate interest, and growing numbers of fans packed the stands on Sunday. There were no Chrysler 300 stock cars in 1960, but Ford, GM, and Chrysler noticed the enthusiasm of brand identity among fans along with the potential for word-of-mouth advertising, and sought combinations of lighter weight and more power to get higher speeds.

While the most powerful Chevrolet of 1960 was 348-powered, Pontiac ran 389s, Dodge and Plymouth had 383s, Oldsmobile had 394s, and Ford ran its 352. In 1959, Ford upped T-Bird performance with the 430-ci Lincoln engine. Its long stroke and slow-moving pistons were designed for smooth, low-end torque to move 5,500-lb Lincolns with the swagger of an ocean liner. A showroom hardtop coupe Thunderbird tipped the scale at around 3,800 lbs dry, so the 430-ci T-Bird gave an instant boost in performance from power-to-weight ratio without significantly changing the weight distribution with the heavier engine. With a 52.5 front/47.5 rear distribution on a 113-in wheelbase, this Bird had good handling and could fly, but the 430-ci brute had little in the way of available performance parts. The racers had to learn their way through it.

Historically, the 1959 430-ci Thunderbird was the first muscle car, as defined by a bigger engine from a larger car line installed in a smaller car. For stock-car racing, the T-Bird offered lots of potential that came at a time when Ford racers needed any help they could get.

Chevrolet and Pontiac engineers quietly kept back-door race shops open to the right people, while Ford boss Robert McNamara shut the door on Dearborn's efforts, complying with the AMA ban of 1957. The general public was not aware of any sort of ban on racing, and GM fans rejoiced when the Pontiacs flew around the big ovals and Chevys took the top two places in NASCAR's point standings in 1960. Meanwhile, Ford sales dropped 30 percent from 1959, but Falcon sales were up 503 percent to over 500,000 units, and that got the boss's attention.

NASCAR disbanded its Short Track and Convertible Divisions after the 1959 season, and the 1960 schedule included 44 races, with convertibles and coupes running side-by-side. Dirt tracks still dominated the schedule, and 8 of Ford's 15 victories were on dirt that year. Unfortunately, that made no impact on sales. NASCAR held races throughout the country, and a win in California had no influence on publicity in the South.

Meanwhile, several tracks featuring NASCAR races in 1958 had closed by 1960, while two new paved ovals (Charlotte and Atlanta) were to be completed late in the season. The schedule was reduced by six races, giving the teams more time to build, develop, and test at a time when factory attention was growing,

The "Win on Sunday, sell on Monday" influence of stock-car racing brought many buyers into new-car showrooms to drive off with stylish and powerful Pontiacs.

38   NASCAR'S WILD YEARS

1960: RACING AND THE KIDS

Pontiac factory catalogs were stuffed with high-performance parts for over-the-counter sales, including cast-iron headers and a host of power-boosting options.

though ever so slowly. But not at Ford. Holman Moody had to weather tough times, working on whatever came their way, from Studebaker Larks to assembling 430-ci Thunderbirds from factory-reject parts purchased at scrap prices. As Holman Moody put together 150-mph stockers, it looked to the outside world like Ford Motor Company was heavily into racing. It wasn't. John Holman used his previous Ford contacts to purchase the parts, including complete bodies and engines, among truckloads of factory-line rejects, to build the Holman Moody stockers. Selling the parts solved disposal problems at the Thunderbird assembly plant in Wixom, Michigan, but the Ford men had no idea who Holman was or what he was going to do with the parts.

General Motors was racing. From 1958 on, Chevrolet had gotten increasingly deeper into stock-car racing through SEDCO in Atlanta, and then through Jim Rathmann's Miami shop. The clandestine marine engine development program accumulated a total of $102,511 through March 1960 and achieved the goal of making the 348 a true 340-hp performer. That engine, although 40 hp under the Pontiacs and 30 mph slower, was to figure in some surprising victories. One was Junior Johnson's victory in the 1960 Daytona 500 in a year-old 348-ci Chevy.

Up in Wilkes County, North Carolina, Junior had become known as a hard-driving wild man who returned from an 11-month, three-day stint in federal prison on a moonshine charge to finish eighth in the 1958 NASCAR points race. When Bud Allman in Conover (just south of Junior's home in Ingle Hollow) heard that Junior was out of jail early in 1958, he called, and Junior signed on to drive a year-old, ex-Holman Moody '57 Ford owned by New Yorker Paul Spaulding. Allman maintained the car, and Junior won six races in 28 starts with 12 top-10 finishes that year. Conover had been one of Junior's bootlegging stops, so he knew the town well, and he was soon back hauling on the "Wilkes County Champagne" circuit at night and racing whenever he could.

The Super Duty 389 with Tri-Power rated at 348 hp and backed by a T-10 Borg-Warner Synchro-Mesh 4-speed transmission set the mark for the street in 1960. In stock-car racing, the single 4-bbl version of the 389 set all sorts of pole records as the fastest of the fast.

NASCAR'S WILD YEARS 39

CHAPTER TWO

Chevrolet styling for 1960 continued the Impala name plate denoting grace and pace with NASCAR-championship-winning performance.

1960: RACING AND THE KIDS

Junior returned home to the North Wilkesboro track in mid-May and thrilled the crowd again with his daredevil driving. Though it was paved the year before, the asphalt of the track broke up, but Junior flew around the oval showing he had lost none of his daring in prison. He built a half-lap lead over the field, then went too hard into turn three and sailed over the embankment, rocked through a patch of high weeds with the throttle wide open, and returned to the track still in the lead. The crowd went wild, then cheered even louder for their local hero when he won. The next month, he won three more races in a row, then returned to North Wilkesboro and won the fall race. His biggest win that year was beating Fireball Roberts on the one-mile dirt track at Atlanta's Lakewood Speedway.

The following year, the Spaulding-Allman-Johnson Ford took to the track with spectacular results. Junior won another five races in 27 starts with 14 top-five finishes. He flipped his Ford in practice at the Hickory Speedway in North Carolina. It somersaulted through the air and landed on its wheels. Junior went on to set the pole and win the race! He was becoming a legend in his own time. Hard charging was what he knew best, and in a 100-mile feature at the Greenville-Pickens Speedway in South Carolina, he lapped the 24-car field, and then lapped them again. At Darlington, a spectacular crash in practice that ripped the car apart looked to be the end of the line for Junior, but he returned from an overnight stay in a nearby hospital the next day and drove a Holman Moody Thunderbird in the Southern 500.

By 1960, Junior had been seen sleeping in racetrack garage areas so often that stories about his laziness abounded, though they were seemingly at odds with his sensational driving. Was Junior a Jekyll-Hyde character, a mild-mannered country boy who became a madman behind the wheel? Or was he just a lazy country boy who could drive fast? The truth was that he wasn't lazy and he could drive fast; he was sleeping by day because he hauled moonshine all night. Being a race driver with a rigorous schedule of testing, racing, and traveling proved to be good cover that got him out of another federal rap, but he had become notorious in legal circles. The feds around Wilkes County decided that the only way to catch Junior Johnson was to put a bounty on his head. There he was, a big-time NASCAR driver with as much as a $10,000 bounty for anyone who fingered him. That amount of money was several years' income for many, but nobody turned him in. Junior was accustomed to taking chances, but he was wise enough to recognize the inevitable; somebody out there would take that money and never have to give his name. The "revenooers" were closing the net on him, so he concentrated more on racing than moonshine, but it took time to offset the family income that his nighttime activities supported. In a few years, his brothers L.P. and Fred would be part of the Junior Johnson racing team. After winning 50 Grand National races by 1965, Junior retired to his Ingle Hollow race shop. The Junior Johnson racing team was NASCAR's top winning team at the time.

Down in Level Cross, North Carolina, Lee Petty signed a lucrative factory contract with Plymouth during mid-1959. Plymouth got the experience of two-time (1954, 1958) NASCAR champion Lee Petty along with his hard charging son, Richard, who had earned his racing miles mostly in the tough Convertible Division. That contract transformed the Petty team – used to running used Oldsmobiles – into a two-car team with the latest factory equipment, and Lee won his third NASCAR championship that year with 4 Oldsmobile and 10 Plymouth wins. Soon to become the Petty blue Plymouths, the No. 42 (Lee) and 43 (Richard) cars soon emerged as the toughest Chrysler factory team.

Oops! Factory team? Well, now we know that the factories claimed that they weren't racing, saying that those good ol' Southern boys made the cars go fast on their own. With Plymouth's sudden emergence as a steady winner and a threat to win on any track, chatter was that wily ol' Lee Petty had seen the virtue of Plymouth's light weight and new big-inch engine.

The Pettys took Chrysler's newly instituted unibody construction in all passenger cars to new highs; the old-style body-on-frame construction was gone. Stiffening the more flexible unibody was a challenge that all the racers had to face in coming years as all manufacturers shifted to unibody construction as a cost-cutting measure. The roll bar behind the driver took on a new function; building a full roll cage from the back end of the front subframe to the front end of the rear subframe tied the whole car together just as if it had a frame. The Pettys were ahead of the wave.

Advertising touted "The Solid Plymouth" with its new 330-hp, 383-ci engine, and the new body design with its giant upright rear wings put Plymouth into the thick of things. It was harder to compete against the well-developed Pontiac 389 than Ford's 352 and Chevy's 348; cubic inches were king. Holman Moody's 430-ci Thunderbird was out there because Ford marketed such a car, so why wouldn't the 413-ci Chrysler New Yorker engine in a Petty Plymouth be legal, too? NASCAR's rule enforcers said it wasn't, citing that strictly stock was strictly stock, and engines had to be available to the public in the configuration raced. Plymouth didn't market such a car, so the Petty cars had to run at a disadvantage to the bigger-inch, more powerful competitors on the big ovals, but they were still tough competitors on short tracks.

The Daytona 500 lineup that year was exclusively hardtops, which had proved faster than convertibles, and on the front row were, what else, Pontiacs. Fireball Roberts and Jack Smith, winners of the 100-mile qualifiers, followed by Cotton Owens and Bobby Jones, also in Pontiacs, gave the 500 a decidedly Pontiac flavor. Known from high school for his blazing fastball, Fireball Roberts set a new pole record of 151.556 mph, over 8 mph faster

CHAPTER TWO

Chevrolet's top-rated 348-ci engine for 1960 came from the factory with 2-3-bbl carbs and was rated at 335 hp, up from 315 with a single 4-bbl carb.

home $19,600, his biggest payday so far, and a big boost toward ending his bootlegging exploits. Johns won $8,600 for second, and Richard Petty got a bigger check than his father ($6,450 compared to $3,650), but over $10,000 for the Petty team was a handsome payout for a Sunday afternoon drive, showing the advantage of a two-car team.

Two weeks later, Richard won his first Grand National feature at the half-mile Charlotte Fairgrounds track in a year-old Plymouth, beating Rex White in a Chevrolet. The two of them were, by then, in a seesaw points battle that heated up as the season progressed. Rex piled on the points with the most wins, six for the season. He backed his victories with 25 top-five and 10 sixth-through-10th-place finishes. Richard's wins, 16 top fives, and 30 top-10 finishes came in more than 3,900 points behind. Ned Jarrett, who would be White's biggest Chevy challenger in 1961, notched the most Ford wins in 1960, five, for a fifth overall in the points. Lee Petty also won five races to finish close behind Jarrett. Bobby Johns (Pontiac) was third and Buck Baker (Chevy) came in fourth. Consequently, the point totals went Chevrolet-Pontiac-Plymouth, in that order, all well ahead of Ford, whose "We Don't Race" corporate position was taking its toll on sales.

Richard Petty's season-long point total would have been higher if it had included his second-place finish in the 400-mile debut of Charlotte's new 1.5-mile speedway late in the season. Unfortunately, he was disqualified for entering pit road through the unsodded infield between the pits and the front straight, which was strictly forbidden in the pre-race drivers' meeting. The track was new and landscaping incomplete, so officials wanted the cars to stay on the pavement. Both Petty cars were

than Cotton Owens' pole of the year before. Both records were set in Smokey Yunick cars, showing that Smokey's inside track to the factory had the edge.

The 500 unfolded with a Big Three shootout like never seen before; Roberts and Smith led early, then Junior Johnson and Rex White in their Chevrolets broke into the lead about mid-race. Late in the race, Richard and Lee Petty made it look like a Plymouth affair. From lap 170 to 191 of the 200-lap feature, a couple of year-old cars made the newbies look like has-beens; Bobby Johns put his '59 Pontiac out front with Junior right on his tail in a '59 Chevy. When Johns' rear window popped out, Junior went around him and stayed in front the final 8 laps to win among the much-faster Pontiacs – in a year-old Chevrolet powered by a 348-ci truck engine. Johns took second, followed by Richard and Lee Petty third and fourth, the highest finish of all the 1960 models. All other competitors were at least one lap down. Junior took disqualified. Two weeks later on Atlanta's new superspeedway, the last points race of the season, Lee and Richard finished sixth and seventh behind Rex White in fifth. Rex had already clinched the Championship.

Where was Ford? The total corporate commitment to racing was just three men who carefully maintained no contact with Holman Moody. Don Frey, Executive Engineer of Ford Division Product Planning, managed to get corporate backing and a tiny budget. He put Dave Evans in charge of the three-man group, along with contracted support from Don Sullivan, the sage of speed who'd been involved with developing Ford engines all the way back to the flathead V-8 introduced in 1932. Sullivan took the 352 to new levels of power and durability with parts designed solely from his know-how, as they had no budget for testing and developing equipment. Bill Innes, a rising managing engineer in the Engine and Foundry Division, took interest and had the parts made. When John Cowley showed up to work on the special project, a heavy-duty suspension for police interceptors, it took several weeks for him to learn the chassis and suspension he worked on was for a prototype car for racing, not a Police Interceptor that was already in Ford catalogs. The Evans-Cowley-Sullivan combination put together their prototype on a shoestring by scrounging and using lots of their own time. To avoid an association with Holman Moody, which would instantly reveal Ford's new interest in racing, the Wood Brothers in Virginia were signed on to crew the 1959 model Ford during "tire tests" at Daytona in August. The driver for the tests, Cotton Owens, came straight from among NASCAR's list of top drivers. Owens topped 145 mph with the 360-hp 352, faster than any lap turned in the previous Daytona 500, and he said he could have gone faster with better suspension. Owens caught the drift and asked about driving a Ford in the next Daytona 500.

The one-car project, an unofficial prototype, was refined and strengthened further during thrashing by Curtis Turner and the Wood Brothers crew. Throughout the fall they ran the car lap after lap around the rough, half-mile dirt oval in Concord, North Carolina. By early November, the NASCAR package was complete and in the catalogs as a kit to modify showroom-model Fords. Testing on Daytona Beach during the winter speed trials almost got the project canceled when it was mentioned in a newspaper story that caught management's attention. Orders were handed down for the team to hastily remove themselves and the car from Daytona Beach. Ford performance had earned few friends in the rough-and-tumble ranks of stock-car racers, but they did sell a few kits. Holman Moody took to the new kit and advertised that they would build a 150-mph 1960 Ford stock car, complete and ready to race for $4,995. What a deal! The Daytona 500 proved otherwise. Of 32 Fords entered, 28 made the starting lineup, most dropped out, and not one came close to winning. The iron-block FE-series 352-ci engine just wasn't durable enough or powerful enough to compete with the proven Pontiacs and Chevrolets.

After the 1959 season, Paul Spaulding retired and Junior Johnson had no ride. Just a week before the Daytona 500, Ray Fox got a visit from John Masoni, who owned the Daytona Beach Kennel Club dog-racing track located next door to the Speedway. He had a car and wanted to race. With so little time, Ray declined. Undeterred, Masoni offered to double the money that Fox received to prepare and race the car. It proved to be a history-making move.

Fox took on the challenge, gathered up his crew from his shop, and called Junior. During testing, Masoni's old '59 was just a smidgen off the pace of Smokey's Pontiac in the hands of Fireball Roberts – about 30 mph! Fox gave the car some more tweaks, and Junior was about ready to hang it up when he discovered something. Cotton Owens was in a Pontiac when Junior happened to nose in right behind him. The two cars rolled on as one with Junior running as fast as the Pontiac! He had discovered a secret that no one knew about, not even Ray Fox, who thought he had stumbled onto something. In fact, it was physics. The aerodynamic envelop of the bigger Pontiac kept the underpowered Chevrolet tucked in its draft; the slower car could keep up with the faster car and didn't require as much fuel. Junior started thinking that he could win the Daytona 500 at Pontiac speed with Chevrolet fuel economy. In the first 100-mile qualifier, Roberts and Owens posted a one-two win, followed by Ford's top entries, Fred Lorenzen and Joe Weatherly. Junior came in fifth, going faster than anyone imagined. In the second qualifier, the Pontiacs of Jack Smith and Bobby Johns led three new Chevrolets. Then, in the wreck-strewn 500-mile race, Junior emerged victorious just as he planned, adding another chapter to his growing legend as the man who could win driving anything.

The new super tracks, secret factory backing, intense driver rivalries, tens of thousands of young fans packing the stands, burgeoning press and radio coverage, and a fast-growing TV audience brought stock-car racing to a new level in 1960. When CBS broadcast its "Sports Spectacular" live from the Daytona International Speedway, the big time had come to the "good ol' boys." Plenty of short-track and dirt-track racing still went on, comprising most of the NASCAR schedule, but the exciting image of 150-mph Grand National stock cars roaring around massive thunder domes was now in the public eye.

So began NASCAR's wildest decade.

CHAPTER THREE

During the 1961 Dixie 400 in Atlanta, #28 Fred Lorenzen got together with #90 Dave Mader. Neither finished the race. (Photo courtesy International Motorsports Hall of Fame)

1961: An Explosion of Speed

During 1961, the '50s era of homebuilt hot rods and garage stockers exploded because of one factor: the introduction of 400-plus-cubic-inch engines. These new engines were, in fact, little changed from previous hardware, but going from 389 to 421 (Pontiac), 348 to 409 (Chevy), and 383 to 413 (Chrysler) had an enormous psychological impact on the emerging youth market. Ford didn't hit 400 ci, but its 390 reached 401 hp. Southern California-style hot rodding had changed; any one could get a factory-built hot rod right out of the showroom for no more than a down payment. That trend revolutionized the industry and put teenagers behind the wheels of the fastest production cars yet seen on America's highways. Aftermarket speed merchants were quick to follow Detroit with equipment to enhance the perfor-mance of any stock engine, and they flourished. Sophisticated hot-rodder tricks spread across the country into every speed shop in the nation.

The ultimate hot rods of the time, AA/Dragsters, topped 177 mph in a quarter-mile that year (Dode Martin, Carlsbad, California in his Chevrolet-powered dual-small-block dragster), while elapsed times dropped to nearly 8.5 seconds ("Sneaky" Pete Robinson, Atlanta, Georgia, also with Chevy power). Stockers were running similar top speeds during 500 miles on high-banked Southern ovals, and the fans loved all of it. Speed was king, and Detroit's new iron turned up the heat several notches.

Pontiac was still the big gun in '61. Rumors of optional high-performance engines with over 400 ci became reality early in the year when the new Pontiac 421 was released. Like the 389 before it, the 421 boasted an array of heavy-duty equipment, available across the counter at any Pontiac dealer, that was the best in the industry. Along with high-performance parts came technical information designed for one purpose: to win races, any race. The kids marveled at the factory hardware and packed into all sorts of racetracks. Since local drag strips held events every Sunday afternoon, while NASCAR races were just twice a year at any one

Young Richard Petty did some of his own mechanic work, here overseen by a stern observer.

NASCAR'S WILD YEARS

track, drag racing received lots more participation that inspired intense tinkering and tuning. Unlike stock-car racing, drag racing spoke directly to hotshoes who wanted to go faster and quicker than ever before, and also unlike stock-car racing, a small fee bought a pit pass at drag strips, so anyone could get up close to the cars and talk to the drivers, too.

On the grassroots level, drag racing was the true enthusiast's sport in America. On quarter-mile asphalt strips all across the nation, drivers tested their down payments and became racers in powerful Super Stocks. New-car showrooms made it possible, proving to manufacturers that "win on Sunday, sell on Monday" was very real for straight-liners as well as the go-rounders. GM was after the youthful performance segment of the market. Pontiac was king of the big tracks in stock-car racing, and Pontiac led the new wave of Factory Experimental (F/X) and Super Stock (S/S) cars in drag racing. The war dance of the Indian generated lots of excitement, driving Pontiac sales up 16 percent in 1960, down 14 percent in '61, then up 35 percent in 1962.

Big-inch engines were fitted into smaller cars. The new engines and the factory experimental cars they powered drew enormous crowds to drag races everywhere and brought about the spectacular rise of the Super Stocks.

Pontiac's 421 was the big daddy of Super Stocks in '61. Pontiac offered more high-performance hardware than any other manufacturer. By simply increasing the bore of the 389 from 4.063 to 4.093 in, and lengthening the stroke 0.125 in, the resulting 421 gained 33 ci and 72 hp in factory rating. The highest-output 389 was 333 hp, while the first-generation 421 went to 373 hp, and then to 405 hp in '62. The 421 was rumored to make 460 hp in stock-car trim. The hot version of the 421 came factory-installed, while replacement parts were required to bump the 389 into its hottest form. The engines were the same dimensions and same weight, thus wherever a Super Duty 389 fit, the Super Duty 421 fit as well.

The Tempest sold well overall, 100,783 units in six models, but the 4-banger didn't. The car was larger than today's compacts, yet smaller than full-size cars, and fit what buyers wanted. They came back for 143,193 more in '62. The first Tempest V-8 was the all-aluminum 215-ci engine shared with Oldsmobile and Buick. In 1963, the reduced-bore version of the 389, the cast-iron 326-ci V-8, became optional. Where the 326 fit, so did the 421, and so the F/X Tempest was born. Adding a 389 produced the sensational GTO, introduced in late 1963.

The factory bought its forged-aluminum pistons from Mickey Thompson Enterprises, and Thompson was one of the first to see the potential of the high-powered Tempest in drag racing. The Tempest used the factory's cast-aluminum headers and the second-generation Super Duty head expressly for the 421 (with new 2.02-in intake valves versus the previous 1.92 inchers). The Tempest developed a hot temper and was bad to the bone.

Drag racers could build a variety of cars from the growing assortment of heavy-duty parts bought from manufacturers, so NHRA(National Hor Rod Association) invented a class for them, Factory Experimental. Classes were broken down by displacement-to-weight ratios: A/FX cars were up to 8.99 lbs per ci (7.5 lbs minimum), B/FX were cars from 9 to 12.99 lbs per ci, and C/FX class cars were over 13 lbs per ci. When the FX cars invaded drag strips, young people came in droves. In A/FX, Mickey Thompson's 421 Tempest was followed by fellow Californians Jim Nelson and Dode Martin, who dropped a 413-ci Ramcharger into a Dodge Lancer. They raced their *Golden Lancer* to sensational wins. Ace Wilson and his 421-powered Royal Tempest from Michigan was another pioneer of the class.

Experimental equipment on Chevrolet's 409 put the Super Super/Stock (SS/S) class cars into B/FX. Don Nicholson and Dave Strickler turned 12.93-second passes in B/FX and 12.97 in SS/S in their 409 Chevys, and the crowds went wild. The top-running Stock-class cars qualified for several other classes and pushed popularity of the Super Stocks even further, and the 421 A/FX Tempest stood at the top of the heap.

Anywhere cars gathered, speed came, too, and aftermarket speed merchants satisfied the voracious appetite of the "new" market with a steady diet of more power and more speed. Much of the movement was driven by enthusiastic kids just coming to driving age at a time when the new-car market dropped big-time. GM sales in '61 were down over 13 percent across the board. Ford was down 11 percent. Chrysler took a beating with sales dipping 37 percent. Since new-car sales were the sources of advertising and engineering funds to support factory racing, what little there was in budgets was reduced considerably. Still, the NASCAR schedule had eight major superspeedway races that year receiving wider and wider media coverage, and the show went on, bigger and better than ever before.

Budget cuts meant tough times at race shops specializing in building the heavy-duty equipment for stock-car racing. Even though stock cars looked like showroom models, they were, in fact, highly modified under the sheetmetal with specialty equipment far stronger than stock pieces. Greater safety was an important cause; if something broke and a car careened into the crowd at high speed, the catastrophe would probably be the end of racing. Not only were the factory men concerned, but also track owners, promoters, car owners, drivers, and suppliers – everyone recognized the importance of keeping cars away from spectators.

One major safety item was the "full-floater" rear ends, or the safety hub. The idea was to have the rear-end housing and hubs support the weight of the car, rather than the axle bearings, which had long been the practice in racing. However, because of the low stresses and mild side loads encountered in everyday driving, manufacturers designed their cars with axles running in a single row of bearings to carry the load. For stock-car racers, full-floating rear axle assemblies from the differential housing to the axle

1961: AN EXPLOSION OF SPEED

Glen Wood went from driving for his brother's team to joining them in building a NASCAR dynasty that fielded top cars and top drivers into the next century. (Glen Wood photo)

housings to the hubs carried the load of the car, freeing the axles to turn the drive wheels. Full floaters achieved the quadruple purpose of preventing a car from careening wildly at high speed when an axle broke; providing much more durable load points with beefier hardware; making removal and replacement of an axle far easier; and making it easy to remove axles so that a car could be towed without the ring and pinion turning. Back in 1961, being able to tow the racers was important because there were none of today's massive trailer/haulers outfitted with living quarters and a machine shop. Few teams even trailered their cars, preferring the low cost of towing.

How did full floaters work? The splined end of the axle in the differential was driven by the ring gear assembly. It applied torque to the drive wheel through the outer hub carrier by means of an axle plate with holes that matched the five-bolt lug pattern. The axle was held in place laterally by this plate being sandwiched between the wheel and hub. Simply removing the wheel and pulling the axle plate from the lug bolts extracted the axle. With the axles out and the wheels on, the car was ready to be towed without the driveline turning at all. Reinstalling the axle was just as easy.

Race shops modified stock rear ends for about $300, making a full floater expensive, but they were good insurance against the cost of crashing a car or, worse, crashing into spectators. NASCAR had made such equipment mandatory the previous year.

Racing at the scorching speeds achieved on Daytona's big tri-oval was new to most drivers. Junior Johnson won the 500 the year before in a low-powered car due in good measure to his ability to avoid the flying debris and twisted hulks of crashed cars. Going 150 mph wasn't new to Junior – he often ran faster than that during late-night moonshine runs. So many of the 68 cars in the starting field were damaged that NASCAR was forced to cancel the next two races because there weren't enough cars to race.

When the Charlotte Motor Speedway, built by Curtis Turner and Charlotte auto dealer Bruton Smith, wasn't ready for the first World 600 in May 1961, the race was rescheduled for mid-June. Unfortunately, the asphalt had insufficient time to cure and came apart on race day. During testing and qualifying, cars threw up chunks of the track, and teams installed grill screens and windshield deflectors to ward off the debris as best they could. Early in the race, Junior hit a pothole, blew a tire, and crashed into what was to be the victory platform. Later, after race officials let the race finish, he was disqualified for the same reason that the Pettys were, driving on the dirt, and Joe Lee Johnson (no relation to Junior) of Chattanooga, Tennessee, won the race in a Chevrolet.

NASCAR let the cars run, then disqualified them and refused payment due to disqualification. That rubbed a lot of drivers and teams the wrong way and intensified the growing rift between track owner/promoters and owner/drivers who claimed that officials did anything to make a buck at the expense of owners and drivers. Turner took to carrying a pistol, and began circulating the idea of unionizing the drivers.

Fred and Rex Lovette of Wilkes County, North Carolina, stepped into the NASCAR scene. They were the men behind Holly Farms, and along with many local investors, they had seen their poultry company grow as fried chicken went from Sunday dinner to nightly fare. Along the way, they pulled the county out of the economic doldrums of the 1950s that kept the moonshine business going. The Lovettes put neighbors in business raising and processing chickens, driving trucks delivering feed and hauling chickens, growing grain and making feed, and working railway feed mills. Even the chicken litter gradually turned the hardscrabble red clay of the county into rich farmland. The Holly Farms racing team, with Junior as builder-driver, received factory backing through local Pontiac dealerships. They emerged in 1961 among the top teams. The crew chief was Crawford Clements, brother of Louie Clements, who was crew chief for Rex White. Fred Johnson, Junior's brother, was in the racing business now and also left the "likker business" behind, sort of.

At Daytona during the first 100-mile qualifier, Junior and Fireball Roberts were fender-to-fender for the lead on the 40th and final lap when a sharp piece of metal on the track cut one of Junior's front tires. Junior's brand, new No. 27 Pontiac spun and collided with Richard Petty's brand, new No. 43 Plymouth,

CHAPTER THREE

wheel broke it, sending it into the windshield. Blood spurted out of his chin, and Junior thought his throat was cut. Climbing out, the first person to come along was "Big Bill" France in his new Buick with a white interior. When Junior told France to take him to the field hospital, France refused, saying that he'd get blood all over his new car. Junior demanded and France relented. Off they went to get stitches in Junior's chin, and France had a job cleaning the blood off the upholstery.

The Pontiacs rolled big-time during both of the 100-mile qualifiers, taking the top three positions in both. Fireball Roberts set a record pole at 155.709 mph in the first race, while Joe Weatherly won the second round at 154.122 mph. Back at the wheel of another Pontiac for the Daytona 500, starting 43rd, Junior added to the clear superiority of Pontiac power by blazing to the front in only 33 laps of green-flag racing. He led a second time during laps 40 to 42, but hot-dog wrappers from the stands floated onto the track and plastered themselves to his grill. His engine overheated and expired; he was out after just 45 laps.

For 1961, "old" cars ruled the Daytona 500 again. At the finish, Marvin Panch and Joe Weatherly roared to a one-two finish driving year-old Pontiacs, and Panch posted the fastest average over 500 miles ever seen in stock-car racing, 149.60 mph. Paul Goldsmith rounded out a Pontiac one-two-three.

With Poncho power under his right foot, Junior went on to win seven Grand National races that year, with 9 top-fives and 22 top-10 finishes, to gather up sixth in the championship points race. Pontiac drivers took 30 of NASCAR's 52 races, surpassing all previous win records. Pontiac was king.

At Martinsville at the end of April, Junior and Rex Lovette schemed to talk by radio with each other while Junior was on the track. Lovette's Holly Farms truck drivers used radios when picking up chickens, and the notion of in-car communications while racing seemed like a good idea. It worked – they were the first known to use such equipment in NASCAR. But as Junior lengthened his lead over the field, Lovette was on the radio yelling at him to slow down to conserve the car. Junior became annoyed and decided that the radio wasn't such a good idea and turned it off. During a late pit stop, Lovette made his point by brandishing a big hammer at Junior who just smiled and patted the top of his helmet, a pre-arranged signal, indicating that his radio wasn't working. He went on to win the race.

Remember Richard Petty going over the wall? The Petty team had a tough time and neither of their cars made it into the 500. Not only did Richard exit the first qualifier with his new Plymouth destroyed, he had glass shards in his eyes and was hobbled by a twisted ankle. While he was leaving the field infirmary after having the glass removed, the white flag was flying for the second qualifier. Then a deafening crash was heard. Lee Petty's Plymouth and Johnny Beauchamp's Chevrolet had tangled and gone over the wall. Lee was not as fortunate as his son. He was near death, and was transported to a local hospital where a mem-

Ned Jarrett ran a points race in 1961, while 1960 Grand National Champion Rex White ran for wins. White won over $15,000 more during the season with seven wins in his Chevrolet, while Jarrett's single victory was a minor 100-miler. Neither driver ran the full schedule of 52 races, White running 47 to Jarrett's 46, and as the season neared the finale, Jarrett nudged ahead of White to take the title by about the total of one race. (Ford photo)

sending it into the outer railing of turn one. Petty went airborne over the railing and into the parking lot below. Junior hit the railing, knocked down a string of posts, then spun down the track and across the apron, coming to a stop by the inside railing. Unbuckling his harness and removing his helmet, he started climbing out just as another car careened toward him. Junior quickly pulled himself back into the car and grabbed the steering wheel. The car hit with a horrendous impact that buckled the driver's side front tire almost back to Junior's feet and shoved the engine into the interior. His grasp of the steering

1961: AN EXPLOSION OF SPEED

ber of the Petty family stayed with him around the clock. His long hospital stay and recovery marked the end of his competitive racing career. Richard and his brother Maurice returned home faced with soldiering on in their father's absence with their new cars in twisted heaps.

The redesigned 1961 Plymouths were a styling and sales disaster. Sales dropped almost 64,300 units, down 37 percent from the previous year. Plymouth stylists' half-decade affair with rear fins ended in 1960. Fins were eliminated entirely on 1961 models that accentuated sculpting around the headlights and tail lights and along the sides. The new styling was rejected by the public. With sales down so drastically, the cost of fielding a racing team was questioned. Further, the changed body was unlike anything on the previous year's stockers and required completely new racecars. Whether or not the fins were stabilizing components of the previous aerodynamic shape remained a question, but the new cars were unstable at superspeedway speeds.

High-speed stability, the ability to stick to the track, and durability were goals of every builder. To achieve success required a lot of testing to properly dial in a car. Now the decision-maker in the Petty organization, Richard took the reins. He had to put a new car on the track, and hurriedly prepared another car to race, but no longer as part of a two-car team. In 41 starts in the 52-race schedule, Richard won just two races that year, backed by 18 top-5 finishes and 23 top-10s to end the season a distant eighth in the points. The Chevrolets of Ned Jarrett and Rex White swept the championship one-two, and there wasn't a Ford in sight.

Although Ford drivers won more races than any other make in 1960 with 15, those short-track and dirt wins simply didn't resonate in the marketplace. Dropping to third on the major win list in 1961 behind Pontiac (30 wins) and Chevrolet (11) meant that Fords were also-rans.

During 1961, the "big-3" made optional high-performance engines available primarily for advertising purposes gained from stock-car racing. Chevrolet's 409, rated at 360 hp, was simply the 348 casting with 4-5/16-in bores rather than 4-1/8-in, and with the sides of the main-bearing webs machined to clear the thicker, heavier counterweights of the new 1/4-inch longer stroke crankshaft. Heads were also machined from 348 castings. While the 1960 348 was the powerplant of the Grand National champion, the 409 succeeded in winning only one race in 1961. (Chevrolet photo)

Somebody at Ford had to decide to get in or get out, but no one seemed able to make that commitment, and Holman Moody was about to slip away. The door of the Holman Moody shop in Charlotte stayed open in 1961 (and the year before) only by taking on any job that came along, such as campaigning a team of Studebaker Larks in compact races. Only Autolite, yet to be purchased by Ford Motor Company as its spark-plug division, was willing to put any significant money into racing. As Holman Moody's principal sponsor, Autolite racing manager Fran Hernandez broached the idea late in 1960 of racing an Autolite Dodge in the 1961 NASCAR season.

Fred Lorenzen was a two-time (1958 and 1959) USAC stock-car champion, but trying to campaign his own NASCAR team on a shoestring with a 1960 Ford produced only 10 starts that year. His season began well enough. He placed third in the first 100-mile qualifier behind the Pontiacs of Fireball Roberts and Cotton Owens, and he finished the 500 in eighth, two laps down. The Pontiacs and Chevrolets were too much to handle during the remainder of the season. The year was so fruitless and exasperating that he sold his rig and returned home to be a carpenter with his brother. By Christmas, he had hung up his helmet.

Back in Charlotte, John Holman and Ralph Moody thought the idea of racing a Dodge might work. Their future with Ford looked bleak, and Plymouth had a long-term contract backing the Pettys, but Dodge had won only one race in four years. Dodge was, however, flush with money from its huge sales year in 1960, which more than doubled its 1959 sales. The prospect of good terms and year-to-year factory financing meant that Holman Moody could make Dodge a top competitor and be off Ford's on-again, off-again yo-yo. Moody called Lorenzen on Christmas Eve and offered him the drive. What better present could an aspiring driver receive?

Handsome Freddie was not only thrilled with the offer, he was amazed that Holman wanted him, a Yankee, over all the

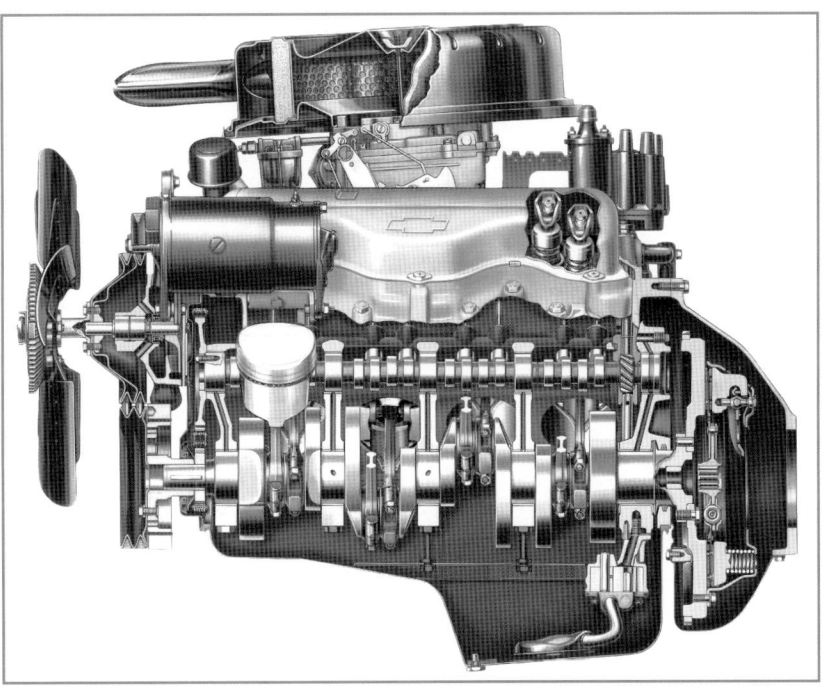

CHAPTER THREE

Above, right and next page: 1961 marked the fading of the finned era and the emergence of performance. Ford's top engine, the 390-ci Tri-Power rated at 401 hp topped Chevrolet's new 409 rated at 360 hp, making a combination of elegance and performance that drew buyers to Ford. In a down year from the previous two years, Ford sales drooped 166,000 units, while Chevrolet lost 413,000 units. Ford's fashionably low and sleek Starliner Coupe was as close to bullet shaped as any car had come.

Southern drivers who had become the stars of NASCAR. Actually, they were all committed: Rex White with Chevrolet; Ned Jarrett jumping from Ford to Chevy; Fireball Roberts with Smokey Yunick and Pontiac; Junior Johnson, Bobby Johns, Buck Baker, Emanuel Zervakis, Jim Paschal, and Edwin "Banjo" Mathews in Pontiacs; and Richard Petty with Plymouth accounted for the top 10 drivers of 1960, all with rides in 1961. But why Fred Lorenzen from Elmhurst, Illinois?

Just 26 years old, Lorenzen was a Ford man, and he was a good driver who was smart and worked hard. He had learned the ropes the hard way, and he was unsigned late in the season when other teams were already testing. Of course he would drive.

Word of the Dodge deal got to Jacques Passino, the newly appointed manager of Ford's fledgling special vehicles program. He acted swiftly to assure Holman that funding was on the way, though he couldn't say when.

Henry Ford II made it happen; the boss saw what was going on and had already taken action. Just before the 1961 Atlanta 500, Henry was in town to meet with southeast region dealers who clamored for Ford's return to racing. Their sales spoke clearly: GM dealers were eating their lunch, and Ford had nothing high-performance to offer. The boss told them that Ford was getting

1961: AN EXPLOSION OF SPEED

back in, and a public announcement a little later referred to the 1957 AMA resolution in part saying:

"...Ford Motor Company feels that the resolution has come to have neither purpose nor effect. Accordingly, we have notified the board of directors of the Automobile Manufacturers Association that we feel we can better establish our own standards of conduct with respect to the manner in which the performance of our vehicles is to be promoted and advertised."

What that meant was what Passino sold to Holman. Ford planned to introduce a new engine in the fall for '62 models, a 406-ci version of the high-performance 390. Factory-rated at 405 hp, it was sure to crank out more than 430 hp with a single 4-bbl carburetor in speedway tune. Further enticement came in the form of a tough new 4-speed transmission. The combination showed that Ford was, ever so slowly, responding to the needs of the high-performance market and racing. More factory effort was being directed toward racing on all fronts, though it still amounted to just crumbs as of midyear.

Passino put Holman in a dilemma – should he get on the Dodge wagon or the Ford wagon? Neither was a sure thing, and throughout the 1961 season, Ford offered little more than promises. The Autolite Dodge deal looked like a top-five package that would, no doubt, lead to deeper factory support after a few wins. But being a longtime Ford man, Holman decided to stay with the promises from Dearborn, and Lorenzen stayed as his driver.

Ford's 1961 stock-car season was dismal, but the Ford men learned a lot, such as Pontiac engines that were fitted with all sorts of illegal parts but NASCAR accepted anyway. The promoters had learned that fan appetite for racing put big dollars into their pockets, and bending the rules to put on a good show drew ever larger crowds. It was just too bad that the Fords weren't fast enough to keep up with the Pontiacs, Chevrolets, and Plymouths. Fan support for favorite drivers increased, almost equaling the fans' admiration for the cars. After all, the Pontiacs had pushed the average speed of the Daytona 500 past the Indianapolis 500, making it the fastest 500 miles on earth.

Then at the end of the season, outside events had a major effect inside corporate Ford. In November, a new United States president, John F. Kennedy, was elected, and he chose Robert F. McNamara to be his Secretary of Defense. McNamara left his office at Ford in January 1962, causing a reshuffling of decision makers, but Henry Ford II was still the top man. The helm of the Ford Division passed over a host of top managers and fell to a young and dynamic Lee Iacocca, who had sailed up the ranks from top Ford salesman in the country to corporate manager before his 36th birthday. Iacocca took the helm of the Ford Division in November and inherited a host of problems. One was the Cardinal, which he thought was the wrong way to capture the youth market. Another was flagging sales, and a third was what to do about racing. The kids were his answer to all three.

Iacocca wanted a new theme for Ford, something exciting that would fire interest in Ford cars again and bring back the kids. "Win on Sunday, sell on Monday" clearly resonated in Pontiac and Chevrolet sales, and he decided that if Ford was to get into the "sell on Monday" part, then Fords had to "win on Sunday." Rumblings of sweeping changes came from his office as racing and engineering excellence proven in competition became Ford's new theme. "Competition Proven" was soon emblazoned on the fenders of Holman Moody cars.

There was nothing better than racing for generating excitement. And that Cardinal...it had to go, but something exciting for the kids had to replace it. Big changes were on the way.

CHAPTER FOUR

Chevrolet promotional photo was part of the make's "See the USA, in your Chevrolet" advertising theme directed at young buyers. (Chevrolet photo)

1962: The Big-Inch Rumble

Ford's sleek '61 Starliner was about as close to bullet-shaped as any car had come, but its lack of power – 375 hp from 390 ci, compared to Pontiac's 405-hp 421 – kept it from becoming a NASCAR threat that year. It sold well, contributing to a total of 710,392 big Fords sold in 1961. Like all new models, the new-for-'62 Ford styling first shown to the public in the fall of '61 showed no vestige of fins but more roundedness on both ends. Buyers drove away with 722,642 Galaxies that year, compared to 1,495,476 Chevrolets, 244,391 Pontiacs, 401,674 Plymouths, and 251,722 Dodges. Many Ford buyers opted for the new 405-hp 406 with three 2-bbl carbs. Like Pontiac's Tri-Power cars, similarly equipped Fords could sip along on the center 2-bbl when cruising, then unleash massive acceleration of big cubic inches on all six barrels.

The kids loved the idea of Tri-Power but a dual-quad setup was the real eye-popper and an even better performer. Drag-racing equipment from the Big Three included new high-performance cams, cast headers, a choice of rear-end drive ratios, close-ratio or wide-ratio transmissions, and that ever-so-popular 4-on-the-floor shifter, and all of it could be bought right off the showroom floor. For the strip, Ford engineers came up with a special nine-piece body kit of fiberglass components, mostly for the front end of the Galaxie, that dropped weight 164 pounds. The factory ET (elapsed time) wars began with one trick car after another. For oval tracks, the Ford men came up with the Starlift, a "fastback" top sleeker than stock that could be bolted on for sedan races or removed for convertible races. The factory high-speed war ratcheted up another notch.

While the lightweights from Ford and other manufacturers were show-cased in drag racing, howls of protest from non-Ford stock-car competitors, said it wasn't a

What the kids wanted was this kind of Chevrolet, a romping, stomping 409 made famous on drag strips around the country and from every juke box and AM radio station that belted out the Beach Boys' hit, "She's real fine, my 409…"

Far more 409s made the drag scene than stock-car racing, and for no more than a down payment, any hotshoe had a hard-running Super Stock. (Gold Dust Classics photo)

convertible because it didn't have the central crossmember in the frame (which would have added considerably more weight): NASCAR banned the Starlift. Bill France and NASCAR stuck to the always-evolving rules, saying strictly stock was strictly that, and if it isn't available to the public, it isn't allowed to run. Ford had promo literature showing the Starlift as an option and even had a car in an Atlanta showroom, although it was a one-off ploy to get lighter cars approved by NASCAR.

However, bending the strictly-stock rule meant drawing more spectators. But it didn't work out that way for Ford; the Starlift option showed up in April and was banned in May.

Ford was closer to matching archrival Chevrolet in performance, but the 8-bbl 409 with a hot Duntov cam sent a lot of Fords home early from drag strips all across the country. Along with Pontiac, GM provided stepped-up performance that left Ford lacking once again, but Dearborn was closer than the year before.

Cars with small badges on their flanks denoting engine displacement drove the kids crazy and created intense rivalries. The 1950s-era hot rods fell from favor as every kid dreamed of driving a hot new 409, 406, or 413. Lee Iacocca, the new Ford Division boss, wanted them in Fords, and he had lots of ideas.

Iacocca came up from selling cars, so he knew what excited the kids – anything with big numbers, or any race winner, since it was talked about right up to the next race. He also recognized that the kids really liked smaller cars that went fast, cars like the stunning XK-E Jaguar. If not the Jag, a powerful Corvette would do – both of them the sort of car that Ford didn't have. Getting into that market required putting Ford's models and marketing in order, and Iacocca set about doing just that.

Ford's team of six racing engineers, led by A.J. "Gus" Scussel, was the beginning of Special Vehicle Operations. The team concluded that Ford's limited re-entry into stock-car racing was not

1962: THE BIG-INCH RUMBLE

Ford's 405-hp 406-ci engine required considerable beefing of the main-bearing webs and cross-bolting of the caps to stay together. This 3-2-bbl ad photo was for the drag racers and the kids who could order this powerful engine as an option. (Ford photo)

world championship racing – never before had any manufacturer jumped into racing so thoroughly, just because the boss initiated a new company image. Iacocca came up with Ford's new corporate motto, "Total Performance," and he backed it with expectations of winning, not just here or there, but everywhere and everything worth winning! He was determined to make Ford the kid's choice, and he had the boss's support.

It was a tough beginning. The new spirit at Ford came to Holman Moody in the form of new cars. Unfortunately they came well after the other race teams got their new equipment, and losses soon proved just how far behind Ford was. Then, NASCAR threw another rules curve by outlawing the Starlift after just one race. The Pontiacs and Chevrolets were faster than ever, and to get some edge, California ace driver Dan Gurney was signed on to campaign a Holman Moody Ford in selected races. By midseason, the Fords improved a little.

Pontiacs rolled in 1962, reigning NASCAR and USAC champions, and the Smokey Yunick Pontiacs raised the bar further when Fireball Roberts took Smokey's black-and-gold ride to a new Daytona 500 speed record for the third year in a row, 158.744 mph in the first qualifier. He then bettered his own 500-mile record by winning the race at 152.529 mph, 27.8 mph faster than Junior Johnson's 1960 win. Roberts drove Yunick's Pontiac to sweeping victories in both of the Daytona races that year.

Up to mid-race, Junior Johnson and Roberts swapped the lead back and forth, making the Daytona 500 a Pontiac shootout, but when Junior left the race, Richard Petty moved up to lead 17 out of the final 50 laps. Roberts led the rest. Even the previously unthreatening Plymouth was faster and more durable than the Fords, which blew their engines due to over-stressed blocks from the punishment of flat-out racing.

The Ford men set to solving the problems of lack of power and durability. By midseason, the 406 block received a beefed-up bottom

working. Furthermore, Iacocca recognized that the Cardinal was the wrong car for the emerging youth market. Unfortunately, it was already in the works, and changing the momentum of a corporation once it was committed was a formidable undertaking because of costs already incurred. Iacocca had to kill the Cardinal by offering a better idea. In the beginning of 1962, Iacocca organized a committee to invent a new car for the kids. When the Mustang debuted on March 17, 1964, it was an instant success. It sold more than any car before except Henry Ford's Model T. The Mustang was definitely a better idea.

Ford exploded onto the racing scene in 1962. Drag racing, road racing, stock-car racing, Indy racing, off-road racing, and

CHAPTER FOUR

Pontiacs took the green at Daytona and roared off to lead all the way to the checkered flag. Not only were their 405-hp Super Duty 421 engines the most powerful in the starting lineup, the entire car, whoever built it, was a 500-mile brute that gave no quarter to competitors. Fireball Roberts, Joe Weatherly, Junior Johnson, and Cotton Owens, all in 1962 Pontiacs, dominated the race, with Richard Petty the only non-Pontiac to lead. Roberts was out front the last 50 laps to set a new 500-mile speed record. (Ford photo)

end with heavy-duty bolts from outside the skirt just above the pan rail into the main-bearing web bosses of the 2, 3, and 4 journals. The cracking that sidelined the Fords at Daytona ceased, but the engine was still down on power. Even so, Ford took its first sweep, one-two-three at Darlington in the Rebel 300, but the fact that Roberts crashed his Pontiac on the second lap was a factor. By the Labor Day Southern 500, Fords had proved little, and the Pontiacs of Roberts, Joe Weatherly, and other Pontiac drivers were unstoppable.

Early in the season, the Holly Farms team announced that it would race a limited schedule, mostly at tracks in Holly Farms sales areas, but Johnson was still a threat driving for other teams. His best race that year was in the Southern 500. Late in the race, he moved to pass Richard Petty, who blew a tire, and Johnson was flagged the winner. But NASCAR withdrew that victory several hours after the race as protests caused a lap recount. Johnson was actually second to Larry Frank in a private-entry Ford that limped across the line with a flat and its suspension broken. Frank was a local driver who'd never won anything of consequence, and here he was not only taking Darlington's crown, he gave Ford its only major win of the year.

Junior was certain that he was leading at the flag and commented later that he could easily have passed Frank had he known he was scored one lap down. Then, in the National 400 at Charlotte, Junior was behind the wheel of Ray Fox's Daytona Beach Kennel Club Pontiac and easily scored his only win that year, dominating by leading 204 of the 267 laps.

For 1962 models, Plymouth planners paid attention to growing public interest in smaller cars. They saw sales recover from

1962: THE BIG-INCH RUMBLE

Smokey Yunick, shown here with Jim Hall of Chaparral Racing, proved his factory connection had the inside lane to the best equipment from the Big-3.

the previous year's disaster by offering smaller new cars with a totally new design. Big-car styling was scaled up from the Valiant with its long-hood, short-rear-deck concept that would become the norm later during the 1960s pony-car era. The surge in Valiant sales looked to match full-size Plymouth sales by year's end. The new Plymouth rode on an 8-inch-shorter wheelbase, 116 in, and dropped almost 600 lbs. For drag racing, the new, lighter Plymouth and Dodge were sensational with their new 413-ci version of Chrysler's "B" engine. But with Pontiac's stock-car 421 cranking out at least 465 hp, the Chrysler cars were 30 to 45 hp down for oval track racing.

A year after Lee Petty's near-fatal crash at Daytona, he was on the slow road to recovery while Richard and Maurice handled the helm of Petty Engineering. They were also on a slow road to recovery because of such drastic year-to-year changes in their Plymouths. Once again, they had to build all-new cars while campaigning their year-old cars in early 1962 season races, as the new season actually began late in 1961. They chose the Savoy, a 2-door post sedan, not the Fury. The Savoy had little sex appeal in the youth market, and in stock-car racing, Plymouth and Dodge were at the bottom of the HP heap, but Richard had learned the lesson of drafting well. When tucked in behind Roberts' blazing Pontiac, his lowly Plymouth wasn't so

lowly after all. In the Daytona 500, he revisited Junior's method from 1960, staying near the front, actually leading on four occasions, and then finishing second overall to take home $10,250.

The Petty Plymouth team was back to two, sometimes three cars, with number 42 most often driven by veteran Jim Paschal, who won four races that year, three in Petty Plymouths. Lee returned to the cockpit for the final laps of his career. He started the Martinsville 250 in April but removed himself early on to let Paschal drive. Richard rolled up a string of second-place finishes throughout the season and put the Petty-blue Savoy in the winner's circle in the North Wilkesboro 400 in April, the first of eight wins that year. Plymouth power in the smaller Savoy was proving a point that would be revisited a few years later when NASCAR went to midsize cars. But during 1962, the combination of driving talent, excellent set-up, and lighter weight made for tough competition on smaller tracks, as shown at Greenville, South Carolina, where Richard won by three laps in the 200-lap feature. For the Southeastern 500 on Bristol, Tennessee's tight oval, the Petty team fielded three cars with Paschal taking the win over Holman Moody's top driver, Fred Lorenzen. Richard ran a close third, while the No. 41 Plymouth driven by Bunkie Blackburn, who had finished 13th at Daytona in a Petty Savoy, rolled in eighth.

Richard looked to be on his way to his first Grand National Championship season, especially when he won three in a row late in the season, but those Pontiacs... Joe Weatherly was the Indian's top gun, racking up nine wins with an amazing 45 top-10 finishes in the 53-race schedule. He tallied 2,396 points more than Richard, who had competed in every event in NASCAR's first $1,000,000 season.

Chevrolet's 1962 409 was significantly improved from the bored and stroked 348 of the previous year. Although displacing the same 409 ci, the '62 version didn't run out of breath at high RPM like the earlier engine. Heads on the new 409 received larger ports, which were raised 1/4 in, and intake valve diameter was increased from 2.066 in to 2.203 in. Exhaust valves went to 1.734 in from 1.72. On drag strips, either engine made a tough Super Stocker, but on the high banks, lack of torque at high RPM was a severe handicap for the earlier engine that was significantly improved in '62. But it was still lacking.

All 409 and 348 blocks were the same except for extra clearance provided in the 409, which got its increased displacement from a 3/16-in-larger bore diameter (to 4-5/16 in) and 1/4-in-longer stroke (to 3-1/2 in). Factory rated at 409 hp at 6,000 rpm with torque of 420 ft-lbs at 4,000 rpm, the dual-quad 409 was tough to beat on the street or strip. Single 4-bbl engines were rated at 380 hp. The 1962 engine came in two versions, early and late. The wedge-shaped combustion chamber in the early engines was at least 90.15 cc, giving a maximum compression ratio of 10.3:1, well under the factory-advertised 11.25:1.

CHAPTER FOUR

Fred Lorenzen, Holman Moody lead driver, could not repeat his 1961 Rebel 300 win at Darlington, but teammate Nelson Stacy rolled across the finish line victorious in the last NASCAR convertible race, then took the World 600 at Charlotte two weeks later in a sedan. Larry Frank won the Southern 500 in his only victory capping Ford's paltry six wins that year. Things would change in 1963. (Tom Kirkland photo)

Rex White wheeled his Chevrolet to a last-lap duel with Joe Weatherly's Bud Moore Pontiac to score the 409's only victory, the Dixie 400 at Atlanta. (Rex White Collection photo)

The shape of the top of the piston contributed to the combustion chamber volume, and early pistons were milled to a plane across half of the top to provide valve clearance, while the crown of later pistons was milled only for intake-valve relief. Combustion chamber volume was also decreased to 83.55 cc for the later engines, giving a maximum compression ratio of 11.04:1. For showroom models, the compression ratio was reduced during factory assembly by using two head gaskets to produce 91-cc combustion chambers. Racers used only one gasket to get more power. And even though spark-plug placement at the edge of the combustion chamber was not optimum, the angle they were placed at to clear the exhaust manifolds proved as effective as similar designs of competing engines.

In late heads, rocker-arm studs were pinned through their cast-iron boss, rather than simply pressed in. But unlike competitors, valvesprings for competition engines were single, not dual, with an inner damper to restrict float. The damper's flat cross-section steel, rolled into a coil, increased valve-closed compression to at least 140 lbs and valve-open compression exceeded 355 lbs when compressed 0.48 in, the lift of the cam. Valvesprings were heat-treated for 30 minutes at 400 degrees Fahrenheit while compressed to 1.15 in order to ensure proper function at the sustained temperatures for hours of racing. Using a new Duntov cam, both intake and exhaust valves were actuated through longer pushrods and slightly improved valve hardware to reduce wear.

Following Pontiac's lead, Chevrolet offered high-performance equipment over the counter by issuing a Regular Production Order (RPO) for new pieces. Cast-aluminum intake manifolds, for example, were redesigned to match the improved heads such that either a single or dual 4-bbl version could be cast from the same basic design. But unlike the standard single 4-bbl manifold, with its partition between the right and left throats, the stock-car racing version came without the partition, an open-plenum design. Another feature of the racing heads was blocked heat risers. Heat risers, important in production equipment to decrease engine warm-up time, were disadvantages in racing because higher temperatures in the intake reduced the volume of air/fuel mixture that could flow into combustion chambers.

Assembly-line exhaust manifolds were also quite different from RPO racing equipment, the latter being cast-iron headers that were not interchangeable from side to side. The new manifolds helped breathing and improved performance considerably.

At a time when competitors were going to dual-breaker distributors to solve high-speed ignition problems, Chevrolet engineers decided that single breaker points were sufficient. Long before electronic ignition, 1960s-era V-8 engines came with points that closed and opened by following the contour of an eight-lobe cam on the distributor shaft that was driven by a gear from one end of the cam. Ignition settings, spark timing, and valve adjustment were arts that tuners used to achieve maximum fire at the precise time to make the most power. Distributor advance and point-gap settings controlled spark energy and timing. Chevrolet marketed its improved racing distributor to replace assembly-line dual-point equipment.

Chevrolet combined all this and more, the latest and best high-performance equipment available from the factory, into a Service Package, PN 3822953. HP, torque, and high-RPM longevity improved significantly over the previous 409, but it was not enough to unseat Pontiac as king of the big tracks. Chevrolets won 14 of the 53 races on NASCAR's schedule, while Pontiac took 22 and the Grand National Manufacturers Championship in 1962.

Pontiac had the most complete catalog of racing equipment available that year. Building on the spectacular success of the 389, the 421 was no more than the 389 overbored 0.30 in and stroked 5/8 in. It was also strengthened a little in its 4-bolt main bearings on the 2-3-4 journals, and fitted with a forged-steel crankshaft with all the goodies. While most high-performance V-8s were considerably over square (meaning they had a larger bore than stroke, such as the 409 B/S ratio of 1.23:1), Pontiac engineers opted for a B/S ratio of 1.02:1, and it worked beautifully, with lots of torque throughout the powerband.

Factory records show that 200 of the 421 Super Duty engines were built in 1962, and between 179 and 200 cars were produced, all intended for racing. Mickey Thompson, with his deep connections with Pontiac Division boss Semon "Bunkie" Knudsen, got two cars. He ran one of them at Bonneville to set several straight-line speed records, then topped 149 mph in

CHAPTER FOUR

Hayden Proffitt waded through some 70 Super/Stock entries to nail down his shot at Stock Eliminator at the NHRA US Nationals in '62 by dusting off the Ramchargers 413 Dodge, then lost to Dave Strickler's hole shot driving the 409 Chevy of "Grumpy" Jenkins.

The 409 was a sensational performer street and strip performer known coast-to-coast in 1962. Factory rated at 425 hp @ 6000 rpm, this dual quad powerhouse was the longing desire of many of the kids. (Alex Gabbard photos)

attempts to set long-distance speed records before a broken rocker arm ended his efforts.

Among his many interests, Thompson managed the Los Angeles Drag Strip where he tested all sorts of cars, such as his side-by-side dual supercharged-Pontiac-powered land-speed-record, 4-wheel-drive dragster, dubbed *The Monster*. His goal was to better his own World Standing Start kilometer and mile records, which required exiting the kilometer at better than 251 mph and the mile at 283 mph respectively. Meanwhile, he turned out an A/FX Tempest, first shown publicly at the February 1962 NHRA Winternationals at Pomona, where his 12.37-second blast put the crowd on its feet with gasps of disbelief. Then, later in the season, the *Golden Lancer* Plymouth team nailed down both ends of the NHRA A/FX record at 12.26 seconds and 118.53 mph. Later in the season, Thompson laid down a stunning 12.22-second pass, and Factory Experimental quickly shaped up to the most exciting class in drag racing.

The 421 also came in two versions. Early engines were fitted with heavy-duty 389 heads with smaller valves, while later heads, PN 544124, came with 2.02-in-diameter intakes and 1.76-in-diameter exhaust valves, both 0.1 in larger than those in the 389. These heads came along just as the NASCAR season got under way, but unlike early heads, factory preparation of the new heads included machining top surface lands and installing steel pushrod guide plates. Since all 421s were competition engines, all came with no heat-riser ports to the intake manifold.

Most high-performance hardware, such as dual-point ignition, was Pontiac's regular heavy-duty equipment, but there were some special parts. Oil was kept under control in a special oil pan that included a windage tray with baffles to keep oil in the sump. Exhaust manifolds also came in two versions, identical castings in either iron or aluminum. The latter, though of considerable weight reduction, proved ineffective on oval tracks for a simple reason: sustained high exhaust temperatures melted the aluminum, and exhaust gases blew holes in them. For about $90, a pair of aluminum headers, PN 543053 and 543054, were among all sorts of equipment that Pontiac sold in its catalogs, and 1962 sales exploded 64 percent over 1961.

The Pontiac counterpart of Chevrolet's engine wizard, Zora Arkus-Duntov, was Malcolm McKeller, and like Zora, he produced a series of cams that have since carried his name. The McKeller No. 10 camshaft used in the 421 was a mechanical-lifter, flat-tappet design that upped the advertised 405 hp emblazoned on NASCAR hoods to around 465 hp, perhaps more, but no one in the Pontiac camp was talking. Engineers could calculate, though, and to push the big, heavy, wide-track Pontiacs to the speeds they regularly turned on the big tracks required a lot more than 405 of the best ponies. Pontiac was America's performance leader, but a team down in Level Cross, North Carolina, was getting better and better at making Plymouths fly.

The combination of smaller, lighter full-size cars from Plymouth and Dodge in 1962, along with improved B-series 413-ci engines, completely changed Chrysler's fortunes in the market and on racetracks. And like its larger competitors, Chrysler Corporation produced two versions of the engine, hot and hotter, and all of them came from the Marine and Industrial Division, which built tougher equipment than the assembly lines. The hot

1962: THE BIG-INCH RUMBLE

Above and below: The smoother, rounder, more powerful Ford of 1962 boasted 405 hp from the new tri-power 406. While Ford fans urged on their favorite make in stock-car racing, taking only six wins that year, they watched the Chevys, Pontiacs, and Chrysler cars lead through the traps at drag races. There wasn't much to brag about. The Ford men were working on sleeker and more powerful cars for the next model year.

for the kids. Sales of the new smaller Dodges and Plymouths with the big-inch engines skyrocketed. Total Dodge sales were up 14 percent over 1961; Plymouth sales rose just 6 percent. Then both took off in 1963; Dodge sales jumped 67 percent, Plymouth advanced 50 percent. Ford sales increased just 4.3 percent, and Chevrolet sales got a boost of just 6.6 percent. And 1964 was even better.

Chrysler's 413s featured an over square bore and stroke of 4.188 in and 3.75 in, respectively (B/S 1.17:1). The new engines differed primarily by compression ratio; earlier compression was 11:1, delivering a factory-rated output of 410 hp at 5,400 rpm, and torque of 460 ft-lbs, while the later engine's compression of 13.5:1 gave it a rating of 420 hp and 470 ft-lbs of torque. They were impressive and made superior Super Stock drag cars. They weren't quite as superior for stock cars, but the Petty cars turned in a stellar year with eight wins and 31 top-five finishes in 52 starts. Dodge and its new Dart 440, however, had little to proclaim in a winless year. Other teams had difficulty mastering Chrysler's torsion-bar suspension.

The cast-iron engine blocks in all Chrysler engines, the 361, 383, and 413, were the same, except for deck height. The 413 had a higher deck height to match the longer stroke, an adaptation from earlier high-bank 383 engines marketed and raced in 1959

engine was a way to get the new high-torque mill into production cars, and the hotter engine was upgraded for racing performance.

The Chrysler 300 had long been recognized as a benchmark of performance, style, and elegance in American motoring, but its weight, size, and cost made it an affluent gentleman's cruiser, not a car

CHAPTER FOUR

Chevrolet 409s became a cult favorite by being the fastest Super Stocks in the nation.

1962: THE BIG-INCH RUMBLE

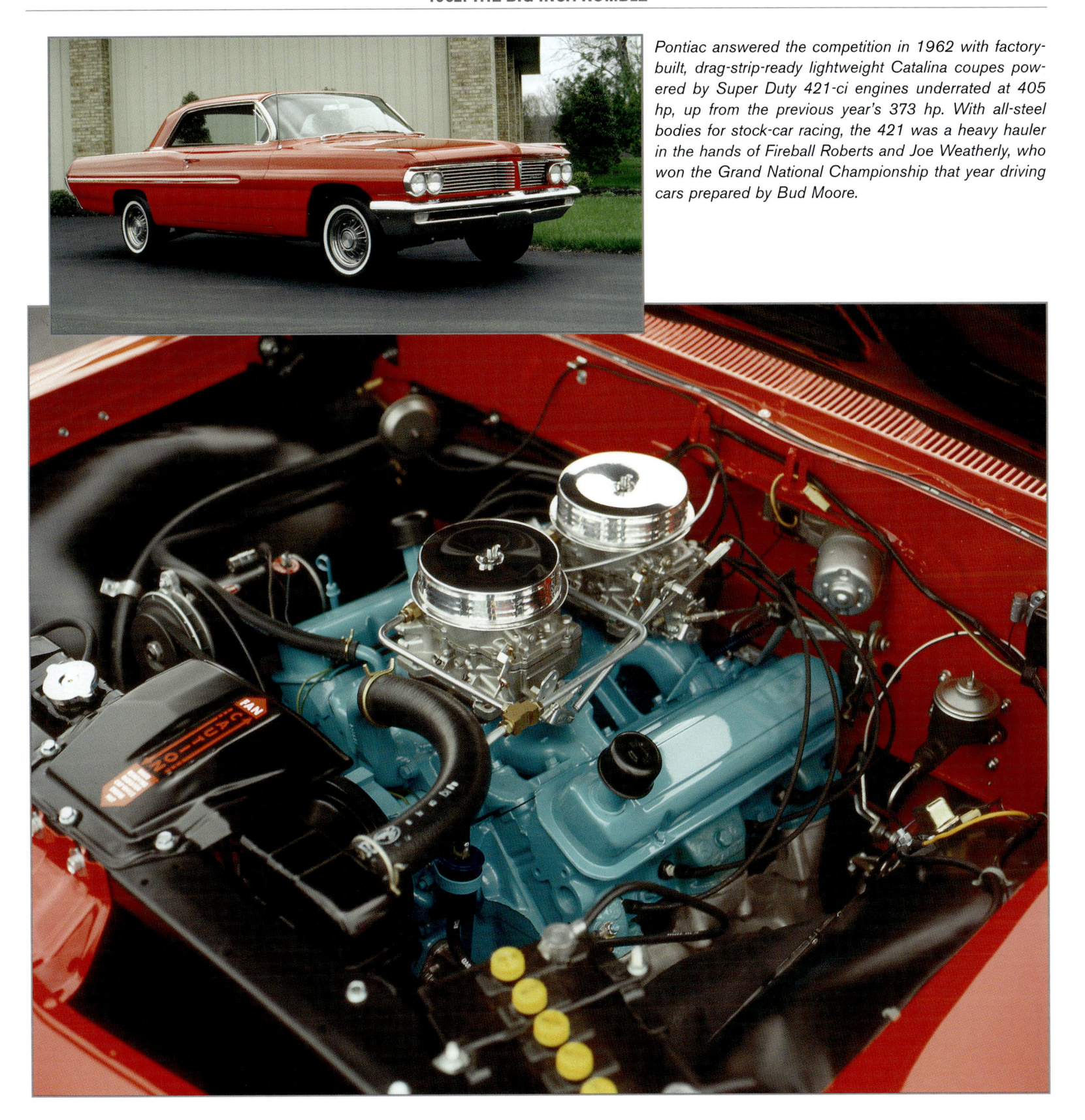

Pontiac answered the competition in 1962 with factory-built, drag-strip-ready lightweight Catalina coupes powered by Super Duty 421-ci engines underrated at 405 hp, up from the previous year's 373 hp. With all-steel bodies for stock-car racing, the 421 was a heavy hauler in the hands of Fireball Roberts and Joe Weatherly, who won the Grand National Championship that year driving cars prepared by Bud Moore.

CHAPTER FOUR

Thrilling Factory Experimental (A/FX) cars burst on the drag-racing scene in 1962. This one was Pontiac's first and is still campaigned among the collection of North Carolina's Bill Blair, whose father won the 1953 Daytona Beach race in an Olds. Factory-stamped aluminum front sheet metal was ultra-exotic equipment that reduced overall weight, making the 421-powered Tempest a formidable stripper.

64　　NASCAR'S WILD YEARS

1962: THE BIG-INCH RUMBLE

and '60. The only other visible difference in the blocks was that the 413s received larger valves that required notches in the top of cylinder bores to clear the exhaust valves. All 413 engines received a forged-steel crankshaft, which was similar to the standard crank. It differed in that it was shot-peened to stress-relieve critical areas such as the fillets between the bearing journals and crank arms, and had extensive flame hardening on the bearing surfaces. The 413's main bearings were much harder copper-lead-tin tri-metal from the Dodge truck line, and thus required hardened journals. The main journals rode in grooved cap bearings that completed the oiling path from the main gallery just under the cam to lubricate the crankshaft and were matched to looser tolerances of 0.001 to 0.0015 in. Rod-bearing design tolerance was 0.001 to 0.0025 in.

A major art in race-engine building is finding the clearances between wear surfaces that permit an engine to make maximum power (by revving freely) without coming apart. For racing, break-in time had to be minimal and output maximized, but break-in time was necessary to ensure properly seated components. The goal was simple: to win a 500-mile race, a freshly assembled engine had to stay together just over 500 miles. Consequently, engines were the heart of racing, and the Pettys were masters.

The 13.5:1 engine, known as the Ramcharger in Dodges and the Super Stock in Plymouths, was strictly for competition. It received forged-aluminum pistons with valve reliefs and piston-to-cylinder-wall clearance of 0.010 in. Until it was warmed up and the pistons were fully expanded, these engines exhibited noticeable "slap," when the piston skirts slapped the cylinder walls. It sounded like the engine was about to come apart. That was just the builder's art at work; when warm, the engine quieted down to let the driver know it was ready to rumble.

Chrysler's high-performance B heads had 25-percent larger ports for improved breathing (the source of power in any engine) and no power-robbing heat risers to the intake. The valves were also 25 percent larger, the 2.08-in intakes were "tulip" design with conical faces, making more substantial stem-to-head flutes for added strength. The exhaust valves were 1.88 in, and were more conventional, but stronger than standard. Both intake and exhaust valves were closed with special, thermally treated dual springs with inner dampers. The solid lifters were 0.001-inch smaller in diameter for added clearance and freer motion, and were driven by a selection of cams with lift and duration for various applications. The 413 was tough.

Chrysler used heavy-duty stainless-steel head gaskets (versus mild steel). While dual 4-bbl carbs were the trick setup for drag racing, circle tracks required a single 4-bbl. Chrysler benefited from its engineering's focus on ram induction, introduced with the impressive but bulky SonoRamic Commando dual-quad setup of 1960. Dual- and single-quad "short ram" cast-aluminum intakes for 1962 delivered more torque above 4,000 rpm

Above and following pages: While Dodge came up short in stock-car racing – no NASCAR wins in 1961, '62, or '63 – drag strips were a very different story. The factory saw its primary PR effort pay off in big ways each time a Dodge Ramcharger blasted down the 1320, more often winning than losing. Dodge sales jumped by 31,000 units over 1961 sales, over $77 million. The horsepower war was rapidly unfolding, and the kids loved it.

CHAPTER FOUR

without the long and cumbersome ram tubes, which prevented the valve covers from being removed with the intake in place. The new dual-plane intake connected the intake valves to the carb throat that was farthest away to get the ram effect at high speeds. These intakes were designed with removable covers to provide access to lifters.

While the wide manifold was impressive, sort of a throne for a Carter 4-throat carb, the most impressive feature of the new engines was their cast-iron exhaust manifolds, which swept up from exhaust ports and arched along beside the valve covers, then swooped down at the firewall. As a result of the width of the B engine, there was insufficient clearance between body and suspension components for standard downward manifolds. The clutch and manual transmission, still a 3-speed in '62, was surpassed in Super Stock drag racing by the first really tough automatic, the TorqueFlite, which was soon to become a renowned Chrysler feature.

In 1962, baby boomers began coming of driving age, showing their interest in all things fast. With ever-larger turnouts at ovals and drag strips, the factories whetted appetites with stock cars showcasing faster speeds than ever before, and more was just around the corner.

PAXTON Superchargers
RAMCHARGER
CHASSIS ENGINEERING
MANCINI RACING
Mopar PERFORMANCE PARTS
RON MANCINI
PIN 3
SS/A
AUTO CRAFTERS
MANCINI BROS.
Wolverine Hallmark
AMALIE
Edelbrock
FLOWMASTER
MSD IGNITION
Mickey Thompson

CHAPTER FIVE

Finally reaching the big leagues in 1963 with a Holman Moody Ford, South Carolina's Cale Yarborough began his rise to three decades of racing and three successive Grand National Championships (1976-'77-'78). (Ford photo)

1963: The Showdown

The spirited rock 'n' roll of the 1950s, with its potent beat, rhythmic bass, and harmonizing lead, was the fast-moving expression of kids who took to dancing as never before. Swing gave way to music made by small groups of kids for kids, boys singing to girls and girls singing to boys, all of them singing about good times and partying. By the late 1950s, California beach music began its sweep across the nation, rolling from jukeboxes, radios, and 45-rpm hi-fi sets everywhere with catchy new sounds. Among all sorts of chart-toppers were Jan & Dean and The Beach Boys; their fresh and vibrant interweaving voices captured young peoples' attention with tunes of fun in the sun. By 1963, hugely engaging hits like "Drag City," by Jan & Dean, and "She's Real Fine, My 409," by The Beach Boys, set the tone of the time. The latter record made a teen icon of Chevrolet's top "W" engine. No better advertisement had ever been produced, and it didn't cost GM a dime.

The early 1960s was a time like no other; surf, Super Stocks, and summertime fun were its expression. Within a few years, that youth-driven vigor would be tempered by the sobering realities of the Vietnam war. In the midst of it all were the cars, the focus of the good times. Each year's new models were awaited with breathless anticipation that the factories fueled with veiled hints, covered cars, and hidden surprises not announced until the release date. Each year brought advances in the HP war that looked like it would never end.

New-car sales surged in 1963. Chevrolet was up 6.6 percent, Ford was up 4.6 percent, Dodge was up 67 percent, Plymouth up 50 percent, and Pontiac up 14 percent. While the good times rolled across America in the fall of 1962, big changes in stock-car racing were just around the corner.

As the 1962 season wound down, the factory men eyed each other's racing equipment and began their plans for the next year. All except Pontiac went to bigger engines. Ford launched its bid to top NASCAR's charts with a 1963-1/2 fastback similar to the previous Starlift hardtop, but with new lines. Engine displacement jumped from 406 to 427 ci, with a "side-oiler" lubrication system within the block. The Ford men were so confident of their tough 427-ci competition engine that it was released into regular production. A total of 4,978 were sold in Ford showroom mod-

While Ford Division fielded race-winning cars that scored 23 victories in 1963, Mercury Division struggled to win just one. Californian Darel Dieringer started the Daytona 500 18th to finish 16th, then won the Riverside road race at the end of the season. (Ford photo)

els advertised as "1963 Fords, America's liveliest, most carefree cars." For the $461.60 option, buyers got a fully equipped dual-quad racing engine, factory-rated at 425 hp. For $34.80, Ford's new and exceptionally strong "top-loader" 4-speed made a sleek Galaxie 500XL Sports Hardtop a hot-rodder's dream for a total list price of $4,065.10. A well-tuned 427 Galaxie could stomp any 409 from anywhere, but only its golden "Flying Thunderbird" emblem near the leading edge of the front fenders, boldly embossed with "427," told the world what was inside. The kids noticed such things, and proclamations of Ford's entry into full-spec racing engines sparked many showdowns.

Chrysler went its 413 one better with 426 ci and more power (425 hp) for 1963 models, and both Dodge and Plymouth Super Stocks were darned near invincible on drag strips. This was not the case on the high banks, as some mysterious iron from Chevrolet caused a lot of grief.

CHAPTER FIVE

Rex White and Louie Clements teamed to win the 1960 Grand National Championship, the second title for Chevrolet (Buck Baker won Chevy's first title in 1957), then finished second to Ned Jarrett's title year in 1962. It would be 11 more years before Chevrolet won again. (Rex White photo)

Richard "Dick" Keinath, Chevrolet engineer, designed the 427-ci Mystery Engine as a clandestine effort deep within Chevrolet engineering. The project was killed in early 1963, then led to the family of Mk IV big-block engines when reintroduced in 1965. (R. L. Keinath photo)

Chevy's high-performance team led by Zora Arkus-Duntov one-upped the 409 W engine with a rarely seen RPO-Z11 dual-quad 427-ci big-block. It looked like a 409, but was faster. The engine came in 55 factory-prepared drag-racing cars. Meanwhile, the NASCAR 409 was dumped in favor of a new and blisteringly powerful 427 that was completely different from the W engine. The new 427 was not an RPO item; it first showed up in testing at Daytona. It was so fast that everyone was talking about it – especially the competition.

Deep in the heart of Chevrolet's engine design staff was an engineer named Dick Keinath who had been involved with high-performance development of both the 283 and 348 engines. He was centrally involved with cast-aluminum engines, heads, and components, which were scheduled for the Corvette but showed up only in Jim Hall's USRRC Chaparrals in 1965, another hush-hush backdoor job that Chevrolet had become known for. Initially, work with aluminum was the corporation's first efforts at making low-cost, high-volume aluminum-alloy drivetrain components for lighter, more fuel-efficient vehicles such as the Corvair.

Meanwhile, Pontiac boss, Semon "Bunkie" Knudsen, was promoted to run the larger Chevrolet Division, and in July 1962, he gave the go-ahead to design a racing engine. The highly unusual Engineering Work Order stated: "Please design an engine per instructions of R. L. Keinath," a completely new engine from a clean sheet of paper. It was dubbed the Mk II and was very secret. No one else in top corporate management knew about it.

The Mk I was Zora's high-performance Z11, and Keinath began with the 409 bore centers and 409 ci. He then designed all-new everything to produce a full-tilt monster mill unlike anything previously available from the Big Three – a staggered-valve competition engine. The top of each combustion chamber was on the plane of the top of the pistons, unlike the 16-degree angle combustion chambers in the block of the W engine. For better induction and exhaust, intake valves were canted 26 degrees, and exhaust valves at 16 degrees, with the combustion chamber in the cylinder head. The splayed-valve heads soon became known as the "Porcupine Heads," and the valve layout was patented in Keinath's name. The engine was unique and required all-new castings poured at GM's foundry and engine plant in Tonawanda, New York.

Since Pontiac's 421 was already in competition and both Ford and Chrysler were introducing 427- and 426-ci engines, respectively, Chevy's men in contact with NASCAR negotiated for engine displacements closer to production engines. NASCAR first ruled a maximum of 6.5 liters (396 ci) for 1963, but by November 1962, the limit was increased to 7 liters (430 ci), so Keinath set to redesigning his new engine to displace 427 ci. That required a longer stroke, and the new version became the Mk IIS (S for stroke). The change required designing and fabricating all-new internals (except for main bearings), and meant modifying drawings, designs, molds, patterns, core boxes, and castings – and the targeted release was the Daytona 500 in February, just a few months away. Unchanged from Mk II to Mk IIS were the free-flowing cast-iron headers, four downward tubes that came together into a flange for bolting on the exhaust pipe. Development team members Bill Howell and Tom Poole ran testing and dyno runs on the engine and showed that the benchmark 409 factory-rated at 425 hp was handily surpassed; the Mk IIS came in at upwards of 600 hp depending on equipment, such as the single 4-bbl intake plenum designs in development.

An entire engineering department and shop, geared to machining cylinder heads, intakes, exhaust manifolds, blocks, and components, worked three shifts, nights and weekends, to meet

1963: THE SHOWDOWN

Over at Chrysler, Virgil Exner resigned late in 1962, causing a shake-up. His replacement, Elwood Engle, had penned the "forward look" of Ford's 1950s-era cars, particularly the early Thunderbirds. As the new Vice President of Design at Chrysler, his influence reshaped the entire corporate lineup and gave Dodge and Plymouth a much-needed freshening, resulting in a sales bonanza. New styling, along with a fabulous "new" engine, the 413-ci B engine taken to 426 cubes and 425 hp, brought buyers in by the droves. The new Stage 3 426 for stock-car racing raised output substantially, and with Engle's more aerodynamic package, the Petty-blue Plymouths were sure to be a force to reckon with.

Richard Petty rounded out the 1962 season with 14 wins in 54 starts, the most wins that season in NASCAR's scheduled 55 races. But it was not enough to capture the Grand National Championship. Joe Weatherly and his Pontiacs took Richard to the wire; just three wins backed by a

Ford's 427-ci stock-car racing engine evolved from the strengthened 406 of the previous year, then received successively improved induction systems to remain a race winner into 1969. (Ford photo)

Keinath's schedule. Cam and crankshaft machining was contracted to Detroit-area shops. Everything needed to build complete engines that were, ultimately, planned to go into production was managed on short-notice production. But because of time constraints, much potential planned in the Mk IIS was compromised, and power was down because of the lack of manufacturing skills and development time. In original as-planned form, the engine would have been even more powerful, and was to be Chevrolet's answer to the full-bore 427 Ford and Chrysler's 426 wedge. Tonawanda records show that components to build 60 Mk IIS engines were built, but that was it.

Later, the Mk IIS rose again as the Mk IV production big-block, though it was simplified and detuned to reduce manufacturing costs. Chevrolet's Mk IV 396-ci big-block was introduced in 1965. It grew to 427 ci in 1967, and then to 454 ci in 1970. The ultimate Mk IV was the aluminum 494-ci Can-Am engine of 1969.

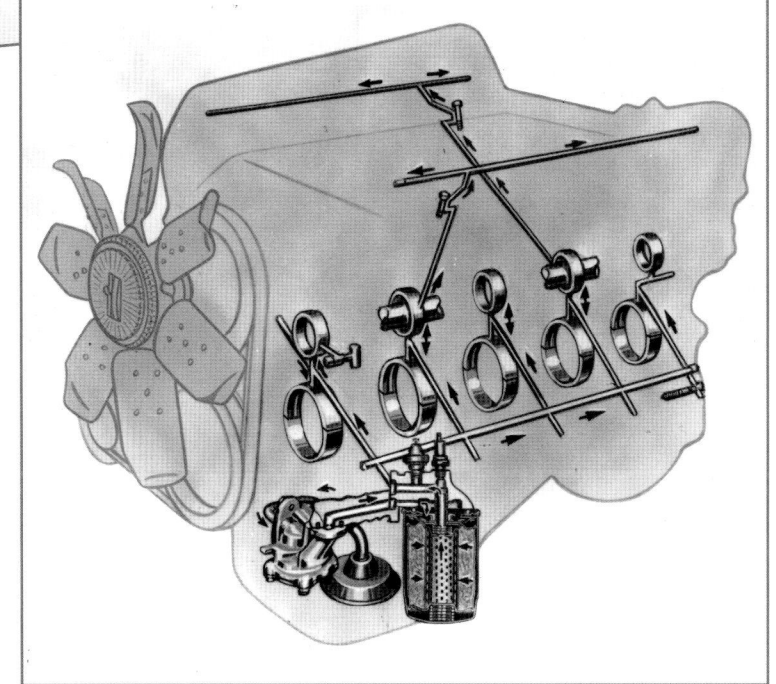

Because of unequal oiling to the cam and rod bearings, Ford engineers designed the "side-oiler" with a side gallery that insured that each bearing got adequate lubrication to endure the stress of racing's high RPMs. (Ford photo)

CHAPTER FIVE

John Holman had much to laugh about with his Fords on a huge roll and Ford Motor Company behind him. He joined with Ralph Moody to form Holman Moody in the 1950s. The team struggled until Lee Iacocca moved into the head office at Ford Division and changed the course of the company. (Ford photo)

multitude of high finishes totaled 2,228 points more and put him ahead of Petty.

Pontiac and its legendary 421 were still the big guns of stock-car racing, but the new engines from Chrysler, Chevrolet, and Ford promised a tougher year in '63, especially on the big tracks that received so much publicity. Because of size and weight, the Indian's edge was diminishing, and even after removing weight in the frame, holing it wherever strength was not compromised until it was dubbed the "Swiss Cheese" Catalina in drag racing, the Pontiac men knew they were in for a tough season. They had no idea. Still, the stock-car season went the way of the Indian with Bud Moore wrenching Joe Weatherly's Pontiacs to take the Grand National title for the second year in a row. Weatherly's late-season switch to Mercury brought Moore to Ford, which would later lead to an internal rivalry and lots of great racing.

There were four teams of blisteringly fast Chevrolets at Daytona testing: Ray Fox and his Daytona Kennel Club entry with G.C. Spenser driving; Smokey Yunick's car with Indy 500 star Johnny Rutherford behind the wheel; Rex White handling his fast Chevy; and Junior Johnson in Fox's Holly Farms-sponsored car. Smokey jumped from Pontiac to Chevrolet at the

Above and facing page: Curtis Turner, featured in Sports Illustrated *(February 1968) as "King of the Wild Road," was a Virginia moonshiner and lumberman turned racing driver. He won his first Grand National race in 1949 to become one of stock-car racing's biggest stars, and Ford's lead driver in the mid-1950s. As co-founder of the Charlotte Motor Speedway, and in need of cash when the new track surface broke up in its first races during 1960, Turner received financial backing from the Teamster's Union to make repairs, with the agreement that he would organize the drivers. Subsequently, Bill France ended their longtime friendship by banning Turner for life, relenting in 1965. With Ford Motor Company backing in the interim, Turner raced the Midwest Auto Racing Circuit (MARC) and USAC with his "Old Crow" trademark. Said to have won 350 races during his driving career, Turner was called the Babe Ruth of stock-car racing.*

1963: THE SHOWDOWN

NASCAR'S WILD YEARS

CHAPTER FIVE

Chevrolet Division engineers turned out two sensational stock-car engines in 1963, the 427-ci Mystery Engine in stock-car racing, and the Regular Production Order Z11 drag-racing special, the ultimate W engine cranking out 425-plus-hp from 427 ci in factory-built lightweight A/FX Impalas.

behest of Bunkie Knudsen, now at the helm of the Chevrolet Division. Smokey gave his Pontiacs to Banjo Mathews, who put Paul Goldsmith in the driver's seat. Indy 500 winner A.J. Foyt drove another hot Indian (among a dozen or more Pontiac drivers), so the Ponchos were sure to make the qualifying races a showdown to be settled in the 500 itself.

The 1963 NASCAR season opened in November '62 with short races in the South. In the season opener at Birmingham, Alabama, the Petty team rolled to victory one-two, Jim Paschal a lap ahead of Richard. Brother Maurice qualified eighth, then crashed, and would race only a few more times before concentrating on the hardware and organization while Richard drove. The next race a week later, a 200-lap feature in Tampa, Florida, the Petty Plymouths reversed their one-two victory with Richard winning, and both drivers outpacing Joe Weatherly's Pontiac in third. The third race, held on the Petty's home turf at the Tar Heel Speedway in Randleman, North Carolina, was a Paschal two-lap victory; Richard's transmission failed. Then came Riverside. The Petty team struggled. Richard's transmission sidelined him again, and Paschal crashed. The NASCAR points leaders rolled back home from the California desert with broken cars. Both were near the bottom of the finishing order and were suddenly no longer the points leaders.

The Ford men showed off their 427 side-oiler fastback sedans in the Riverside 500 in Riverside, California, a 2.7-mile road course and new venue for NASCAR. Goldsmith and Foyt were in Pontiacs on the front row, but Holman Moody signing Dan Gurney proved to be a good move because the left-turn boys had few skills in road racing. Though it was considerably different than racing sports cars, Gurney got the hang of driving a big, hulking sedan, and set the fastest qualifying time. He ran away with the win, only temporarily engaged by Parnelli Jones at the wheel of a Bill Stroppe Mercury that lost its transmission about midway. The win was the first of five Riverside victories in a row for Gurney and the first of 10 straight Ford wins in Riverside's desert showcase. Gurney's was the first major win by a road racer in NASCAR and another credit to his phenomenal abilities and influence on American racing, detailed in *Indy's Wildest Decade*.

That victory gave the Ford men reason to be confident in their new equipment. Then came Daytona and a host of surprises. The Holman Moody Fords in the hands of Fred Lorenzen, Nelson Stacy, Larry Frank, Gurney, and Ned Jarrett (having moved over

74 NASCAR'S WILD YEARS

1963: THE SHOWDOWN

five in either of the 100-mile, 40-lap qualifiers. Richard topped the team's effort, finishing 12th in the first round, while Hurtubise finished 17th. In the second round, Paschal's engine failed, dropping him to 28th. In the 500, only Richard finished, sixth, two laps down from the winning string of Fords, which finished first through fifth. Hurtubise's engine failed, and Paschal's ignition went sour. To win the big one, Chrysler needed more power, and back in engineering, a new hemispherical head for the B engine was in the works.

What happened to the fast Chevys? Smokey Yunick (interviewed in 1989): "...we started callin' it the 'Mystery Engine' because they were half-assed in racin'. They wouldn't admit it.... I had all of 'em right here. I've always remembered 42 sets of parts for 42 complete engines. Every engine that got raced got raced out of here to whoever run a Chevrolet... It was a joke. We were way faster than anything else... I had a long talk with him [Knudsen] 'bout ten days or two weeks before the race, and I tried to get Knudsen to withdraw the cars. Don't run 'em' cause it was a phony deal. I finally got him to agree with me. Then, when he presented it to NASCAR, they didn't want him to pull out. We were working around the clock; didn't know if we were in or out. We were puttin' them in and out of the dynamometer tryin' to patch up problems. Now, we're down to about three days before the race, we're all qualified and Knudsen agrees, 'We are withdrawing the cars.' Finally, at five o'clock in the mornin', Knudsen called saying, number one, we are going to race the engine, and number two, we are going to take two engines down to the Chevy dealer for Ford to pick up, and they are to be there at eight o'clock in the morning."

The Z11 was often mistaken for the 409 but was a very different engine. When examined closely, the Z11 induction system was unique and employed a ram-type manifold with individual runners to the heads rather than the large plenum of the 409.

from Chevrolet) made a solid team. Stroppe Mercurys driven by Jones, Troy Ruttmann, and Rodger Ward showed up, and another team, the Wood Brothers of Stuart, Virginia, with Marvin Panch driving, meant that Ford was there in numbers.

The handsomely restyled Dodge and Plymouth cars with stepped-up performance were tougher than ever, but Dodge was still searching for a first NASCAR win since its one win in 1956. The new 426 wedge B engine had teething problems, including overheating. Only the Petty team proved to have a handle on what it took to win the Daytona 500, but even with three cars and USAC ace Jim Hurtubise signed to drive, the Petty team could not get close to a top

Dodge and Plymouth blasted onto the drag-racing scene when the "Big Go West" (NHRA Winternationals at Pomona, California) looked like a Chrysler-fest. The new 426 engines (Ramcharger in Dodge, Super Stock in Plymouth) dominated Super Stock Eliminator with the final round for Stock Eliminator a face-off between the Ramcharger Dodge and the Golden Commando Plymouth, both cars with deep factory connections. Dodge (Al Eckstrand driving) won with a sizzling 12.44-second run at 115.08 mph, having set the low ET for stock class at 12.12 seconds. Both were automatic-transmission cars.

NASCAR'S WILD YEARS 75

CHAPTER FIVE

Handsomely restyled Plymouths were matched with the new-for-1963 Super Stock 426 wedge engine rated at 425 hp. The combination was good for Plymouth's best NASCAR year from 1949 through 1966, 19 victories in 1963, the only challenger to Ford's 23 wins that year. Plymouths were the terror of short tracks, with Richard Petty taking the Virginia 500 at Martinsville and the Staley 400 at North Wilkesboro, among others, to finish second to Joe Weatherly (Pontiac) in the season-long points race.

76   NASCAR'S WILD YEARS

1963: THE SHOWDOWN

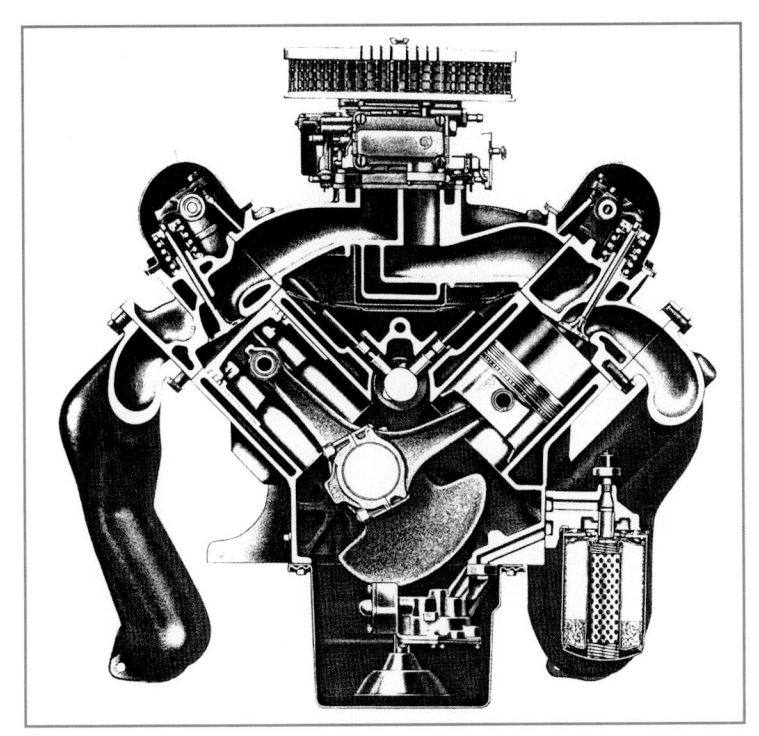

Although the narrow heads of the FE-series engines tended to boil the cooling water in them because of marginal cooling capacity, the engines proved durable and competitive in every form raced. (Ford photo)

Ford's corporate commitment of "Total Performance" called for engineering excellence that was proven in competition. High-performance cars were sold through dealerships, along with a broad range of technical information for building engines and cars for any application. (Ford photo)

The showdown concerning the new Chevy engines shaped up into a media heyday, and Bill France loved all the attention. Chevrolet racing manager Vince Piggins delivered the hastily assembled engines, mostly from reject parts, and Chevrolet was in the Daytona 500 with five factory teams and a host of private entries who struggled to keep up with the rapid changes. France couldn't have orchestrated a better media feeding frenzy.

The 100-mile qualifiers were a Chevrolet romp and everybody was screaming about the mysterious engines that made so much power. Nothing could get close to them. They exceeded 165 mph, while everyone else struggled to get to 160. Junior Johnson set a new qualifying record at 164.083 mph and later said his Chevrolet was "the most superior car I ever drove." USAC star Johnny Rutherford was new to Daytona's high banks, but immediately drove Yunick's Chevrolet to the front to win the second qualifier.

The Petty team, the Pontiac teams, the Ford men, and Cotton Owens' struggling two-car Dodge team (with a fast-rising new driver named David Pearson) were all stung. Petty's early successes meant nothing, and Ford's terrific showing at Riverside (with equipment available to the public) was being upstaged by a secret racing engine no one had ever seen before. NASCAR, always on the prowl for anything to bolster spectator turnout, was so delighted to have factory teams back for the first time since 1957 that rules were bent for the Chevrolets. Strictly stock wasn't strictly stock at all. If it brought more paying fans and the press, it was okay – and the Ford-Chevrolet showdown brought enormous coverage. Try as the Fords did, Rutherford set the fastest pole yet seen at Daytona, an astounding 165.183 mph, and the duel was on for race day.

Rain delayed the race for two hours and the first 10 laps were run under caution to dry the track, but that didn't hold back the Chevrolets and Pontiacs. Junior charged to the front, only to drop a valve on lap 26. It went through the piston, and made a great conversation piece for Dick Keinath's desk. Paul Goldsmith drafted Johnson early on, a switch from the technique Junior used in his low-powered Chevrolet to win the 1960 Daytona 500, but Goldsmith left a few laps later. The new leader, Bobby Johns and his Pontiac, ran out of gas while leading around the 300-mile mark, and the Fords moved to the front.

The wily Wood brothers had their driver – 6-ft 5-in "Tiny" Lund, a replacement for Marvin Panch, who had been injured in a crash a few days earlier – draft faster cars to conserve fuel. He stayed with Lorenzen and Jarrett at the front getting slightly better fuel economy, a few laps per tankful. With 40 laps to go, Lund roared out of the pits with a full load and no need to pit again. He rejoined the Ford train, and with a few laps to the finish, Lorenzen and Jarrett pitted for fuel, giving Lund the lead. Going into the banking, Lund's engine sputtered out of fuel, and he backed off the throttle a little, hoping to make his fuel last to the finish. Nursing the engine around the track to the last lap, his engine died in the fourth turn, and he coasted toward the checkered flag. Catching one last gulp of fuel, the 427 blasted to life, and he

NASCAR'S WILD YEARS 77

CHAPTER FIVE

Above and facing page: Ford's first major stock-car win in 1963 was Tiny Lund's victory in the hotly contested Daytona 500. It was also the Wood Brothers' biggest win, the start of a long winning tradition with Fords. (Ford photo)

1963: THE SHOWDOWN

sailed across the line 24 seconds ahead of Lorenzen. Ford's top-five sweep of the Daytona 500 was its biggest victory in stock-car racing.

Buttonholed after the race about their new and mysterious engine, General Motors executives, embarrassingly, knew nothing about it. Shortly thereafter, the clandestine efforts of Chevrolet and Pontiac were revealed, and the head office issued a corporate-wide edict – "We don't race," and anyone attempting to do so or having any involvement with racing would be terminated. The Chevy men put the Mystery Engine on the shelf, gave their teams what was available, and tucked there hands in their pockets.

The 1963 season had just begun, and only Petty's team of Plymouths was left to challenge the Holman Moody Ford team and the rapidly rising Mercurys. Ford surged into the points lead with 23 wins that year, compared to 6 in 1962, and won over half of NASCAR's total payout. Mercury took its first win since 1956, and Chevrolet dropped from 14 wins in 1962 to 8 in 1963, hampered as the season progressed by a lack of parts and development.

Along the way, Junior Johnson became the "Last American Hero," so described in word and film, for what the public saw as his effort against Ford's "steamroller." He and Chevrolet were the moral victors, combating Ford's massive corporate effort. The intense Ford-Chevrolet rivalry between Junior and Lorenzen was the talk of the circuit. Junior won seven of Chevrolet's eight wins that year in 30 starts, while Lorenzen won six in 29 starts.

In the World 600 at Charlotte, the Ford-Chevrolet duel between Johnson in his white-and-red Chevrolet and Lorenzen in his white-and-blue Holman Moody Ford saw Junior in the lead for over half of the laps. With two laps to go, Junior was well out in front, when a fan tossed a bottle out of the stands. It splattered into glass fragments on the track just in front of Junior, cutting a tire. The necessary pit stop to change rubber put him second to Lorenzen at the finish.

There was no such luck for the Ford team in Atlanta in the Dixie 400, as Junior ran the last 33 laps in the lead and won. He backed it up in Charlotte at the National 400, leading for 209 of 267 laps. He trounced Lorenzen in the final 30 laps, winning by 12 seconds, leading the Fords of Panch and Fireball Roberts, who were now in the Ford camp.

For his efforts that year, Junior took home $67,350 in winnings, while Lorenzen topped NASCAR's all-time win list with $112,660. This was the first time a stock-car driver topped $100,000 in a season. His showmanship made him stock-car racing's newest golden boy.

The success of Fox's private-entry Chevy, campaigned so competitively against Ford's factory-backed multicar team, fueled fierce rivalries among the kids and sparked intense brand loyalty far greater than any ad campaign Chevrolet could have come up with. But by season's end, all the Chevys and Pontiacs were also-rans in Ford's first year of Total Performance. Ford Motor Company closed the 1963 season in a return to Riverside, the Golden State 400, with a sweep. Darel Dierenger took the victory to post Mercury's first win in years.

Meanwhile, besides the hard-fought Ford-Chevrolet rivalry, Richard Petty and Joe Weatherly were in a duel to the finish. Weatherly drove for eight different teams that year, coaxing mid-marker cars to unexpected finishes. He took his three wins in Pontiacs early on, then switched to Mercury late in the season. Petty scored 14 of Plymouth's 19 victories, but Weatherly scored enough points in the last race to be Grand National Champion for the second year in a row.

The next year, a competitive Chevrolet was nowhere to be seen in NASCAR, except for Wendell Scott's private entry winning in a minor race. Dodge roared onto the scene with a hard-charging David Pearson behind the wheel.

CHAPTER FIVE

Fireball Roberts switched to Holman Moody Fords in mid-season and won the Firecracker 400 at Daytona along with the Bristol 500 and the Southern 500 at record speed, 129.78 mph. (Ford photos)

NASCAR'S WILD YEARS

REX WHITE

This is the story of Rex White's career in stock-car racing, as told by Rex himself.

"I worked in a gas station in Silver Springs, Maryland, and a guy came along wanting to put a poster in the window to advertise races every Friday night in West Lanham. I said, 'Sure.' I looked at that poster week after week; didn't have the money to go. Finally, I got up enough money, and along with my wife and my brother-in-law and his wife, we went to the races. The first racecar I had ever seen went roaring around that track, and I said, 'That's what I want to do.' And I didn't stop until I got to racing.

"Soon after that, I met Frankie Schneider in West Lanham, and I helped him in the pits on Friday nights – take axles out and change the tires so he could tow the car on the flat down the highway. When his helper got drafted into the Army, he asked me if I wanted to go racing, and I said, 'Sure!' That was 1951.

"Frankie was from New Jersey and ran the Sportsman and Modified circuit. At some of the racetracks we ran three carburetors in Modified, sometimes we ran one in Sportsman, depending on the race. They were 1937 and '39 Fords with modified engines and chassis, larger wheels, full floating rear ends, roll bars. Usually, we had one roll bar right behind the seat. A lot of the cars had an old seat out of an airplane and an old aircraft seat belt. Back then, we didn't have belts we could buy.

"In 1953, we parted ways, and I got to know a guy who had pinball machines and jukeboxes. He helped me get a car together, and we went racing. We started at West Lanham, and we ran in New Jersey, Delaware, Pennsylvania, places like that. I started out on pavement, but later on, I ran dirt and asphalt. We ran any kind of racetrack that had a race. The only change we made to the car was the tires. We ran treaded tires on dirt and slicks on pavement.

"We knocked around in our old car for about a year, not doing very good. Then, in the winter of '53, I built a new racecar, a '37 Ford with a flathead V-8. We had a bunch of mechanical troubles starting out and didn't get going for about a month; had engine problems, my father died, and I took some time off for that. I came back and flipped the car, tore it all to pieces, got hit laying in the racetrack upside down, got my face cut up. I rebuilt that car in a week and came back and won the race at West Lanham Speedway. That was the first race I ever won. It was a Modified race and several of us run as Sportsman. The reason why we did that was, if you were paid $275 to win, you got an extra $75 if you were running one carburetor, plus you didn't have to buy alcohol if you ran gasoline. You were better off to run one carburetor if you could run up front. I beat a guy running three carburetors and alcohol that night. The next night, Saturday night, I won in Manassas, Virginia, and the next day, Sunday afternoon, I won in Marlboro, Maryland. I had a clean sweep that weekend. The car was very plain, it wasn't painted, I had masking tape on it for a number, it was X; it wasn't a show car of any kind, but it always looked good taking the checkered flag. That brought me a lot of attention and kicked off my racing career.

"I raced at Wall Stadium in Belmar, New Jersey, and Wilmington, Delaware, and Allentown, Pennsylvania, and Marlboro and West Lanham and didn't do too bad the next year. But, I think I only won three races that year because of mechanical troubles, one thing or another. In 1955, I took off to go racing in the Carolinas where, supposedly, all the hotdog drivers were, the Myers brothers, Curtis Turner, Glenn Wood. I run the whole season down there, and got a lot more popular. In the winter that year, I went to Florida to run the winter circuit with Fireball Roberts, Bobby Johns, Al Keller, and I won seven races down there. Then, I got called up to Bowman Gray Stadium in Winston-Salem, North Carolina. Alvin Hawkins was the promoter at Bowman Gray, and he asked me if I'd like to drive a new car at Daytona. 'Why sure,' I said. 'I'd be glad to.' He told me he'd bring the car to Daytona. I kept running my car in south Florida, then went to Daytona in February to drive the new car, a 1956 Chevrolet. It was supplied by Pioneer Chevrolet in Yadkinville, North Carolina. Well, they didn't know anything about racing. They took the hubcaps off of it, put a roll bar in it right behind the stock seat, and put a seat belt in it. That's the way they brought that car to race at Daytona. That was strictly stock, and that's the way we raced it; didn't do very good, finished twenty-second and got $60.

"That race led to running the whole Grand National season in '56, driving for the same dealer, and I finished 11th in Grand National points. I won a race that year at McCormick Field in Asheville, North Carolina. It was a baseball diamond where we raced around the field. There was also a half-mile track there called Asheville-Weaverville. It was a nice racetrack, high banked. Later on, there was another racetrack down on the river, three

CHAPTER FIVE

Chevrolet poured more attention and development into the sensational Super Stocks of drag racing than stock-car racing and produced as many as 57 RPO-Z11 stripper specials, complete cars powered by the 427 W Mystery Engine, but very different from the Mk IIS that went stock-car racing. (Henry Gabbert photo)

racetracks in Asheville, and I won races on all three of them. I did most of my own mechanic work and towed to thirty-seven races by myself. I did well enough that I wanted to go race at the Flat Rock Speedway in Michigan.

"I'd raced Chevrolets all this time, and the factory was helping drivers such as Bob Welborn, Possum Jones, Jim Reed. I was driving for a dealer, but I couldn't get any help from the factory. So, I took a week off and worked on the chassis, got the car looking better, and went to Flat Rock Speedway where I'd be racing before the people from GM. I set the pole and beat all the hotdogs.

"Mauri Rose was in charge of all the racing at Chevrolet, and he came over and asked me, 'What do you need?' I told him, 'I need everything.' He wanted to know if I had a truck, so I called my owner who had a farm, and he sent a cattle truck up there and we loaded it with parts from GM so we could go racing the rest of the year. At the end of that year, Chevrolet formed a racing team and opened a garage in Atlanta, called it Southern Engineering Development Company (SEDCO) and planned to field a factory team. They invited me to come to Detroit, and I had lunch in their cafeteria with Ed Cole. I had bought a Robert Hall suit, and I thought I looked pretty good until I sat down with them two hundred and three hundred dollar suits. I got hired and went to work for Chevrolet the first day of November 1956 and got $650 a month to drive plus expenses, and I got a job working in the shop as a welder-fabricator and got another $650 a month for that. So, I was rich. I had more money...I'd never made money like that before.

"We started out pretty well at Daytona, and we had a car to finish second (Johnny Beauchamp, '57 Chevy). I installed the roll bar, shocks, and sway bars in every car there – my car, Buck Baker's, Speed Thompson's, Johnny Bearchamp's, and the convertibles of Possum Jones and Bob Welborn.

"We ran the new Chevrolet fuel injectors, that dog-house sort of glorified carburetor put out by Rochester, but NASCAR outlawed them after the race. So, we went to one carburetor. I don't know how many races we run, but on June 15, Chevrolet closed the racing division. That was a terrible blow to me. Before they closed it, I won two races and Frankie Schneider, who I got to be my partner on short tracks, won one short track race, and I won one. With no warning at all, we all came to work one day at SEDCO there at the East Point, Georgia, garage right on the line with Hapeville near the Ford plant, and they'd locked the gate on us and told us we were fired. They gave us a racecar and a tow truck and what few parts we could get.

"After that, Jim Rathmann in Miami was the factory's man when they started the marine engine development program where they could hide development of the 348. Frankie Delroy was the first person hired to be head of Chevrolet's racing team, but he was not the man for the job. He had me out buying used parts to build cars for a racing team. We didn't have any equipment to speak of; I built my cars out of my own tool box. We knew by Daytona that if we didn't get some new management, we were done. So, they fired Delroy and hired Rathmann, and he started spending the money like it was water. I was working in the shop on spindles and hubs and designing a new car, a nice short-track car for me and Frankie Schneider. Rathmann fired me, saying I couldn't work in the shop and race, too. He said I couldn't draw two salaries. They shunned me and wouldn't let me in the shop, so I told the two boys working for me how I wanted the car built. They built my car and brought it to Manassas, Virginia. I had never seen the car in finished condition. I went out, warmed up, and came back in to change the bite a little bit, change the air pressure in the tires, and sat on the pole. In the race, I lapped the field, including the factory Fords, Marvin Panch and Jim Reed who was a Ford hotdog and Bill Amick from California. I also lapped Frankie, my teammate, and won the race. I'd never beat him on the racetrack, and he wouldn't go to dinner with me after the race. I won two races for the factory team, all of them were black- and - white post cars. Then the gates closed in June.

"I went on racing on my own the rest of the season and wound up 21st in Grand National points. I raced a lot more races in 1958 and finished seventh in points and won two races. Then in 1959, Chevrolet dabbled back into racing a little bit, and they gave me a car; nothing but a car. So, I built it for racing and was struggling to do everything. Well, the Chevrolet racing team had hired Louie and Crawford Clements, brothers from Owensboro, Kentucky, and after the team got disbanded, Cotton Owens hired Louie. They weren't working too well together, so I hired Louie, and we ran the circuit in 1959 and won four or five races, I think, and finished tenth in points.

"We wound up the next year with two cars and started chasing points. We got one car and one spare engine, so with the

1963: THE SHOWDOWN

For 62, Chrysler engineers turned up the heat with two versions of the 413 equipped with new high performance hardware that made Dodge and Plymouth Super Stocks tough to beat. (DaimlerChrysler Historical Collection photo)

In top form with a compression ratio of 13.5:1, the dual quad 413 was factory rated at 420 hp @ 5400 rpm, a relatively low revving engine with rather closely matched power and torque curves, torque peak at 470 ft-lb, making a broad power band and a tough competitor.

engine from the '59 car, that's what we raced the entire year. We didn't start out to chase points, but with two cars, one for dirt and one for asphalt, we moved up in points during the season toward the championship. I won more races than anyone else that year and finished the season over 3,900 points ahead of Richard Petty to win the Grand National Championship.

"I went to work for Chevrolet at the Mesa, Arizona, Proving Grounds in 1960 and worked with Zora Arkus-Duntov testing cars and engines and got paid for that, right up to the winter of 1962 when they came out with the 427. I worked with Duntov on the Stingray Corvette with the 'tear drop' roof on it and test-drove the car. He was in engineering. Vince Piggins and Paul Prior were the Chevrolet men in charge of racing out in the field at the time. Zora did have a lot to say about things, and he loved that 348 and 409, but Vince and Paul were the people we had most contact with.

"The 348 was designed as a truck engine. It was never designed to race. In '57, we ran the 283. In 1958 when the 348 came out, I built one for a guy, but it just wasn't a good car. A '57 with the 283 could beat it. Duntov and Chevrolet stuck with that engine, trying to make it powerful enough to race until Duntov came along with idea of going to the 409 for 1962. It was not a good racing engine, either. It just wouldn't pull horsepower like the Pontiac 389.

"In 1960, Ned Jarrett ran a Ford he sponsored mostly by himself and did pretty well. Vince Piggins told me one day that they wanted to sponsor another car and asked me who I would recommend. I recommended Ned, and he got a car and some pieces and parts for the next year. We didn't get any money, but it put Ned in business for 1961, and he beat me for the championship. I beat myself, really, because I tried too hard to win. I wasn't interested in chasing points again; I should have, but I wanted to win by going down the straightaways like the Pontiacs. I was sick of the 348s and 409s because I couldn't do that. Then, Ford began to get ahead of us with Holman Moody. They could get more power than we could, and it paid off in the long run.

"In 1961, since we had to have a car owner, I formed a partnership with Louie Clements where he was the car owner. That lasted until 1963 when we dissolved the partnership. I was the only driver to ever win on a superspeedway with the 409. That was the Dixie 400 at Atlanta (averaging 124.896 mph). We built the engine and the car, but the 409 was so sensitive to temperature – hot day, cold day, it just ran different. On a hot day with bad humidity, it just didn't have any horsepower. The factory guys ran them on the dyno and corrected everything and said, 'Boy! We're pulling 380 horsepower!' I told Duntov; I said, 'You correct everything on the dynamometer, but when I go down the back stretch at Daytona, the only correction I can do is press the pedal to the floor.' I did that, and the Pontiacs went on by.

"In 1961, I run second to Ned Jarrett in Grand National points, and in 1962, I finished fifth. Then, in the winter of 1962, we began to get factory help again, and I built two cars. Bill Howell in Chevrolet engineering got us the new 427 soon to become known as the Mystery Engine. Bill worked for Dick Keinath, the engineer who designed it. That was a beautiful engine. I went to Mesa and did all the testing with the engine, different exhausts and rocker arm setups, and I ran over 177 mph; that was fast back then. It had good water circulation around the valves and combustion chambers and would develop unbelievable horsepower. We made 529 horsepower with a single 4-bbl carburetor. But the factory was running way behind. We

CHAPTER FIVE

Pontiac's bid for drag-racing fame in Super Stock was with the 421-powered Catalina with a holed chassis, the "Swiss cheese" lightweight package with aluminum components.

Pontiac's Super Duty 421 reigned supreme in NASCAR during 1962 and '63 with Joe Weatherly taking championships both years.

didn't have enough engine pieces to test good at Mesa, so we ran what we had. They kept saying, 'Be here tomorrow. Be here tomorrow. Be here tomorrow.' New parts didn't show up, and we ran out of time for Daytona. But that 427 was a good engine. At Daytona, I led twice with a blown head gasket; went into the pits and poured water on it, and still got back in the lead. Down the backstretch, I could go by Tiny Lund's Ford (the Wood Brothers 427 fastback) and nearly suck the paint off his car.

"Right before the race, we were trying to put enough pieces together to get Ray Fox a car and some others. I negotiated the deal for Ray; got him a tow truck, his cars, his money, the very same deal that I had. Smokey hadn't got a car yet, and we had some stuff we had hauled from the Proving Grounds where we blowed engines and was trying to put together a good engine to run the 500 with in my car. We used the heads off one of the engines but didn't check them with a straight edge. We had domed the heads a little bit and didn't know it. We put them on the engine and blew a head gasket during the race.

"Finally, Smokey got one of the test cars. Chevrolet didn't usually let their test cars out from the Proving Grounds, but he got one that I had built for testing. He set it up for the 500. That car was a surprise to me when he popped up with it, but Smokey was big in General Motors racing and went right to the top while I had to work my way up from the bottom. He and 'Bunkie' Knudsen were great buddies from back when Knudsen was at Pontiac and Smokey did so well with Pontiacs. When Knudsen went to Chevrolet, Smokey went with him. Smokey added some more bars to the roll cage, but he run the same hubs and spindles that I had built out at the Proving Grounds. We set up test cars, never planned for them to make it to the racetrack, and everything was assembly-line hardware, fenders, bumpers, A-frames that we reinforced; everything came from the factory. They were stock cars, and I had only one shock mounted at each wheel, so Smokey added the second shock. Johnny Rutherford was his driver, and he could drive. I run second to him in the second qualifying race for the 500. Junior Johnson won the first 100-mile qualifier in Ray Fox's car.

1963: THE SHOWDOWN

1962 and '63 Grand National Champion Joe Weatherly moved from driving Bud Moore's Pontiacs to his Mercurys around midseason 1963 and diced with Darel Dieringer during the Southern 500 to finish behind the Ford of Fireball Roberts. (Ford photo)

"During the 500, that was the only time I could pass anybody whenever I wanted to and just go to the front. That 427 engine developed horsepower at any racetrack at any RPM you wanted to run. You could turn it, too, 7,000, 8,000 rpms briefly, and it held up. With the 409, if you turned it 500 rpm more than it should be, off comes a rocker arm and the pushrods are bent. The 427 had the same rocker-arm ratios as the Pontiac, only it had a better cylinder head and it pulled a lot more power.

"Then, things went crazy at the factory. They spent a lot of money in that program, from back in the previous summer and all the testing we did, then kicked the props from under it. Somebody big must have got to somebody for it to stop like that. All of a sudden, 'We're out of racing,' they told us. That was a big blow to me again and changed my whole view of doing politics and racing. From then on it was an up-and-down cycle of hiding this or getting that from somebody, keeping everything under the table. People weren't dumb; they knew where the stuff came from.

"Seven or eight days before the race, a truckload of engines arrived in Daytona, but before they were unloaded, Chevrolet backed out of racing. I'd built a new shop, hired people, and was looking forward to a great year, and they came along and kicked it right out from under me. They wouldn't unload those engines. So, since we couldn't buy them anywhere, we were out of engines. We found out later that Holman Moody made NASCAR stick to the rules that said no experimental engines; engines had to be available to the public, and NASCAR made Chevrolet sell two of those engines to Ford. Bubba Farr had a '63 Chevrolet with a 409 in it, and he said, 'If you're giving Holman Moody two of 'em, I ought to get one.' They did let him have an engine, but after the race, they took it back. Holman Moody went right over to Smokey's and loaded up those engines. Chevrolet didn't get them back.

"Piggins and Prior and Howell came down to Daytona and hung around a few days before the race, but come race day, they were gone. Chevrolet had four of the 427s in the 500, my car, Smokey's, Ray's, and Bubba Farr's. (Rutherford finished ninth, four laps down. Rex finished 14th, six laps down.) We ran until July in that Chevrolet and struggled, using head gaskets over and over, because you couldn't get any parts for the engine. We kept pulling the engine down, afraid we would blow it, but it kept on going. I ran second in the World 600, probably the best finish we had with the 427. Then I went with Mercury. I dropped to ninth in Grand National points that year.

"That was a bad deal because Mercury wasn't a good racecar. I could have went with Plymouth, since neither of them offered any money, just cars and engines, but with the Plymouth I had to start with torsion bars and learn the ropes of how to make a Plymouth handle. So, I made up my mind that Chevrolet would never dump me again and went with Mercury because Bill Stroppe had the cars already built. By the end of the year, 1963, we hadn't done any good, and I got disgusted with the whole thing and dissolved the team. The next year, I ran four races for Bud Moore in his Mercurys and was going to have a factory deal, but since I was the low man on the totem pole, the budget cuts got me out. However, Chevrolet lived up to everything they said they would do.

"In 1965, I ran Sportsman all summer, run 32 races and won 20 of them with ten seconds in a '55 Chevrolet. At the end of 1965, I got out of racing and went to work with a Chrysler-Plymouth dealership."

CHAPTER SIX

Pop Eargle built this "automobile rotisserie," which allows much easier access while building a car. The '64 Dodge shown has a roll cage welded in to strengthen the unibody and protect the driver. (Photo courtesy International Motorsports Hall of Fame)

1964: Wedge Versus Hemi

Ford was offering its best equipment to anyone wanting to buy it, but many teams were racing old equipment against Holman Moody, the Wood brothers, and Stroppe factory teams, although Stroppe primarily ran USAC. As the new season loomed ahead, prospects were dismal for non-Ford teams. However, the rumors of Chrysler reintroducing the legendary Hemi became reality, and both Plymouth and Dodge were suddenly highly competitive.

Lee Petty had recovered substantially from his near-fatal crash at Daytona in 1961. He directed much of Petty Engineering, now Petty Enterprises, and even got back into the driver's seat during the season for one last go-round. The NASCAR season began in late 1963 with Richard driving the four races before the road race at Riverside. He ran the 426 wedge that had proved so successful during the 1963 season. The wedge was packaged in the new, more slippery 1964 Plymouth Belvedere hardtop, rather than the Savoy. The combination was a substantial performer, but still off the pace of the Fords that won the first two rounds, the second a road race at Augusta, Georgia, taken by Fireball Roberts. Wendell Scott scored Chevrolet's only win that year in the third round, and Richard Petty took the fourth.

The new season opened with a spread of victories, but at Riverside, the Fords rolled, and Gurney won again. This time he led a one-two Wood Brothers team sweep with Marvin Panch, rather than Holman Moody cars. Once again, Parnelli Jones was his only competitor in a Stroppe Mercury, and once again, Jones exited early and Gurney ran away with the race. Fireball Roberts finished third, Bill Amick placed fourth in a Mercury, and Ned Jarrett came in fifth, giving Ford another top-five sweep.

Along the way, catastrophe struck. Two-time Grand National Champion and the famed "clown prince" of NASCAR, Joe Weatherly, was trying his best in an ill-handling Stroppe Mercury that was well off Gurney's pace. He went off course at turn six, smacked the wall broadside, and was killed. Gloom fell over the Ford camp and all of NASCAR, especially among the many fans who admired Weatherly and his talent for driving some less-than-top-drawer cars to victory.

Paul Goldsmith races his #25 '64 Plymouth at Atlanta International Raceway. After crashing at the Atlanta 500 earlier in the year, Goldsmith finished third in the Dixie 400. (Photo courtesy International Motorsports Hall of Fame)

NASCAR'S WILD YEARS

CHAPTER SIX

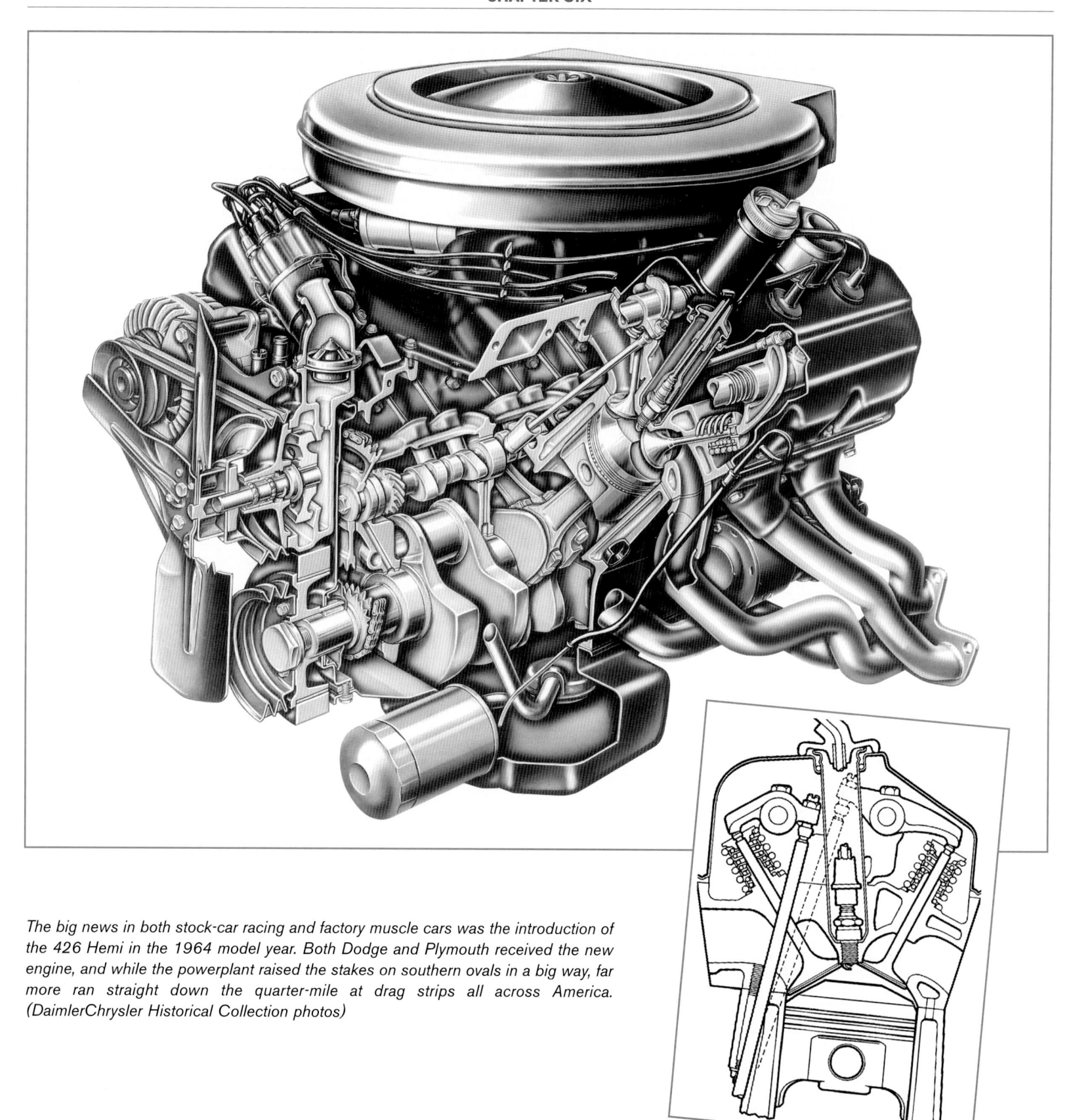

The big news in both stock-car racing and factory muscle cars was the introduction of the 426 Hemi in the 1964 model year. Both Dodge and Plymouth received the new engine, and while the powerplant raised the stakes on southern ovals in a big way, far more ran straight down the quarter-mile at drag strips all across America. (DaimlerChrysler Historical Collection photos)

1964: WEDGE VERSUS HEMI

Fred Lorenzen and his #28 Holman-Moody Ford finished 13th in points in 1964, entering just 17 of 62 races. (Photo courtesy International Motorsports Hall of Fame)

Chrysler Corporation made its Daytona 500 debut of the 426 Hemi highly visible with flaming red Plymouths and Dodges with white-and-gold lettering. Paul Goldsmith added a record Daytona 500 pole of 174.91 mph to the fast-growing reputation of the Hemi.

The season went on, back to Daytona, with the Ford camp replete with top drivers. Even Rex White, a staunch Chevrolet man, had moved over to Mercury. Among Ford's roster at Riverside was Junior Johnson driving a Ray Fox Ford, but when people looked around after the race, they were strangely absent.

Stroppe had set up an operation in Atlanta with Darel Dieringer as lead driver. Bud Moore put together a Mercury operation in Spartanburg, South Carolina, and signed rookie Billy Wade as backup to Weatherly. With Weatherly's demise, Wade moved to top driver and White became de facto second team because of getting parts through Moore, although he operated independently.

As in 1963, Daytona held many surprises, and Ford found itself once again battling NASCAR's bent rules. Chrysler hatched a plan after seeing Ford's rebuilt reputation and its surging sales brought by racing. Its old Hemi, removed from production in 1957, had won two straight championships in the Kiekhaefer Chryslers back then and was, in early 1964, the reigning king of drag racing, with no competition in AA/Fuel Dragster. Factory engineers had been quietly working on a new version of the B engine with hemispherical combustion chambers, and by Daytona, the first of the new engines was sent to Petty Enterprises.

The new Hemi had been a long time coming. A review of Society of Automotive Engineers (SAE) papers published from 1951 on proved that Chrysler's engineers had not been sitting on their hands. In pursuit of an overhead-valve design, a DOHC, hemi-headed, inline 6-cylinder engine had been designed by 1951, but its chain-driven cams and supporting hardware were deemed too expensive for a production engine. The simplified single cam-in-block pushrod design became the FirePower V-8, introduced in 1951 after 8,000 hours of dyno testing and over a half-million miles of road tests. It didn't lose its hemispherical combustion chambers, which gave it as much as a 20-percent increase in output over conventional wedge designs and much better valve placement.

Original work on the inline-6 during the war years led to inline-8 engines, but as displacement increased, the advantages of a V-8 emerged. Chrysler, looking to provide clearance for crankshaft rotation on its over-square OHV V-8 design (B/S = 1.06) dating from July 1945, realized the advantages of the new, compact engine. The increased friction of the larger bores could be offset with reduced-friction materials. With improved thermal, mechanical, and volumetric efficiencies inherent in the new design, there was no need for higher-energy fuels or a substantial increase in compression ratio, as required by all other designs, to make big power. Chrysler focused future efforts on V-8 engines, producing a 330-ci Hemi in January 1948. The new engine validated their enthusiasm for the design.

James C. Zeder, Vice President and Director of Engineering Research at Chrysler, reported in his SAE papers that tests of the new Hemi V-8 showed that a compression increase from 7.5:1 to 12.6:1 increased horsepower at 4,000 rpm from 210 to 270, with no significant increase of thermal loss. Hot rodding with multiple carbs and improved exhausts delivered 310 hp. The tests showed excellent performance with indications of substantial untapped potential. Zeder concluded, "We are assured, therefore,

CHAPTER SIX

The #54 Plymouth of Jimmy Pardue had a little trouble here, but he finished fifth in points for 1964. (Photo courtesy International Motorsports Hall of Fame)

that when high compression becomes desirable or fuel quality makes it possible, this cylinder head will respond to increased demands better than any other combustion chamber with which we are acquainted."

By 1963, racing fuels and high-compression engines were the norm, and Chrysler revisited the Hemi when the wedge engine needed a boost. Their effort was heavily influenced by a group of engineers, some of them working on Chrysler high-performance engines, who built a car for weekend drag racing. They formally organized themselves as the *Ramchargers*, and set to doing what hot-rodders do best – figure out how to go faster. Their early attempts at improving power from a 354-ci Dodge truck Hemi resulted in the long-tube ram induction that Chrysler put into production as the cross-ram 413 of 1961. The *Ramcharger* name had been adopted for the Dodge 426 wedge engine of 1963, and when the new 426 Hemi was released in 1964, the *Ramchargers* were the hottest team in town. They quickly reset the quarter-mile record book.

Fred Lorenzen (outside of No. 99) is seen here on his way to sweeping both races at Martinsville, 1964. He leads Junior Johnson (No. 27). Among Ford's 30 wins that year, Ned Jarrett had the most with 15. Three of Lorenzen's eight wins were on major tracks—Atlanta, Darlington, and Charlotte. (Murray Grant photo)

1964: WEDGE VERSUS HEMI

While stock-car racing was a strong focus, Chrysler Corporation sent more of its new 426 Hemi engines into drag racing across the nation and earned enormous enthusiasm as the "est" (fastest, quickest, toughest, strongest). Dave Strictler's famous Dodge was just one of a host of Hemis that dominated Super Stock, Modified Production, and match racing throughout America. (D. Randy Riggs photo)

Parnelli Jones at the wheel of Bill Stroppe's factory-backed Mercury. The Lincoln-Mercury Division traced its factory-backed efforts to the Lincolns of the Panamericana, in which Bill France competed with Curtis Turner, then to 1957 with Tim Flock and Billy Wade in stock cars. But it would be the 1970s before the make wrote its name in the record books of NASCAR in a big way. Although equipped with the best equipment, and filled with both driving and mechanical talent in 1964, Stroppe's efforts came up short against the southern boys. Part of the Mercury factory effort shifted to Bud Moore's Spartanburg, South Carolina, shop that year, but the Mercs were just too heavy to be competitive. (Ford photo)

Restyling produced more pleasing cars for both Plymouth and Dodge in 1964, and showrooms reflected wider public interest as sales picked up. The restyling also worked better on the racetrack; with a lower, more bullet-shaped nose and sloping rear window, the new cars had better aerodynamics.

Quietly testing the new 426 Hemi on Goodyear's five-mile test track in San Angelo, Texas, was a familiar duo, Ray Fox and Junior Johnson. They tested the Hemi against the fastest car from

NASCAR'S WILD YEARS

CHAPTER SIX

The street Hemi was rare in 1964, but a few got out in the Dodge Polara and Plymouth Fury, rated at 415 hp with a single 4-bbl carb and 425 hp with duals.

the 1963 NASCAR season, Ray's well-beaten Mystery Engine Chevrolet. Once durability was increased, the Hemi engine pushed the aerodynamically improved Plymouths and Dodges over 185 mph – about 20 mph faster than the Fords were running at Daytona.

Once finalized, the first engine let out of the factory went to Petty Enterprises, and testing at Daytona immediately got the attention of the Ford men – another Mystery Engine? Just as the year before, no one had seen such an engine, but NASCAR bent its strictly stock rules once again to get the factory teams to battle it out on Daytona's high banks. Rules said that 1,500 engines had to be built, or at least be scheduled to be built, for it to qualify, but Petty Enterprises had the only such engine seen publicly. Instantly, another duel unfolded between the factory men, with Bill France in the middle trying to work a compromise to bring in more paying spectators. The new Hemi rapidly turned into headlines, and the headlines proclaimed another David-and-Goliath showdown with Richard Petty as the much-cheered underdog against the might of Ford Motor Company. There were also the Dodge boys with Junior Johnson and David Pearson to consider. They were tough to the bone. The Daytona 500 shaped up to be a three-way shootout that started in the qualifiers where a host of fast Hemis proved how tough they were.

However, the Petty crew had problems with the new Hemi. Even after cobbling head gaskets that didn't leak, they had to add about 100 lbs of lead to the rear bumper to hold down the light rear end of the Plymouth so the Hemi could put its enormous power to the ground.

Junior Johnson (Dodge), Buck Baker (Plymouth), and David Pearson (Dodge) rolled in one-two-three in the first round of qualifying. Paul Goldsmith (Plymouth) set a sensational new pole record of 174.91 mph, almost 11 mph faster than Johnson's 1963 record. Bobby Isaac (Dodge), Jim Pardue (Plymouth), and

CHAPTER SIX

Ford produced thousands of 427-powered Galaxies with 410 hp (with a single 4-bbl) and 425 hp (with dual quads). By far the rarest in 1964 was the 427-powered Lightweight Galaxie, an order-only drag-racing special that was factory stripped and lightened, and delivered ready for the strip.

94   NASCAR'S WILD YEARS

Richard Petty (Plymouth) paced the second round one-two-three, and Ford was shut out. Petty was the fastest second-round qualifier at 174.418 mph. Chrysler Hemis commanded the top seven starting positions of the Daytona 500. Ford screamed foul to no avail, even though its cars met the letter of NASCAR regulations, and Chrysler was obviously cheating with an engine that it said was going into production. The Hemi did make it to production, but only 493 were built that year, mostly for drag cars and a few street cars. Plymouth got 246 while Dodge received 247, and their cars were both lighter and smaller than the big Fords.

Another proposal from the Ford men caught France off-guard; they wanted to run the new single-overhead-cam 427, the soon-to-be-legendary SOHC Cammer, thus revealing that Ford's engineers hadn't been sitting on their hands, either. The reasoning was simple: if Chrysler could run a mystery engine, Ford should be allowed to do so as well. France declined and ignited a cheating war with tricks that technical inspectors could hardly keep up with. Even so, the Daytona 500 was a lost cause for Ford and a spectacular victory for Chrysler and the new 426 Hemi. Plymouths and Dodges led all but two laps, with Petty in front for the final 48 laps to easily win at a record speed of 154.334 mph. The Plymouths of Pardue and Goldsmith followed for a one-two-three romp, and Petty was on the way to a Grand National Driver Championship and $98,810 in winnings. He started all 62 of NASCAR's scheduled races and won 9.

Two spectators at Daytona were Henry Ford II and Lynn Townsend, President of Chrysler Corporation. After the race, Ford told Charles "Chuck" Patterson, head of Ford's North American Operations, what he thought of Chrysler's win. Almost the next day, a twofold plan emerged; Holman Moody undertook fitting the 427 to the lighter, smaller Fairlane, while the engineers back in Dearborn developed a lightweight, high-revving valvetrain and an improved induction system – the High Riser. The Fairlane didn't handle well and was shelved for the time being, but the new 7,000-rpm valvetrain and induction system worked wonders. Ford's cars now had well over 500 hp for the first time. However, just prior to receiving the new equipment, Lorenzen's Holman Moody Ford handled Bristol's tight high banks so well that he led almost the entire 500-lap race to shut out the Hemi clan. Chassis and suspension setup held some secrets, too.

The next big oval race was at Atlanta. With the new valvetrain and more power from the second-generation 427, the notorious High Riser with its high-port heads and ram-type manifold, Lorenzen was unstoppable, building a two-lap lead over Bobby Isaac's Dodge. He took his third straight Atlanta victory, this one among high attrition that left only 10 of the 42 starters running at the finish. Aiding his drive was a trick chassis and suspension set up by the Holman Moody crew, and quick pit stops,

the key to more time at speed. Improved road-holding enabled Lorenzen to drive deeper into turns and go through them faster, dropping lap times.

More tricks included bodies shifted on the chassis for improved handling in left turns, lowered suspension with different right-left setups, droopy noses for better air penetration, movable chassis weights for shifting the roll center, and anything that could be kept secret from NASCAR's inspectors.

Tires were suddenly inadequate for the power of the new engines and the speeds they produced. Both Firestone and Goodyear were unprepared for the major increases in speed, about 20 mph over the previous year, and surviving the punishment of 500 high-speed miles proved difficult. Billy Wade, the sensational young driver who took four wins in a row late in the season in a Bud Moore Mercury, was killed in a crash testing tires at Daytona. Jimmy Pardue, who finished second behind Petty at Daytona in a Plymouth, was also killed while testing tires at Charlotte.

Other safety issues rose, some challenging NASCAR's insistence that cars run as manufactured equipment. Assembly-line gas tanks were required, not bladder-type fuel cells that other racing venues had already adopted. That rule cost Fireball Roberts his life at Charlotte during the World 600 when he crashed backward into a retaining rail, flipped, and was trapped, strapped into his car as its roof filled with a pool of gasoline. Junior Johnson, Ned Jarrett, and other drivers stopped to help, pulling him out of the burning wreck, but a month later he died. Another of NASCAR's top stars had gone.

While debates and arguments flourished, Ford's predicted sweep of the NASCAR crown turned into another season-long shootout for Richard Petty, this time with Ned Jarrett. Lorenzen won 9 races, 6 straight in one stretch, but Jarrett's 15 wins as Ford's short-track ace was tops among Ford's 30 wins. Running in two fewer races than Petty likely cost him his second championship. Petty's possibilities were clearly influenced by his dropping out of several short-track races because of rear-end failures. Chrysler rated the Hemi at around 500 hp, though the Ford men claimed it exceeded 600 hp. With its massive torque, it showed the weak link in the driveline by breaking it. Rear ends needed to be beefed up for racing with a Hemi.

Ford won four of eight races on the big ovals, while Dodge and Plymouth evenly split the other four. Jim Paschal took the World 600, proving that Plymouth and the Hemi had long-distance durability. As the season progressed, Dodge proved a bigger threat by racking up 14 wins versus Plymouth's 12, and Mercury added 5 to Ford's tally.

Petty's first championship contributed to Plymouth's showroom sales boost of 15.1 percent over 1963, while Dodge brought in 19.9 percent better sales. Ford sales took a leap of 149,000 units, while Chevrolet sales for 1964 dipped 188,600 units. This was a substantial downturn of nearly a half-billion dollars from

B/NSS
1
DODGE
RAMCHARGERS
CHASSIS
ENGINEERING
CRANE
Cams
MSD

From deep within the Dodge, a group of engineers applied their knowledge to building super-quick drag machines and built a name for themselves – the Ramchargers. Dodge adapted the name and marketed its top-performing engines as the Ramcharger. Many of drag racing's stars of old have returned to nostalgia racing, and returned to championship form.

the upward trend of the previous three years, when racing fast Chevys was a marketing tool. "Win on Sunday, sell on Monday" really did work in the new-car marketplace.

Trouble for the Hemi was just ahead. By season's end, safety issues prompted major changes in NASCAR's rules, and efforts to slow the cars resulted in Bill France banning both the Hemi and Ford's High Riser 427. The Ford men applauded the return to sanity in racing, but Chrysler racing boss Ronney Householder issued a proclamation that neither Plymouth nor Dodge would participate in any further NASCAR racing unless the rules were modified.

Richard Petty went straight, straight down the quarter-mile in 1965. While diehard Plymouth and Dodge NASCAR teams won only six races that year, Ford won 48 of the 55 events.

RAY FOX

The following is the story of Ray Fox's career in stock-car racing, as told by Ray himself.

"In Salem, New Hampshire, they had a big board racetrack there, and when I was about seven years old, the Indianapolis 500-type cars came to race there every year. I went to watch them, and that put racing in my mind. Then with all the people racing on the Beach, Malcolm Campbell and people like him out to set world records [the combined two-way average of 276 mph in the measured mile, March 7, 1935], I just had to come to Daytona Beach. I got out of the service in 1946 and came to Daytona. I met Fireball Roberts and Marshall Teague, and I went with them to different racetracks, like Jacksonville and Savannah, Pompano

CHAPTER SIX

Ray Fox (center) looks over a racing exotic. (Ray Fox Collection photo)

1964: WEDGE VERSUS HEMI

Ray Fox had a great talent for building cars and engines for stock car racing. He had has hands into all kinds of cars, including Pontiacs, Chevrolets, Fords and Dodges. (Photo courtesy International Motorsports Hall of Fame)

Darlington's Record Club for 1964 lists speeds by make to show that Ford's 427 wedge was almost a match for Chrysler's 426 Hemi under NASCAR rules. David Pearson posted the fastest lap for Dodge at 135.98 mph; Richard Petty ran 136.82 mph in his Plymouth; Fred Lorenzen posted 135.73 mph in a Holman Moody Ford; and Darel Dieringer ran 134.42 mph in a Stroppe Mercury. Shown is Fireball Roberts in a factory-backed entry just prior to crashing with David Pearson's Dodge at Atlanta. (Ford photo)

NASCAR'S WILD YEARS 99

CHAPTER SIX

Indy 500 winner (1961, 1964) A. J. Foyt brought top billing to NASCAR. He entered eight races to win the Firecracker 400 at Daytona. (Ford photo)

Beach in Florida, and other races in Florida. I raced a Hollywood supercharged Graham. It didn't do too well because of falling apart, but Fireball and Marshall did well with their cars, and we had a lot of fun. That was strictly stock racing before NASCAR or any organization. We raced at places that held races, and we'd go run them. Dirt tracks; all of them were dirt tracks.

"I had been with Fish Carburetor for a long time, and when Mr. Fish died, in 1959 I believe, they left the shop to me and paid me $75 a week to help me get going in building racecars. My first involvement with factory racing was with Betty Skelton and Campbell-Ewald, the advertising people for Chevrolet. The factory had just come out with the 1960 Corvair and they wanted to promote it as an economy car. I set up the car to do the test at Daytona, going round and round the track. There were two hundred entries, and I won with ninety-six miles to a gallon. The Chevrolet guys said, 'Sorry, we can't advertise that!' I got paid, and that was it.

"I wanted to do something different in racing, so I built a car to set the world closed course speed record on asphalt, out here at the Speedway (Daytona). The track was new at the time, 1960 I think it was. I built a '55 Dodge with a 392 Hemi engine and a blower on it, and LeeRoy Yarbrough drove it to set the record at a little over 182 miles per hour. That was fast back then.

"In NASCAR that year, the dog racing track out beside the track and I got involved with a '59 Chevrolet. The dog track owned it, and I set it up. Junior Johnson drove the car and won the race, the Daytona 500, the second race that was run on the track. That race was really something out of this world. I worked hard on that Chevrolet engine, and it ran fairly decent, but drafting had a lot to with winning the race. Toward the end, Bobby

1964: WEDGE VERSUS HEMI

Ford's secret weapon was the 427-ci single-overhead-cam (SOHC) Cammer engine developed in 1964. At more than 600 hp with a single 4-bbl carb, this engine was to be Dearborn's attack on Chrysler's Hemi. (Ford photo)

Chrysler engineering developed the 426 Hemi of 1964 as a step up from the 392 Hemi of the late 1950s, an evolution of the 331-ci engine of 1951-'56, the first production form of a decade of hemispherical combustion-chamber development by the Corporation. (DaimlerChrysler Historical Collection photo)

won at Atlanta (setting a new record of 125.23 mph that stood until 1966), and we went to Daytona for the Firecracker 400, and David won that race, too (setting a new record of 154.29 mph that stood until 1968. In 1961, Pontiacs won 30 of 52 NASCAR races).

"The '59 Chevrolet and the '61 Pontiac were strictly private entry cars, no factory connection whatsoever. The dog track owned the cars, and I built them and ran them out of my shop in Daytona Beach. The dog track also owned the 1962 Pontiac, and we did pretty well that year, too. [Pontiacs won 22 of 53 NASCAR races that year.]

"I got involved with the 1963 'Mystery Engine' Chevrolets because I had done so well with the Corvair. Chevrolet decided to go racing, and I signed a contract with them for so much a year, but as the year went on, they got out of the contract. We kept on racing with the parts they had sent me and did the best we could. Junior Johnson drove for me and did very well at the beginning of the season, but the parts we had wore out after a while. Junior won the first qualifier before the Daytona 500 [setting a new record at 164.03 mph that he surpassed the next year at 170.78 mph driving Ray's 426 Hemi Dodge, a record that stood until 1967]. In the 500, the car was fast, but it didn't hold up; valvesprings was our biggest problem. Junior did well wherever we ran the car that year, probably ten races. He won seven out of eight Chevrolet wins that year [including the Atlanta 500 and the fall 500 at Charlotte]. We won

Johns was leading the race in Smokey's Pontiac, and when he went through the turns, Junior was right behind him, right on his tail, and it sucked the back window out of Johns' car. He fell back and Junior went by. Junior ended up winning the race. His driving made the most of that race.

"The dog track wanted to run a Pontiac the next year, and I built the car. It ran a 389 engine and single 4-barrel. Darel Dieringer was supposed to drive the car, but he had a contract with Goodyear and they wouldn't let him. Someone said, call David Pearson. He was just beginning and had driven a few dirt-track races. He came down and did a great job. We went to Charlotte for the World 600, and he won the race. I went on from Charlotte to win five superspeedway races that year. David

CHAPTER SIX

David Pearson and Richard Petty line up for a night race with stone guards and driver shields in place. Cotton Owns (second left), owner of Pearson's car, looks on during a pit stop. Short tracks, dirt, and night racing were fast fading from NASCAR's schedule. (DaimlerChrysler Historical Collection photo)

With the factory Chrysler teams raising the bar at the beginning of the 1964 season, it looked to be a tough year for Ford and lead driver Lorenzen. But peeling off five wins in a row – culminating with a victory in Darlington's Rebel 300 at record speed, 130.013 mph – the No. 28 Ford and its crew showed they could also fight tough. (Ford photo)

102 NASCAR'S WILD YEARS

1964: WEDGE VERSUS HEMI

Mercury Division racing boss Fran Hernandez and Fred Lorenzen catch up on the latest in racing news – Ford's romp toward 30 wins that year. Even though Lorenzen was the top driver among great talent in Dearborn's garage, he failed to crack the top 10 in NASCAR's point race in 1964, even though he won eight races, half of his lifetime record to that year. (Ford photo)

about all of Chevrolet's wins that year. I built up cars from the parts I had left over from what Chevrolet sent me, two or three cars, so I had other drivers, too. Some races, I'd run two cars, some races, three cars.

"Zora Duntov was Chevrolet's inside man, and he supplied the ferocious cams for those engines, but I didn't do much of anything with the factory men. I built the cars and raced them. After Chevrolet got out, we were on our own. Even though the Chevrolet 427 was sort of a secret engine, it was a hell of a good engine, and mechanics could fix it and make it run better. It had more power over a better RPM range than previous engines, and we ran a lot of races with that engine. Usually, Junior qualified on the pole; many, many times he was on the pole.

"For 1964, Dodge wanted to get into racing. When the Hemi came out, it was really something. It was by far the best engine. There wasn't much of a comparison between the Chevrolet 427 and the Dodge 426 Hemi. The 1963 Chrysler engine was not the Hemi, but it ran fairly good. [Richard Petty won all but three of Plymouth's 19 wins that year. Dodge had no wins.] We went to a five-mile course in Texas in late November 1963, where we had Thanksgiving dinner while we tested the cars. The Chrysler people were there,

Cotton Owens (facing the camera), helps out on a pit stop for David Pearson's '64 Dodge. Pearson finished third in overall points for the '64 season. (Photo courtesy International Motorsports Hall of Fame)

but my Chevrolet out-ran the Dodge by ten miles per hour around that five-mile track. Then they decided to bring the Hemi in. That engine was very potent.

"Those engines were supplied to us by the factory. We didn't have anything to do with developing that engine, but every engine we ever got we had to do a lot of work on to make them last for racing. We put the engines together from parts they sent us and tuned them and made new components sometimes, like pistons, to increase performance. The previous Chrysler 413 engine had cross-ram manifolds, but the Hemi didn't have anything like that. They came with the carburetor on the top of the engine and was bolted to an aluminum intake. We ran those engines mostly with a single 4-barrel carburetor, but they could be set up with two 4-barrels. The earlier Hemi, the 392, was the same and had two 4-barrels, but the new Hemi was a 426 and a lot better. It was really something. I worked on the 392 for customers in my shop, but I didn't race that engine.

"Our biggest problem back then in blowing engines was valvesprings. They just didn't hold up, and a valve would get down on a piston, and that was it. Even with dual valvesprings and a divider between them, they didn't hold up, and we did a lot of trying new springs and parts like that to see what would last. [Dodge won 14 races in 1964, having won 1 in 1956 and 1 in 1960.]

"The next year, NASCAR screwed around with the engine rules so much that I got out. Ford and NASCAR got together and the Hemi had to be reduced to 405 cubic inches. So, I had pistons made, then they changed the rules again, and I got disgusted with the whole thing and got out. I ran a Dodge with the wing on it in 1970; Buddy Baker drove it, among other drivers, but I didn't do much and quit in 1972."

1964: WEDGE VERSUS HEMI

David Pearson (#6 Dodge) and Fireball Roberts (#22 Ford) got together during the Atlanta 500. Fireball Roberts started just nine races during the 1964 season. (Photo courtesy International Motorsports Hall of Fame)

NASCAR'S WILD YEARS

CHAPTER SEVEN

Following the Mystery Engine episode at Daytona 1963, Chevrolet Division, along with all of GM, pulled out of stock-car racing, the result of Dick Keinath's superbly powerful 427 Mk IIS that dominated the qualifying races. That engine went through various design changes to become the Mk IV 396, introduced in the 396 Chevelle in 1965. (Chevrolet photo)

1965: Shaking the Rules Tree

Bill France was so sure that Chevrolet would get back into racing that he wrote new rules for 1965 to favor the make. By eliminating the Hemi, the High Riser, and Chevrolet's Mystery Engine, France leveled the playing field in favor of mass-produced engines, bringing the hardware back toward strictly stock. In doing so, he ignored the rapid advances that the factories made in heavy-duty hardware and their ability to put together special-edition packages of the best high-performance equipment. The Ford 427 Galaxie Sport Hardtop was a prime example; it sold almost 5,000 units in 1963 alone. Special editions were strictly stock, too, strictly speaking, but what France had in mind was along the lines of what had been showroom stock, and the fans were not interested. The kids wanted the "ests" – the latest, the fastest, the quickest, the hottest, the baddest, the wildest, the biggest numbers. They looked to drag racing and found the most powerful engines stuffed into smaller cars.

France, in his continual attempt to write rules to keep a lid on ever-rising costs, also overlooked the potential of the rapidly increasing craftsmanship mastered in race shops across the country. The ability to build better "stock" cars that were not only faster but more durable and safer than factory-built cars soon became a central issue in what was strictly stock and what wasn't – in particular, tube-frame cars. NASCAR's entries hadn't actually been strictly stock since the 1950s, and every allowance given by the rule makers since then resulted in cars further from stock. By necessity of mass production, the factories built road cars, not race cars, and the race shops had become adept at taking an assembly-line body shell and making a race car of it. Now France seemed to be trying to withdraw the allowances that had made 1964 the best year of racing NASCAR had ever seen. And stock-car racing had a fast-growing competitor: drag racing.

Rather than legislate out the factory's best efforts, drag racing promoters embraced the "ests" and created classes for anything anybody wanted to race. Factory Experimental, A/FX in particular, quickly became the most sensational type of car from anywhere, and the factories were heavily involved. With Chrysler out of NASCAR and GM not returning, left-turn racing was an all-Ford show in 1965, and promoters saw attendance rapidly

Down at Holman Moody in Charlotte, John Holman cranked up Ford's 427 wedge to show around 525 hp. All that power was needed to compete with Chrysler's 426 Hemi, until the fast Dodge and Plymouth stockers were removed from competition by corporate decree. (Ford photo)

decline. They screamed at France to change the rules to bring back the factory hardware. By then, Ford was racing everywhere in the world, and all of the factory men had turned their attention to drag racing's phenomenal growth. The pay-off was in sales.

Despite NASCAR's claimed influence on sales, the big three saw spectacular sales growth in 1965 with only Ford involved in stock-car racing. In particular, the kids paid enormous attention to the new generation of smaller cars stuffed with big engines,

CHAPTER SEVEN

One of Holman Moody's Fords raced by Fred Lorenzen in 1965 was found and restored to better than original racing condition, seen in recent years parading at various tracks.

Developed from the 405 hp 406 of 1962, Ford's 427 side-oiler with dual quads, factory cast-iron headers, and cross-bolt mains proved highly successful in every form of racing the Ford men went after. (Ford photo)

quickly dubbed muscle cars. Ford's sensationally popular Mustang, introduced as a 1964-1/2 model, sold 883,600 units by the end of the year. The Mustang alone accounted for over 2 billion dollars in new Ford sales in its first 18 months. To see them go fast meant going to drag races where the 10 Holman Moody-built A/FX Mustangs, mostly with the 427 Cammer power, were

Opening the new year with another win at the Motor Trend 500 at Riverside, Dan Gurney continued his Ford roll in road racing, driving for the Wood Brothers team in 1965. (Ford photo)

national sensations. There was also a host of Falcon and Fairlane drivers jamming gears behind 427 wedge power. Fierce competition from anything running a Hemi made thrilling shows, and the occasional Chevrolet match racer added a little spice. Enormous crowds of spectators flocked to drag strips all across the nation and snatched up newsstand magazines that highlighted the latest and best.

Pontiac's GTO, introduced in late 1963 with the 389, was another market sensation. Buick's Skylark and the new shared-platform Chevrolet Chevelle and Oldsmobile 4-4-2 emerged as market-niche cars with big sales numbers in 1964 and 1965.

So, who needed NASCAR? Chevrolet didn't – with sales up 22.3 percent over 1964, "We don't race" was working fine. Chevy ventured into the muscle car market with the Mk IIS-derived Mk IV 396-ci big-block stuffed into the small Chevelle. Ford had blown the top off sales with the Mustang, and new big Ford sales were up 21.1 percent. Dodge and Plymouth were doing very well with their Ramcharger and Super Stock big-blocks in their smaller and lighter "big" cars, up 8.4 percent and 18.9 percent, respectively. Drag racing was eating NASCAR's lunch.

Richard Petty fielded two Petty Engineering Hemi-powered Barracudas with Plymouth backing. The first one, dubbed *Outlawed*, and a later, improved version *43 Jr.*, were 10-second, 140-mph strip burners. These factory-based cars were the newest type of strip teasers, and match racing lit up attendance everywhere.

Match racing shootouts were intensely exciting showdowns between the latest and most powerful equipment from the Big Three, and fan support was enormous. Fast Fords, Plymouths, and Dodges were everywhere, and A/FX Pontiacs were still the king of performance at GM, but largely second-tier entries compared to the faster iron from Ford and Chrysler. Oldsmobile had some new GTO-size 4-4-2s with their big inch engines topped with a blower and fuel injection that were just made for tire burning. Even though they weren't national-caliber winners, they made for sensational drag racing. The kids loved every minute of it and couldn't wait for more.

While NASCAR teams were hampered by rules, drag racing became the showcase for unlimiteds – anything anyone wanted to build had a place to race, and the wilder the better. Fords, Chevys, Mercurys, Dodges, and Plymouths lined up in best-of-five or best-of-seven Sunday-afternoon match races that were instant crowd pleasers. Match races with local and famous drivers from around the country were hyped in radio broadcasts to area youth: "Come Sunday, see the biggest and best racing on the planet! Be there!" And they did.

Off-road, special-edition Super Stock cars like the 427-powered '64 Ford Thunderbolt, and Factory Experimental lightweights from Mercury, Plymouth, and Dodge, could be purchased race-ready from dealers. Match race cars were a step up. Nitro-burning unlimiteds in Super-Experimental Stock advanced

CHAPTER SEVEN

On a brilliant southern California day, Ford power ran Riverside's road course largely unopposed. Darel Dieringer (No. 06), Parnelli Jones (No. 15), Fred Lorenzen (No. 28), Junior Johnson (No. 27). (Ford photos)

rapidly, and eventually became funny cars. Stock-car racing was on notice; the most exciting racing in America was in a straight line. The craze swept across America like a wildfire and showcased the most innovative and creative racing seen anywhere. High-HP cars were in abundance at every event, many with more than 1,000 hp. The kids loved it all, and dealers counted their money. Stock-car racing had little to crow about.

After experiencing phenomenal growth in 1964, drag racing in 1965 was even better. With two major nationwide sanctioning bodies, the NHRA (National Hod Rod Association) and the AHRA

1965: SHAKING THE RULES TREE

(American Hot Rod Association), along with a host of regional and local organizations, the sport exploded in popularity. In just one weekend, over 130,000 spectators attended the NHRA National Championships held in Indianapolis to watch more than 1,100 entrants compete for a handful of Eliminator trophies and national stardom. The manufacturers of whatever components a winner ran – tires, spark plugs, gasoline, shifters, and tachometers, to name just a few – trumpeted the success in advertising across the country. Drag racing reached fantastic heights unimaginable just few years earlier, all because of the kids and their insatiable appetite for speed.

By then, drag-race engine builders had learned that factory assembly lines produced compromise engines. As the techniques of engine assembly and performance enhancements spread into speed shops everywhere, factory hardware was improved by

Continued on page 113

A. J. Foyt (No. 00). (Ford photo)

The Holman Moody garage at Daytona. (Ford photo)

NASCAR'S WILD YEARS 111

CHAPTER SEVEN

Lorenzen and Johnson dueled during the second 100-mile qualifier for the Daytona 500. Johnson took the win in the closing seconds of the caution-delayed race. Darel Dieringer won the first round. Average speeds for both races were well off the pace of the 1964 races because of Chrysler's pullout, which made the 100-milers at the 500 a Ford fest. Lorenzen took the flag after 133 laps, rather than the scheduled 200, because of rain, and led an 11-car Ford parade. (Ford photo)

Factory drivers Curtis Turner (No. 41), Fred Lorenzen (No. 28), and Dick Hutcherson (No. 29) in a Ford freight train at Charlotte. This was typical of 1965 races. In hopes of bringing back spectators, Bill France allowed Turner back into NASCAR, but even Turner's hard charging could not shine the lost luster of Chrysler's boycott. Lorenzen, Hutcherson, and Turner finished in that order on the superspeedway that Turner brought into existence but lost to bankruptcy a year after opening. Lorenzen won both Charlotte races that year. (Ford photo)

Curtis "Pops" Turner won the debut race at Rockingham, the American 500. He held off hotshoe Cale Yarborough in the closing laps to show that he could still whip the youngsters. (Ford photo)

112   NASCAR'S WILD YEARS

1965: SHAKING THE RULES TREE

Lorenzen started 17 races in 1965, won 4, and took home $77,965 for the season, adding the Daytona 500 and both races at Charlotte and Martinsville to his growing total, which would be cut short by early retirement. (Ford photo)

Continued from page 111

blueprinting engines to design specifications and tighter tolerances. By 1965, a host of hot rodder's tricks were the norm in taking a factory engine to its full potential. Speed shops turned out equipment better than the factories, and fans got to see it all week after week. In a few years, engine men began producing their own engines, each one a work of art that went far beyond assembly-line engines. The best engine builders became famous for building the ultimates: Keith Black, Donovan, Alan Root, and many others as time went on.

Power got to the ground through increasingly wider, stickier racing tires that evolved with the more powerful cars. Every piece of the car came under scrutiny to be lightened, strengthened,

A. J. Foyt made his second-in-a-row victory in Daytona's 1965 Firecracker 400, another of Ford's 48 wins that year. (Ford photo)

Marvin Panch set the pole for the Rebel 300 at Darlington, but Junior Johnson took the win. It was the first of Ford's sweep at Darlington that year, Ned Jarrett winning the Southern 500. Both Jarrett and Johnson won 13 races, but Jarrett ran more races, 54 to Johnson's 26, to win the Grand National Championship. (Ford photo)

NASCAR'S WILD YEARS 113

CHAPTER SEVEN

Marvin Panch won both races at Atlanta, then scored a road-racing victory at Watkins Glen as NASCAR widened its schedule in search of spectators. (Ford photo)

Jarrett's point total of 38,824 was 3,064 ahead of Dick Hutcherson to win the 1965 NASCAR title, Jarrett's second title year. (Ford photo)

With NASCAR on hold due to outlawing the Hemi, Dodge- and Plymouth-backed factory teams in drag racing ran factory-built lightweight Super Stocks that made sensational quarter-milers. Plymouths opened the season with Super Stock and Stock Class championships in NHRA's Winternationals and closed the season by winning the NHRA World Finals. NHRA's 1964 National Champion Roger Lindamood and his Color Me Gone *Dodge, shown here, had the latest from the factory, a favorite to win wherever they raced. (D. Randy Riggs photo)*

shifted, or removed. Altered-wheelbase A/FX cars with bodies moved back on the wheelbase were enormously popular, and they sprang up all across the nation. Although none of the advances in drag-racing factory cars were breakthroughs, steady evolution to go faster and quicker made the most exciting cars in America, and stock-car racing took it on the chin. NASCAR even went into drag racing with officially sanctioned events in 1966!

Although NASCAR had little to offer in its 55-race schedule but an all-Ford show, that year served notice of a fundamental change. While drivers had always been a major focus of NASCAR, the cars were the main attraction in the early 1960s. The kids believed that if they could get into one, they could be a big-time driver, too. Herman Beam ("And there goes Turtle Beam," the announcer said) was an example. A long-time east-

1965: SHAKING THE RULES TREE

Ford Motor Co. created an enormous stir in American automobiles when the Mustang was introduced as a 1964-1/2 model. Although a "pony car" by stock-car racing standards, Mustang was later to play a significant role in NASCAR's ever-changing rules. (Ford photo)

Wood Brothers Fords, and every other team of Fords and Mercury win 49 of the 55 Grand National races held that year. Only one of those victories belonged to Mercury. Chevrolet was shut out the first time since 1954, having won just one race in 1964. Plymouth also won four, while Dodge took two. All the big races were taken in a Ford romp, and all but one of the midsize tracks were swept by Ford as well. The exception was David Pearson's victory at a 500-miler at Richmond Fairgrounds.

ern Tennessee racer, he raced a 427 Ford in 1963, keeping lap count and notes on a pad strapped to his leg. His wife was chief of a crew made up of volunteer friends. His style of racing was going around the apron as fast as he could to rack up lap money. From 1960 through '63 he drove in 153 races to take home $40,550. He finish 11th in Grand National points in 1962. For 1964, he retired from driving to become a team owner. He signed on a hard-charging driver from South Carolina named Cale Yarborough and taught him how to race on dirt. Both of his cars were wrecked, and Herman was out of racing. It was a tough business.

Promoters of Daytona's giant speedway hailed it as the "Biggest... Finest... Fastest" racetrack in the world, now with stronger retaining walls in the turns instead of the guardrails. However, overall spectator appeal was down in 1965 from the previous banner year. NASCAR estimated that over 9,000,000 spectators watched the 1,182 sanctioned races in its seven classes held on 114 tracks in 19 states and Canada in 1964. The Grand National division for late-model stock cars posted $1,193,939 in winnings over 62 races that year. Spectators who did attend in 1965 watched Holman Moody Fords ("Ford stock-car racing headquarters"),

The notion of pulling for a non-Ford underdog was the beginning of much stronger focus on drivers. Fans tended to see the cars as more or less equal, making achievements more the product of driving talent rather than the hardware they drove. The intensity of make loyalty began to wane from the level it had been at from 1960 to 1964.

The primary issue facing NASCAR in 1965 was the question of who controlled stock-car racing, the sanctioning body or the manufacturers. The factories produced what sold, even in compromised form, so the rule-makers had to write rules to accommodate what was available, or write rules that race teams could use as a guide to build competitive cars. Stock-car promoters finally got Bill France to relent. In late 1965, he produced a maze of rules for the '66 season that reinstated Chrysler's Hemi, but only in 405-ci form, and on tracks over 1 mile long. Ford could run its SOHC Cammer in full-size Fords, but only if they weighed over 4,000 lbs. The Ford men grinned; they were certainly not going to do that. Chevrolet offered its venerable 409 in 1965, then went to the new Mk IV 427 in 1966 and had a potential competitor, but "We Don't Race" wasn't about to put a dime into racing, at least officially. What came out the back door was another story. Plymouth and Dodge came back with a vengeance and made a tough year of it. Meanwhile, NASCAR went straight.

CHAPTER SEVEN

Few of the actual stock cars made famous during the 1960s have survived. From near complete neglect and destruction in an old racer's junkyard, this Holman Moody 427 Ford has been saved and beautifully restored to better than as-raced condition.

The Ford 427 fender badge.

116 NASCAR'S WILD YEARS

1965: SHAKING THE RULES TREE

With the SOHC 427 Cammer intended for stock-car racing but ruled out by NASCAR, Ford sent its most powerful production engine into competition across America in A/FX Mustangs built by Holman Moody and raced in top classes. In its first NHRA Winternationals meet, and racing against Chrysler's Hemi in all sorts of configurations, Bill Lawton nailed down the A/FX title in his Mustang at 128.20 mph in 10.92 seconds. This restoration of the original Don Nicholson car shows Ford's quarter-mile threat of 1965.

CHAPTER SEVEN

Engine Evolution

During the first decade of NASCAR, "strictly stock" meant racing engines could be nothing beyond what was available to the public. Stronger internals, higher-performance components, and closer attention to assembly tolerances were about all that was allowed among a host of tricks that builders got past inspectors. Factory-produced engines were just lightly modified for racing until NASCAR's second decade, when Chrysler changed the equation. In 1964, the Hemi was brought back in updated 426-ci form. The new engine surpassed all competitors with wedge-shaped combustion chambers, and only Ford responded. With its single-overhead-cam (SOHC) 427 of 1964, Ford upped the ante even further. Unfortunately, NASCAR didn't permit the engine into stock-car racing until much later, and even then, weight penalties made it uncompetitive. So, after NASCAR's 1964 ban against Ford's SOHC engine, Chrysler teams raced with the advantage of the Hemi, while Ford engineers continued to improve the wedge-head FE-series 427 until management authorized a new engine.

To combat the Hemi, Ford replaced its most successful racing engine of the era with an even better powerplant. The highly proven 427 wedge won in every form of racing where it ran, but with the 1968 Tunnel Port revision, it was at its ultimate state. By then, Ford engineers applied their know-how to the thin-wall casting 385-series engine displacing 429 ci. The Boss 429 featured cast-aluminum heads with semi-hemispherical combustion chambers, an efficient single 4-bbl induction system, and hardware designed specially for racing. The new engine was capable of being expanded to 494 ci for the flourishing Canadian-American (Can-Am) Challenge Cup Series, where Chevrolet's 427- and 494-ci Mk IV engines ruled.

These big-block Chevrolet engines were derived from the ZL1 427 and LS6 454 Mk IV, which were derived from Dick Keinath's Mk IIS of 1963. Deep within Chevrolet, advanced engine design and development were conducted by a small group directed by Zora Arkus-Duntov, who completed several exotic engines based on the small-block and big-block. When both Chrysler and Ford ceased production of their big-block engines in the early 1970s, the Mk IV Chevrolet replaced them as a NASCAR championship engine (it was still used as a truck engine), as proven by Benny Parsons. Parsons drove L.G. DeWitt's 427-powered Monte Carlo (the first year of the nameplate) to the title in 1973.

Ford's answer to Chrysler's 426 Hemi, introduced in 1964, was the SOHC Cammer 427, which was not permitted by NASCAR. Shown here is "Sneaky" Pete Robinson, a capable engineer who developed the cam-drive gear train that replaced the factory-installed chains. With his mods, Robinson raced his SOHC-powered slingshot dragster to 200 mph in the quarter-mile from around 1,000 hp. (Ford photo)

The Hudson Hornet Twin H-Power was the first factory-produced multiple-carburetor engine permitted in NASCAR racing (1953). The 7-X racing engine, an inline-6 flathead, produced 210 hp and achieved 112 mph, producing 21 victories that year.

Ford's overhead valve Y-block, introduced in 1954 displacing 239 ci, went to 272 ci in '55 racing form and was claimed to produce 225 hp. Thunderbird power won three races that year.

Chrysler's 345-ci Hemi of 1956 produced 355 hp, more than 1 hp per ci, and proved almost invincible on major NASCAR tracks with 22 victories.

118 NASCAR'S WILD YEARS

1965: SHAKING THE RULES TREE

Ford's Engine and Foundry Division developed advanced engines in hopes of selling its ideas to management for production. This single-overhead-cam 302-ci engine was on the dyno in 1963, but never made production. (Ford photo)

Arkus-Duntov's crew at Chevrolet produced their own Tunnel Port 427 with single overhead cams on the Mk IV big-block that showed 660 hp at 6,800 rpm on the dyno. Like the SOHC small-block, it sat on the shelf. (Denny Davis photo)

Zora Arkus-Duntov and his engineers in the advanced engine group, Cal Wade, Fred Frincke, and Denny Davis, turned out a stunning array of exotic engines ready for production or racing if called up. This 377-ci small-block with roller cam followers, hemispherical combustion chambers, a single overhead cam, and a compression ratio of 11.03:1, cranked out 545 hp at 6,000 rpm with 512 ft-lb of torque at 4,800 rpm, delivering 1.45 hp per ci. (Denny Davis photos)

After Ford released the SOHC 427 for production, Chrysler engineers went back to their drawing boards and produced this double-overhead-cam 426 Hemi. When NASCAR ruled the SOHC Ford out, Chrysler immediately stopped development of this engine. (Chrysler photo courtesy of John Mahoney)

In 1969 Ford replaced the FE-series 427-ci engines with the Boss 429 specifically for stock-car racing. It was a hemi-head development of the 385-series thin-wall casting big-block, and won the NASCAR championship that year. (Ford photo)

Chevrolet did not compete in stock-car racing, but did release this all-aluminum RPO-ZL1 big-block that exceeded 535 hp in factory tune in 1969. Expanded to 494 ci with fuel injection at 740 hp, it was the dominating engine in Can-Am racing through the early 1970s. (Chevrolet photo)

NASCAR'S WILD YEARS

CHAPTER EIGHT

To combat the advantage of the Hemi, even with reduced displacement, NASCAR ruled that smaller-dimension cars with wedge engines were allowed based on new ci-per-lb rules, and Ford responded with the 427 Fairlane late in the season. Several teams built cars to the formula that allowed light weight and small engines. Bobby Allison campaigned a 327-powered Chevelle to three wins in 34 races. Meanwhile, Holman Moody built new 427-powered Fairlanes to the new rules as a result of season-long disputes over what was legal and what wasn't. In the biggest upset of the season, Darel Dieringer won the Southern 500 in an independently prepared 427 Mercury Comet, the counterpart to the Fairlane. (Ford photo)

NASCAR'S WILD YEARS

1966: Frantic Fanatics

American racing in 1966 was a phenomenal extravaganza like never seen before. New organizations, new classes, new cars, new tracks, new everything, made the most exciting year of racing anyone ever thought possible. Ford's advance into world-class racing on every front earned Dearborn spectacular victories, with more to come. Rivalries intensified as the factories returned to stock-car racing at the end of the 1965 season. However, Ford walked out over another rules dispute early in the season, but its car-point total for 1966 brought its fourth consecutive make championship. Ford earned 1,047 points, and Plymouth snatched 633, while Dodge brought home 632. One-time NASCAR dominator Pontiac had just 8 points for the season, while Chevrolet independents gathered 232 points.

The reason Ford won was clear: there were more Fords raced than any other make.

Racing amplified admiration for drivers, and legends were made. Drivers rose from greasy wrenches to hometown favorites to national heroes. Stock-car drivers like Fred Lorenzen, Junior Johnson, David Pearson, and Richard Petty were considered at least one-third of the winning combination; the car and the crew made the other, less visible, two-thirds.

Make loyalties still ran high in 1966, but with so many high-powered cars on the road, especially following the spectacular 1965 sales years, all makes sold fewer cars. Chevrolet dropped 27 percent. Ford was off 10.5 percent. Plymouth and Dodge were down 6.1 and 2.9 percent, respectively. Although sales were

After NASCAR allowed the Hemi, the Chrysler teams came back to the high banks with a vengeance, combining for 34 victories on the 49-race NASCAR schedule. "Join the Dodge Rebellion" was the advertising slogan of the Dodge teams in which David Pearson ruled supreme, winning 15 of 18 Dodge wins in 1966, Chrysler Corporation's one-two-three championship year in NASCAR. (DaimlerChrysler Historical Collection photo)

NASCAR'S WILD YEARS

121

CHAPTER EIGHT

Chrysler's 426 Hemi raised the bar in automotive high performance everywhere it raced. Factory rated at 425 hp in showroom models, the Hemi was capable of 600 hp in racing tune. (DaimlerChrysler Historical Collection photo)

down, fan support of racing grew, and NASCAR broadened its base into drag racing.

For 1966, NASCAR sanctioned around 30 drag strips, mostly in the East. NASCAR fielded a three-pronged attack: a Championship circuit, a Grand Stock circuit, and a Fuel Dragster circuit. Each series was modeled on the Grand National series points-building system. There was a season-long championship with an end-of-season payoff that gave drivers financial incentive to win meets and work toward the championship. Big-time promotion by NASCAR and track owners brought the best cars and drivers to the top drag strips, all featured in much the same way as stock-car racing. The plan was to attract fans in growing numbers. It was, in fact, almost a carbon copy of NHRA racing but with more money. Many of NHRA's top competitors were lured by big bucks, but rather than having a class with a "run whatcha brung" flavor, NASCAR drag racing was pitched as the very best, and the mediocre need not apply. This policy brought about NASCAR drag racing's demise, because drag racing was America's grassroots sport. Fans and participants at all levels felt like they were a part of the sport – everyone could race, not just top-gun elites.

The season opened with the Winter Championships in Deland, Florida, then moved northward for NASCAR's first Summer Championship held at Dragway 42 in West Salem, Ohio. The purse was $20,000 in cash, and it drew over 500 entrants, mostly from the East. Though it wasn't as big as some NHRA events, many of the top cars and drivers were there, along with a host of teams with factory connections. In the Ford lineup was "Sneaky" Pete Robinson with his SOHC Cammer-powered Top Fuel Dragster fitted with new aluminum heads. Ford's engineers turned them out and reduced the weight of the car by 120 lbs. Chrysler's Hemi was on hand in abundance, resulting in a spectacular SOHC-versus-Hemi shootout for top honors that brought the fans to their feet.

Among the few West Coast entrants was "Slick Nick" Marshall, who qualified the Marshall-Vermilya AA/FD slingshot rail dragster with a 7.481-second blast at 215.3 mph. Robinson set low ET at 7.480, a mere thousandth of a second quicker, and both waded through the field of 16 number-one bracket qualifiers to the big showdown for Top Fuel Champion. Marshall pulled a holeshot on Robinson and led through the lights to win, while the Ford snapped a couple of rods that punched through the block. Marshall received a healthy $3,300 for the win, and gained points toward the Championship title. Robinson had to get another engine.

In the stock-bodied classes, the final round pitted Ford engineer Dave Lyall's fiberglass '65 Ford Falcon against Ken Vogt's '66 Mercury Comet in fuel-burning Unlimiteds. Lyall took the trophy with Ford power. In the class that corresponded to A/FX in NHRA racing, the final round was taken by Tom Sneden and his factory lightweight Dodge Hemi over the similarly lightweight *Virginian* Hemi Plymouth; Ford need not apply. The *Ramcharger* team was there among many top stockers, making the class a Hemi-fest, the result of Chrysler's "big splash" strategy of getting the Hemi on as many strips as possible.

While some round-track promoters complained that NASCAR was straying from its roots, the lack of spectators at oval tracks caused by Chrysler's pullout the year before proved to be a financial disaster. NASCAR reduced the number of races from 55 in 1965 to 49 in 1966. Once again, the Hemis rolled, and Ford pulled out.

Petty won the 1966 season opener in a year-old Plymouth, and Dan Gurney took the 500 at Riverside again in a new Holman Moody Ford. The third round of NASCAR's go-round schedule brought the teams to Daytona, and the Petty-blue Plymouth was the first entrant for testing and qualifying. In the 100-mile qualifiers, the Hemis ruled, and by race day, Petty was on the pole with a new record, 175.165 mph. Only two-time International Motor Contest Association Champion and Ford factory driver Dick Hutcherson was close, with a 174.317-mph qualifying speed in his Holman Moody Ford. In the 500, Cale Yarborough tried to make a race of it in his Ford by leading several laps, but he finished second. Richard's victory proved the Hemi to be nearly untouchable – he took the checkered flag a lap ahead of the entire field. The fact that the race was shortened two laps due to rain had no influence on the outcome.

All the other factory teams, four Plymouths and five Dodges, had problems and didn't mount much of a challenge. Besides being unstable at high speeds, the Chryslers had problems with overheating, cracking blocks, and explosions in the huge plenums of the single 4-bbl intake manifolds. The intake was designed to flow massive volumes of air and fuel to feed the engine, but having so much fuel in the large plenum chamber produced occasional explosions during start-up. NASCAR officials ruled that hoods on the Chrysler entrants had to be closed prior to ignition.

Strangely, the Hemi, now with more than a year of development, had teething problems, and the new Dodge Charger with its slippery fastback top proved unstable at Daytona's high speeds. The car was too aerodynamic. Stylists and engineers had penned attractive lines for the showroom that produced negative downforce, or lift. NASCAR certainly wasn't going to allow nonproduction spoilers on the trailing edges of the cars; no sir, not even for safety. If it wasn't on production cars, it didn't get to race, sort of, and while engine pieces were hidden from view, spoilers were obvious. France eventually relented and allowed spoilers for the Dodges, but no other cars.

Tires were another issue. Three of the Fords were put out with windshields smashed by rubber chunks that rolled off the rear tires of leading cars. The cars were faster than ever, especially the Hemis, and everyone knew that blow-outs at such speeds were disasters in the making. So, both Firestone and Goodyear introduced racing tires with inner liners and a growing variety of compounds for any need, the softer and stickier type having the chunking problems. NASCAR also finally mandated fuel cells instead of as-manufactured gas tanks, a safety improvement that was long overdue. Brakes were also upgraded with recommended, not mandatory, dual master cylinders. Factory unibody construction was permitted to be braced and reinforced, an art that the Pettys knew well. The minimum ground-to-hoodline distance was set at 31 in. Crash helmets, seat belts, and shoulder harnesses were also all required.

Meanwhile, Chrysler showed up with intakes not found in factory catalogs, while everything Ford raced was available to the public. Bill France had made another of his interpretive strictly-stock rulings. To be competitive, other teams did everything they could to get more speed, and several of the Fords were

CHAPTER EIGHT

Ford's 427 of 1966, the Medium Riser, was the third evolution of the engine introduced in the fall of 1962 and was still competitive. In a flip-flop from the previous year when Chrysler pulled out giving Ford the season, the new rules unleashed Chrysler's Hemi and Ford pulled out to concentrate on drag racing. (Ford photo)

Richard Petty won nine races during the 1966 season. That was good enough for a third place finish in overall points. (Photo courtesy International Motorsports Hall of Fame)

NASCAR'S WILD YEARS

1966: FRANTIC FANATICS

The Petty Plymouth and the Yarborough Ford head the starting lineup of the Daytona 500. Plymouth and Dodge took both rounds of the 100-mile qualifiers. They finished in the same order, one-two, with Yarborough a lap down to Petty in the 500. (Ford photo)

lowered so far in the front that the bumper blocked half of the lower headlights. NASCAR inspectors let the Plymouths and Dodges through with never-seen-before equipment, but anything that the Ford men tried was stopped cold. Lowered suspensions were ordered raised to proper height, but clever mechanics turned to other devices, such as carbon blocks in coil springs that held the car up until they broke and fell out on the racetrack, lowering the car.

Smokey was doing big things with the Chevelle, but once the 396 Chevelle was on the market, followed by the 427 in late 1966, he wasn't the only one. People started to recognize the combination of Chevrolet's hot 427 porcupine Mk IV engine in a small car. The Chevelle quickly became a Late-Model Sportsman and Modified standout in the hands of other drivers, particularly Bobby Allison of the rapidly rising "Alabama Gang." Bill France thought the stage was set for Chevrolet's return to NASCAR, but it didn't happen. Ford's withdrawal didn't have the disastrous effect that Chrysler's pullout of the year before, because so many Fords were still running.

When Petty won the 1966 season opener at Augusta, Georgia, he picked up where he left off in 1964, and the Ford men saw their chances of a winning season going down the drain. In the next round, Dan Gurney's driving ability and a seasoned 427 Ford took the 500-miler at Riverside over the more powerful Hemis. When the Plymouths and Dodges dominated the 100-mile qualifiers at Daytona and Petty won the 500 going away, the rules and the season ahead were clear to the Ford men. Ford withdrew from the remaining short-track races to protest Chrysler's

Smokey's Chevelle

For Chevrolet, the small-block had become by far the most popular V-8, now the hot-rodder's choice. This was a goal for Chevrolet set by Zora Arkus-Duntov a decade earlier. The new-for-1965 "porcupine-head" 396 was only a distant descendant of the one raced in 1963. The drag racers, in their never-ending quest for more power at low cost, overbored the 396 1/8 in and lengthened the stroke 1/4 in to make 454 ci. Fitted with the good stuff and fuel injection, the 454 rose to set the 1966 NHRA elapsed-time record in B Modified/Sports Production (Corvette) at 11.02 seconds. In a few years, the factory was turning out 454s by the thousands.

The 454 was not seen in NASCAR. Bill France was firm; any engine in Grand National racing had to be a production item available to the public in showroom cars, sort of. Even though the 427 Mk IV porcupine was in production during late 1966, and proving stout in Stock-class drag racing, it proved to be no more than a backmarker against the Hemi. With Ford's withdrawal, several top drivers found other rides, and Curtis Turner, allowed back into NASCAR in 1965, got behind the wheel of Smokey Yunick's trick Chevelle. Yunick had been involved in the Chevelle program from its beginnings.

Smokey: "Knudsen took me down to R&D and showed me this Chevelle and asked me what I thought. I had the car put on scales, with front sheetmetal off, and the second day, after I got through looking it over and measuring, I said, 'I don't like it worth a shit. The engine's too far forward and too high and so on.' [The project engineer] said, 'Just what I thought. Why don't we fire all these engineers and hire you to design the thing!'"

Knudsen had the hand-built car, the only one in existence at the time, shipped to Smokey's Daytona Beach garage, where the engine was moved down and back. Testing was arranged, and the car was shipped to the Firestone proving grounds in Mesa, Arizona, in bitterly cold weather. The project was so secret that Firestone gave all its 300 or so employees time off, and Yunick and test driver Mike Roe went to work and got the car up to about 180 mph. Also being tested was GM's new transistor ignition. When the engine lost its spark and died, frantic phone calls flew back and forth until an engineer showed up and disassembled the distributor, but couldn't find a thing wrong with it. Once the distributor was back together and installed, the car fired and testing resumed. Why the ignition had quit went unresolved, but Smokey's Chevelle was born in 1964.

Smokey: "From a performance point of view, the chassis on the Chevys was horrible. The brakes were horrible. The transmissions were bad. The cars were really ill-handling cars. So, we got a deal ["We Don't Race" – remember?] where they agreed that we would try to do it right and give us enough latitude to do it. I got them to build the chassis up there in Chevy R&D under Frank Winchell and Jim Musser. They were the two head knockers in Chevy R&D. After they wasted about a half a million dollars and run us out of time, we finally had to bring the car down here (to Daytona Beach) with about ten of their guys. We finally got the thing finished up and run it in the race (the Daytona 500).

"[Mario] Andretti was gonna drive it in the Daytona 500. He'd never driven a stock car on a fast track before, and he run it into the ass end of a parked car out there and bent it up so bad we couldn't fix it, so we couldn't enter it."

---

non-showroom equipment, and they petitioned France to correct the bias in the rules.

As a result of the vast differences in what the Big Three produced, along with midyear special editions and competition-only models, equitable rules were nearly impossible to write. Drag racing had no such difficulty. Even though Ford built and sold about a thousand SOHC Cammers, none were installed in production cars, and the factory had no plans to install the engine in anything, so NASCAR's offer to let the engine into stock-car racing under extreme handicap was not acceptable. Hemi engines were formidable in smaller and lighter Plymouths and Dodges, but the Cammer in a full-size 4,000-plus-lb car had no chance. So, why spend the money? France wasn't about to let Dearborn get an edge that would lead to a repeat of the dominance of 1965. However, his rules gave the Hemi the edge, and that's exactly what happened.

Ford was building assembly-line dual and single 4-bbl 427-powered Fairlanes and Mercury Comets, which were closer to the Plymouths and Dodges in size and weight. But France continued to require single 4-bbl carbs and full-size cars. He eventually relented and allowed dual quads on 427 wedge engines in full-size cars. When the final rules were set, they had never been so confusing. Three classes were legal: full-size cars with 430-ci engines, a 4,000-lb minimum weight and a 119-in wheelbase; intermediates on a 115-in wheelbase with either 430-ci engines and 4,000 lbs or 405-ci and 3,500 lbs; and compacts running 115-in wheelbase and 335-ci engines and 2,500 lbs. And for a car to be legal, at least 5,000 had to be produced. Ford produced more than enough 427s, but Chrysler was nowhere near meeting the 5,000-units rule. To run the Hemi on big tracks, the engine had to be in the full-size Plymouth Fury or Dodge Polara. Smaller cars raced on other

1966: FRANTIC FANATICS

Ford drivers had a tough year in 1966 stock-car racing. The occasional win on a major track, such as Rockingham, was small consolation for what the Ford men thought were unfair rules. (Ford photos)

Even hard-charging Curtis Turner could not put Ford on top.

NASCAR'S WILD YEARS 127

CHAPTER EIGHT

The Hemi

By 1966, the Hemi was well-proven in all forms of racing and was available in showroom models as well, although significantly detuned. Like the Chevrolet Mystery Engine and the Ford SOHC Cammer, the Hemi was an engineer's dream, brought about by a directive handed down in December 1962 to build an engine that could dominate NASCAR's big tracks and drag racing's top classes. The design of the new engine began in January 1963; the first engine was running on a dyno on December 6, 1963; and proof of the design was Petty's win in February 1964. That's just 15 months from concept to victory. The directive called for 426 ci to meet NASCAR's 430-ci displacement rule. The goal was to have a single 4-bbl carburetor version for stock-car racing, plus a more powerful dual quad version for drag racing. The 426 Hemi was built on Chrysler's well-proven Hemi engine of the 1950s, with an almost identical splayed valve angle and combustion-chamber configuration. Engineers built on the technology that had, by then, become widely accepted as the most powerful available – except overhead cams, but they got deep into a DOHC Hemi once they found out about Ford's SOHC.

The Hemi and B-engine cylinder blocks, both of 426 ci, were very similar, except that the Hemi required oil drain-back holes in the bottom corners of the deck plane on each side. Early testing revealed cracking along the Hemi's right-bank bore walls, and new blocks were cast during the first week of February 1964 with water-jacket cores reduced to increase the wall thickness. So, solving the cracking problem reduced cooling flow and contributed to overheating problems that the Hemi became known for. The block that Petty raced to victory in Daytona was of the improved design and was cast just 13 days prior to the race. To go from molten iron to a complete, race-winning engine in less than two weeks (including delivery time from the foundry to various shops to Petty) shows that Chrysler's engineers and machinists spent a lot of overtime to get the engine out the door in time for the 500.

Close attention to breathing, always the key to making power, produced as near to an ideal induction system, combustion-chamber shape, and exhaust system as any manufacturer had accomplished in production cam-in-block form. Plans called for turning out several hundred drag-racing engines as soon as possible to make the "big splash." Successes in 1964 proved the Hemi very big indeed.

After the first run of several hundred Hemis was completed in 1964, a second run was made for 1965. The new engines included stronger heads, improved valvetrain components, and a number of weight-reducing components. NASCAR's restrictions didn't help the Hemi at all, as cast-iron production components were required.

The Hemi was available in four forms: 404- and 426-ci track engines, 426-ci street engines, and 426-ci drag-racing engines. The Hemi came with all the good stuff, but more was available, such as cast-aluminum heads that saved additional weight in drag racing (not permitted on oval tracks), and dual-plug heads (also not permitted on oval tracks). The top performer was the drag-race engine, which delivered about 600 hp at 6,500 rpm on factory dynos. Oval-track engines of 404 ci delivered about 550 hp, while 426-ci versions put out around 580 hp. Dual-quad street engines with 10.25:1 compression ratio were factory-rated at 425 hp. Strip and track engines ran 12.5:1, but the racers quickly found more power.

tracks had to run the 426 wedge engine, not the Hemi, or the 426 Hemi reduced to 405 ci with dual 4-bbls. Ford's 427 wedge in Fairlanes and Comets, and Chevy's staggered valve porcupine 427 wedge in Chevelles, could also run dual 4-bbl carbs.

The rules were much more complicated than they had been in the past. Many builders followed Smokey Yunick's philosophy: "If it ain't in the rules, it's okay," and an explosion among all kinds of trick cars appeared in NASCAR inspection lines.

On April 15, Ford withdrew its factory-backed teams, and Chrysler had a field day that year taking all but a few of the top races. General Motors didn't return as France hoped, although a few drivers made a good showing in minor races with the Chevelle. Even though NASCAR once again had a limited show, Ford independents made a go of the season winning 10 races, largely the result of thorough development from the previous year. Dick Hutcherson won at Bristol and North Wilkesboro in his Ford, Darel Dierenger won the Southern 500 in a Bud Moore Mercury Comet, Lorenzen took the Old Dominion 500 at Martinsville in a Ford, and Curtis Turner won the second 500-mile race at Rockingham to salvage a respectable year in terms of PR and advertising. Ford man Marvin Panch went over to Dodge and won the World 600 at Charlotte.

Since Plymouth and Dodge waged their own war at the top of NASCAR's win list, fans were treated to driver and inter-make rivalries with stiff competition. It was a good show after all. What looked to be another Petty year became a David Pearson and Dodge showcase, as Plymouth racked up 16 wins to Dodges 18. Pearson's season-long point total soared past Petty, who finished third with eight wins

1966: FRANTIC FANATICS

in 39 races. Pearson's 15 wins in 42 races in his Cotton Owens Dodge established the young driver from South Carolina as a contender. He won his first of three NASCAR Championships. Rookie of the Year James Hylton handled a year-old Cotton Owens Dodge to consistent high finishes, and second place in Grand National points, despite winning no races.

The duo of Pearson and Petty made 1966 a tough year for anyone else to finish higher than third. While Petty had deep, long-term connections with the factory, Cotton Owens' garage put Dodge in the forefront of NASCAR for the first time. Owens had been with Dodge since the introduction of the Hemi in 1964 and finally made it pay off.

As the season progressed, the Dodge Charger's aerodynamic problems were less dramatic on shorter tracks, and the Hemi's power, Pearson's driving, and Owens' preparation proved to be a formidable combination. To protest the rules, the Ford men cobbled

Just five years from his first Grand National win, David Pearson's 1966 season was sensational – 15 wins in 42 starts to take the season by storm and give Dodge its first NASCAR Manufacturer's Championship. (Ford photo)

CHAPTER EIGHT

Broadening its base from stock-car racing into drag racing in 1965, NASCAR held a season-long points race in '66 covering four national events, although all were east-coast strips. The purse was $125,000 in addition to a touring circuit structured somewhat like stock-car racing that ran at about 30 strips. Bill Lawton won NASCAR's Winter Championship at the Deland, Florida, airport that year. He took the Grand Stock Eliminator title in competition among the eight lowest elapsed-time qualifiers in class. Lawton's Mustang was the stretched-wheelbase, fuel-injected SOHC 427 version of the A/FX Cammer that won the NHRA Winternationals at Pomona, California, the year before. Holman Moody built eight of the stretched cars for Ford's campaign in top classes of full-bodied cars capable of 8.5 seconds and 170 mph in the quarter-mile. (Ford photos)

NASCAR'S WILD YEARS

Zora Arkus-Duntov led Chevrolet's finest efforts in engine development during the mid-1960s. His High Performance Team of Cal Wade, Fred Frincke, and Denny Davis (left to right around Zora) designed, built, and tested exotic fuel-injected V-8 engines based on the small-block and Mk IV big-block. Both types of engines were built with variations including hemispherical combustion chambers, overhead cams, multiple spark plug heads, and cast-aluminum hardware. It was all experimental – none of it saw the light of day. (Denny Davis photo)

up the most outrageous car ever seen on NASCAR's circuit. Junior Johnson showed up for the August race at Atlanta in a Ford that was quickly dubbed the "Yellow Banana." The top of the 1966 Galaxie had been radically chopped, and the car had a decided down-at-the-nose incline. The tail was swept up unlike any showroom car. France was so delighted to have a factory Ford that it sailed right through inspection, to the dismay of every other competitor. Strictly stock – sort of. When Cotton Owens was directed by inspectors to raise the front of Pearson's car 1/4 in, he trailered the car in a justifiable huff and left. NASCAR was so hungry for factory competition that it had gone ridiculous.

The Yellow Banana was a one-race wonder and made no impact on racing, but it had a major influence on NASCAR's rule book. Nose-to-tail body silhouette templates along the centerline of the cars were instituted, and have remained an inspection component ever since. Smokey Yunick's next Chevelle had a similar and profound effect on the rules, forecasting the direction of stock-car racing. Tube frames emerged as replacements for factory stampings among all sorts of speed shop built "half-chassis" cars, but they were initially dismissed wholesale by France.

Since fan focus in NASCAR was shifting toward drivers and away from the cars they drove, the season was less about the cars than the young gladiators who drove them. Whether or not the factories were involved was less important to fans than watching favorite drivers in action, and NASCAR saw the advantages of close finishes. Rules, therefore, were France's attempt to constrain cars to close, high-speed racing, where advances in technology were of little interest and were restrained from creating runaway wins. Drag racing, not NASCAR, was the showcase for the latest in factory hardware, but late in the

CHAPTER EIGHT

Buddy Baker, son of Buck Baker, is shown here talking with crew chief Ray Fox (above) and driving his #3 Dodge Charger. Baker drove a #3 Dodge in a few races in 1966 and then in quite few more in 1967.

season, factory Fords quietly began returning to the ovals.

The Ford men had come to the conclusion that trying to meet NASCAR's rules was impossible, so they led rather than followed. Utilizing the intermediate rules, Bud Moore built a Mercury Comet in his Spartanburg, South Carolina, shop with a full-size front clip. Nothing like it had been built by the factory. Holman Moody built similar Fairlanes. Shop-built "half-chassis" cars had arrived, and NASCAR inspectors rejected them. France finally recognized the obvious, and let them race, rather than have Ford completely withdraw. What resulted was shop-built chassis/suspension designs harkening back to the days of full-frame production cars. This, of course, foreshadowed the custom-built tube frames that NASCAR later allowed, and has raced ever since.

Regulations for 1967 noticeably dropped references to "production-based" hardware, but they maintained silhouette, ride height, and class specifications. Stock-car racing finally emerged into the modern era. The cars were no longer assembly-line cars converted to racecars, they were now race-shop produced. The new cars were becoming high-speed rides for their highly publicized drivers.

1966: FRANTIC FANATICS

Dodge introduced the seductively rakish four-bucket-seat Charger in 1966. The design carried over into 1967, and was advertised as the "...new leader of the Dodge Rebellion," offering "a big, bad 426 Street Hemi" as optional. The Charger was the only Dodge offered to the public with the Hemi, and only a few were actually built. In the hands of David Pearson, Dodge won the NASCAR championship.

CHAPTER EIGHT

1966: FRANTIC FANATICS

Above, left and facing page: Plymouth options for 1966 were the Hemi Satellite or the Hemi Belvedere, and like the Hemi Charger, the cars came with heavy-duty suspension, larger brakes, and either the 4-speed or TorqueFlite automatic. Richard Petty ran third in NASCAR points to David Pearson and James Hylton, giving Chrysler's top performing cars a one-two-three knockout blow to Ford.

CHAPTER NINE

Above and facing page: Fred Lorenzen capped his career with a final victory in Daytona's second 100-mile qualifier, setting a new record at 174.583 mph. He beat Junior Johnson's 1964 record of 170.777 mph in Ray Fox's Hemi Dodge. Lorenzen ran the entire race nonstop, the first driver to accomplish that feat, and NASCAR changed the twin races to 125 miles the next year so that at least one pit stop would have to be made. Lorenzen retired with 26 Grand National victories to match Rex White's record. His retirement made an opening for David Pearson to move from Dodge to Ford and for Bobby Allison to move up from an independent to a factory team, subsequently winning the American 500 at Rockingham in Lorenzen's Ford. (Ford photos)

1967: New Beginnings

When Fireball Roberts died as a result of severe burns complicated by blood poisoning and pneumonia following his crash at Charlotte's 1964 World 600, Junior Johnson blamed himself. He and Ned Jarrett were dueling early in the race in a bunched field. Junior hit a bump, bounced off of Jarrett's car, and both of them spun off the track. Behind them, Roberts dove to the inside, also spun off the track, and slammed backwards into the inside wall, flipped, and was trapped in his burning car. Jarrett got to him first, but by the time he and Junior got him out, Robert's life was in question. Soon thereafter, Junior began thinking of retirement.

The following year, having achieved about everything he'd set out to do except being an owner, Junior moved into the owner-driver category, and proceeded to win 13 races in 36 starts, one of the best win records on the books. With Holly Farms' backing again, and the shop actually located in the firm's poultry plant in North Wilkesboro, North Carolina, Junior's driving talent and car preparation proved to be among the best. He began the season winning a Daytona 500 qualifier, and he finished it in a flourish, winning two of the last six races. A sweep of Ford victories shut out the dismal season for Richard Petty and David Pearson, as Chrysler had withdrawn. Junior returned midseason to Darlington for the Rebel 300. He dominated the race with memories of being denied the Southern 500 victory in 1962 on his mind. The reason? Darlington was his favorite track, the most challenging on the circuit, and to win the Southern 500 was the pinnacle of the season for him.

Darlington's not-quite-oval layout wasn't a problem to the 1950s-era cars, but with the much higher speeds in 1965, cars had problems with its egg shape. The sharper west turns (the point of the egg) required special driving techniques, and Junior invented a special Darlington car to meet the challenge. Going into turn three at straightaway speeds sent cars high on the track into turn four. To make it out of turn four with high speed meant rubbing the rail along the top of the track. The fastest cars earned their "Darlington stripe" by grazing along the rail, then rocketing off into the front straight. That grazing took its toll on cars by pushing in the sheetmetal against tires. Many drivers were in awe of the track for what it required of drivers and what it did to cars. To win at Darlington meant facing stock-car racing's toughest challenge – surviving the track that had become known as "Too Tough to Tame." Junior installed springs inside the body so that the sheetmetal could be forced in by the rail, and then be forced back out away from the tires by the springs. It was another of his tricks and worked beautifully.

Throughout his shortened season, Junior's hard-charging driving style put him in the front of most races he entered. He dominated some, and crashed in others, but always walked away. He was a member of Ford's official factory team, which was a who's who of NASCAR: Fred Lorenzen, Ned Jarrett, A. J. Foyt, Marvin Panch, Curtis Turner, Dick Hutcherson, Cale Yarborough, and Junior. Between Junior and Curtis Turner, these "old men" of stock-car racing were legends in their own time, earning respect with their gutsy driving. Fittingly enough, Junior's last win was at North Wilkesboro where it all started. For that first race long ago at just 16, Junior was careful not to beat the son of the track's owner. When he left as champion of North Wilkesboro's asphalt track in 1965, winner of 50 Grand National races, he was hailed by the crowd who acknowledged the passing of the guard. But Junior wasn't through. He soon

NASCAR'S WILD YEARS 137

Glen Wood and crew check over the dual-quad 396-powered Ford driven by Cale Yarborough in the Motor Trend 500 at Riverside. Parnelli Jones won the race in a Bill Stroppe 396 Fairlane. (Ford photo)

became the winningest owner in the sport and brought many young drivers to stardom.

Junior's first season as an owner, 1966, began with the last race of the 1965 season when Junior hired Bobby Isaac to drive at a local asphalt short track. Isaac, who came from nearby Catawba, North Carolina, set the pole and battled Jarrett for the win but finished second. Jarrett won the race and his second Grand National Championship – the first was in a Chevrolet, this one in a Ford. Isaac was a tough young driver made in Junior's mold. He emerged in NASCAR and soon became a force of his own, winning the Grand National title in 1970 driving for Dodge.

1967: NEW BEGINNINGS

Five years after tooling up for the Mk IIS 427 Mystery Engine that first raced at Daytona 1963, Chevrolet Division released a new 427, the Mk IV, which evolved from that first 7-liter engine.

Ford's pullout early in the '66 season recalled Junior's cars and equipment, and both he and Isaac were out of business. Isaac went looking for another ride, and reluctantly, Junior climbed back into the cockpit of another Ford for eight races. He scored few points while putting some rivals behind the wheel, Lorenzen, Foyt, and Turner in particular. Holman Moody supplied cars and equipment to a number of teams, and for the 1966 Dixie 400 Atlanta race in August, John Holman asked Junior to build a fast car for Lorenzen. Under the Holly Farms banner, the Yellow Banana rolled onto the speedway and into controversy as described earlier.

Meanwhile, Smokey Yunick arrived with his similarly groundbreaking Chevelle for Turner. Lorenzen went out early, and France sent word to Junior not to bring the Banana back. The engine failed in Turner's car, and both drivers, each having led the race early on, were out. These two cars signaled the changes to come, as NASCAR's rules evolved from stock to modified.

Finally, the rule book squabbles that nearly ruined the sport seemed resolved to the point that teams got back to racing. In the opening round of the 1967 season, the Pettys were back with new cars, and Chrysler had a stable of top talent and fast cars.

Chevy's high-performance L88 Mk IV 427 engine with aluminum heads proved to be a brute in production Chevrolets. Smokey Yunick made the cast-iron L89 into a NASCAR performer shown at Daytona in late 1966. (Chevrolet photo)

CHAPTER NINE

Yunick put Curtis Turner behind the wheel of his very trick Chevelle during testing late in 1966. During the first 100-mile qualifier for the Daytona 500, Turner ran one lap. Then, on pole day, February 12, Turner stunned both the Ford and Chrysler factory teams by setting the pole at a record 180.831 mph, the first over-180-mph pole and over 5 mph faster than Petty's Hemi Plymouth pole the year before. Turner took the lead on lap 82, then later on lap 173 the engine blew, leaving the Fords of David Pearson, Mario Andretti, and Fred Lorenzen to battle for the last 76 laps. (Smokey Yunick photo)

1967: NEW BEGINNINGS

The Fairlanes of Darel Dieringer (No. 26) and Cale Yarborough (No. 21) lead the Dodge Chargers of LeeRoy Yarbrough (No. 3) and Bobby Isaac (No. 71) in the Firecracker 400 at Daytona. Yarbrough won on a final-lap pass to get by Dick Hutcherson, who retired at the end of the year with 14 career wins. (Ford photo)

During pre-season tire testing at Daytona, LeeRoy Yarbrough brought Cotton Owens' 426 Hemi-powered Dodge Charger through the 2.5-mile course at 184.426 mph to set a new closed-course speed record, although the car wasn't strictly NASCAR legal. Suitably prepared for NASCAR, Yarbrough aimed the bullet-shaped car at Daytona's $5,000 fastest-qualifier money, but missed when Curtis Turner put Smokey Yunick's Chevelle on the pole at 180.831 mph. A Chevelle!

Holman Moody's lead driver, Fred Lorenzen, lost interest in racing during the mid-1960s and probably retired too early. His comeback in 1970 was widely heralded, but inauspicious. (Ford photo)

NASCAR'S WILD YEARS 141

CHAPTER NINE

In the opening round of the season, the Petty-blue Plymouth rolled into the winner's circle at Augusta, Georgia, to begin an astounding season. Then, at Riverside, USAC star and Indy 500 winner Parnelli Jones ran away from the field in a Ford Fairlane, and the year ahead didn't look so favorable for the Hemi. In the third race, Florida's LeeRoy Yarbrough put his Hemi Charger out front to win Daytona's first 100-mile qualifier at 163.93 mph. A. J. Foyt was the lone spoiler in a top-nine Chrysler sweep, finishing second in a Ford. In the second qualifier, Richard Petty was the lone spoiler in a Ford first-through-sixth sweep, Lorenzen winning with a new record of 174.58 mph in a Holman Moody intermediate-sized 427 Fairlane. That was his final victory before retiring. Petty's fifth place was ahead of Mario Andretti in another Holman Moody 427 Fairlane, and the 1967 season looked to be a dandy. It was!

Yarbrough takes the low groove by Ford teammate Dieringer on his way to winning Daytona's July 4 fireworks. Yarbrough ran only 16 races in 1967, taking two wins, and doubled his winnings from the previous year with consistent high finishes. (Ford photo)

LeeRoy Yarbrough in a Dodge (No. 12) won the first 100-mile qualifier at Daytona at 163.934 mph, then blew his engine on lap 71 of the Daytona 500. Tiny Lund, winner of the 1963 Daytona 500, drove a Petty Plymouth to fourth, the highest Plymouth finish. A. J. Foyt (No. 27) blew his engine on lap 46. (Ford photo)

142   NASCAR'S WILD YEARS

1967: NEW BEGINNINGS

USAC star Mario Andretti, in this Holman Moody 427 Fairlane, drove a dominating 112 laps in the lead to win the Daytona 500, his first Grand National win in seven starts. He then went on to win the Yankee 300. (Ford photo)

For the first time in years, Chevrolet power had returned to big-time stock-car racing, or so it seemed. The Chevelle came to fruition at Daytona 1967. Yunick modified the prototype Chevelle that Mario Andretti was to drive in the 1966 Daytona 500, but Andretti wrecked it. The car sat for the year in Smokey's shop where it was repaired and developed further for the '67 race. A few of Smokey's tricks included close-fitting bumpers to aid aerodynamics, fuel lines routed through the roll cage to increase volume, and a cleverly crafted front bumper that was a couple of inches deeper so it could serve as an air dam to smooth airflow over the car, rather than under it. Yunick signed Turner, a long-time friend with a winning attitude and a heavy foot, to drive. Since Smokey's only interest was winning the Daytona 500, not campaigning for points, it was a one-race deal. Turner put the black-and-gold No. 13 car on the pole, surprising everyone except the owner and the driver.

Smokey: "It was gettin' towards the end of the race, and we come in for a pit stop. It was a bad pit stop. Turner got from about a lap ahead to about three-quarters a lap down. Just before he left, I hollered at Turner, 'Don't try to get it all back in one lap!' We'd agreed that he wouldn't turn it over 6,600 or 6,800 (rpm), and I knew that it would turn about four hundred more. But I was afraid he'd forget, so I just warned him again. Just what I was afraid of happened. He turned it loose, and if you'd go over there and look at the lap speed, it would probably be about 184 mile an hour. Broke a rod, and that took care of that one."

The Daytona 500 had its first competitive Chevrolet in years, but with trailing smoke and a stream of oil, Smokey's Chevelle exited the battle. Yarbrough rolled into the lead for a few laps in the world-record-setting Charger, but Andretti and Lorenzen dominated the final 40 laps. Andretti led for the last 32 laps to secure the 427 Fairlane's first major victory.

But trouble was brewing. Chrysler's racing boss, Ronney Householder, saw Lorenzen's 100-mile qualifier win without a single pit stop for either fuel or tires, and concluded that trickery was afoot. Householder stewed; had the Ford men found something? The Chrysler camp complained loud and long that Ford's engines were illegal, that NASCAR inspectors were letting the

During May 1967, David Pearson started as a Holman Moody team Ford driver, finished second in the World 600, then trailed teammate Dick Hutcherson's win in the Dixie 500 at Atlanta, setting a new race record of 132.286 mph. Pearson scored two wins that year in 22 starts. (Ford photos)

Fords through, and Householder threatened to pull out. The Ford men had, indeed, found something – the fifth-generation 427 FE engine. Lorenzen had simply drafted the Dodge Chargers and reportedly ran only half throttle.

When Andretti won the Daytona 500, Householder steamed and the Petty crew was so disgusted with their new '67 cars that they installed new sheetmetal on Ol' Blue, the car that had been so successful toward the end of the previous season. In the next round, Richard won by two laps, and Ol' Blue just got better and better as the season went on.

In the next 10 races leading up to Darlington, Petty won four and David Pearson took two for Dodge, racing out of Cotton Owens' nine-man garage in Spartanburg, South Carolina. Householder's continual complaints against Ford fell on deaf ears. This was racing, finally. The rules were written as equitably as possible, which led to real competition, not the lopsided affairs of the two previous seasons.

NASCAR's new Compact Class, with its smaller engines, was similar to the SCCA's Trans-American Sedan Championship (Trans-Am), which began in 1966 and was instantly popular with the kids. Ultimately, the "Baby Grand" series became NASCAR's Grand American Sedan series, but it received much less attention than Trans-Am. The purpose of Grand-Am was to serve as a farm system to bring talented young drivers up the experience ladder to Grand National. Fueled by the popularity of the musclecar and factory support, Trans-Am was the hottest series of small-sedan racing ever seen. With so much racing going on in 1967, a farm system for stock-car racing simply wasn't needed, so the Grand-Am series dwindled away due to lack of fan support. Trans-Am was exciting; Grand-Am wasn't.

Only full-size cars and intermediates were legal for Grand National (with minimum weight of 3,500 lbs and 9.36 lbs per ci), so the playing field was finally level. The Hemi was held in check with a single 4-bbl carb, while the other big-inch wedge engines could run dual 4-bbls. For safety and strength reasons, frames could be reinforced, with an emphasis on a strong driver roll cage to connect the front and rear tub frames into a unit. For the first time, race shops could fabricate their own chassis, as long as they fit manufacturer dimensions. The minimum hood height was

The Holman Moody team and its new driver, Pearson, worked well together. Later in the year, when Dick Hutcherson retired from driving, he was hired by Holman Moody to manage the Pearson team toward a Grand National points championship. The moves were proven when Pearson swept to the title in dominating fashion. (Ford Photo)

1967 NEW BEGINNINGS

The Wood Brothers completed Ford's stable of top NASCAR teams, and with Cale Yarborough behind the wheel of the Virginia car, two more victories were added to Ford's slim total of 10 wins in 49 races. Yarborough won the Firecracker 400 at Daytona and the Atlanta 500 to give Ford some bragging rights amid Plymouth's 31 victories that year, which included Richard Petty scoring the highest point total ever achieved in NASCAR – over 6,000 points ahead of second place. (Ford photo)

lowered to 27 in, but no trick bodies were allowed. Each entry had to conform to profile templates, and tricks to lower the cars once on the track were ruled out. Disc brakes were also allowed for the first time. It all added up to make the 1967 season the beginning of the modern stock-car racing.

Back in Dearborn in 1966, the Ford men found 30 more hp in the latest version of the 427 with the Tunnel Port induction system. The first 427 of 1963, the Low Riser, had been replaced by the High Riser of 1964, and then the Medium Riser of 1965. The SOHC hemi-head 427 was released as a competition-only engine. Each of these engines was more powerful than the one before it. The Tunnel Port was the final, most powerful version of the 427. Its advantage came from larger round ports and matching intake passages that produced a ram effect. The Tunnel Port was Ford's main stock-car competition engine until it was replaced at the end of 1968 with a new hemi, the BOSS 429. The BOSS was derived from the 385-series engine, not the FE-series like the various 427s, which dated back to the 352 of 1958.

Holman Moody installed a 360-ci Ford truck crank in the High Riser to get a fast-revving 396, the engine that Lorenzen raced at Riverside in a Holman Moody Fairlane. The Fairlane

Richard Petty gained the Grand National points lead by winning the Carolina 500 at Rockingham in mid-June, his 11th victory of the season and almost half of the races run up to that time. His winning speed of 104.68 mph stood as a Rockingham record until he improved it with 116.12 mph in 1970. Petty won both rounds of the Darlington races among an astounding record of 27 victories in 48 starts, a record still unsurpassed. Petty exceeded $150,000 in winnings, another first for a NASCAR driver. (Ford photo)

Mercury's bid for stock-car racing victories was not productive in 1967. Sam McQuagg was Bud Moore's lead driver, but Mercury ended the season winless for the first time since 1963. (Ford photo)

"Back door" racing was Chevrolet's way of doing business in 1967. Here, racing boss Vince Piggins (right) and competition coordinator Paul Prior (middle) chat with drag-racer Wally Booth. (Paul Prior photo)

was lightened 300 lbs according to the displacement rule. This reduced fuel consumption, made tires and brakes last longer, and produced faster cornering. It was a formidable combination, even if the 396 was running just 515 hp, compared to the 580-hp 427 used in 4,000-lb cars. Parnelli Jones proved the setup by trouncing everything on Riverside's road course in the first round of the year.

Chrysler and Ford split the first eight races of the season, but with Ford taking the big track wins. Prior to the Atlanta 500 in early April, Householder laid down the law; if NASCAR didn't correct the rules favoring Ford, all the Chrysler teams would withdraw from the Atlanta race. NASCAR didn't budge, and all the teams ignored the boss. It was time go racing and stop bickering. Cale Yarborough added insult to Householder's bruised pride by taking his first major victory as a Ford factory driver. This began his long and fruitful career of driving Fords and Mercurys for the Wood brothers.

The first 15 races were split almost evenly between Ford and Chrysler power, and the 1967 season showed promise of real competitive racing. No one predicted the Petty roll to come. Ol' Blue and Richard stormed to 27 wins in 48 starts – 10 in a row in a late-season stretch! It was a spectacular season by every measure, the best individual season on record, unmatched to this day. Richard emerged as "The King" of NASCAR that year with a total of 75 career wins by the end of the season, surpassing his father's 54. His winnings exceeded $130,000 for the season as he took his second Grand National Championship. Excitement had returned to stock-car racing, and Householder zippered his complaining. With 31 Plymouth wins backed by 5 Dodge victories against Ford's 10, he had nothing more to say.

Strangely, the reason that the year-old Petty cars were superior to the new cars was never explained. Whatever the reason, Richard Petty and his '66 Belvedere in '67 sheetmetal were a dominating combination never seen before or since.

Throughout the year, NASCAR gained new momentum, and fans roared with satisfaction. No longer would the factories push around the sanctioning body, but neither would the cars ever again be strictly stock. Winning cars were custom-built to look like factory cars, but ran tweaked factory engines dialed in on race-shop dynos. Team owners, car builders, drivers, and NASCAR had reached an accord, and the factories moved to the second line behind the teams. NASCAR required the manufacturers to produce 500 examples of a car for public sale, but engines didn't have to come in the model raced. This gave the teams more latitude when building cars, and special cars for particular races became the norm. Finally, the task of building the best racing cars from the best available factory equipment had been handed to the teams.

Even though Ford drivers won about half the races on the big tracks in 1967, losing the season to Plymouth was difficult to take. Back in Dearborn, stylists penned a slick new fastback Fairlane called the Torino, to be introduced in late 1967 as Ford's new midsize model for '68. Ford was back with its well-honed Tunnel Port 427 the next year.

Back in North Wilkesboro, Junior and the boys took a look at the car and saw a winner. All that was needed was an aggressive driver, and Junior found just the driver he was looking for in LeeRoy Yarbrough. Signed on late in the '67 season from Cotton Owens, Yarbrough turned in a best of third in three starts in '67, and then rolled in 1968.

1967: NEW BEGINNINGS

Ford's Lincoln-Mercury Division went after top-draw drag-racing in a big way with three factory-backed Comet teams, NHRA World Champion Jack Chrisman, "Dyno" Don Nicholson, and "Fast Eddie" Schartmann. The Comets were first-generation funny cars, full fiberglass lift-up bodies over tube frames that were actually short-wheelbase dragsters running nitromethane. Blown and injected SOHC Cammers cranked out the power to virtually dominate the class while producing some of the most exciting drag racing ever seen. (Ford photo)

NASCAR'S WILD YEARS

CHAPTER NINE

Above, right and facing page: Only a handful of 427 Fairlanes made it into Ford showrooms in 1967, and those that did were most often put on drag strips where they ran Super Stock. Factory-rated at 425 hp, their 427-ci side-oiler engines were capable of 525 hp. Underrating output for insurance purposes didn't fool anyone. John Elliot of Canada won the NHRA Winternationals Super Stock title in his father's 427 Comet.

1967: NEW BEGINNINGS

In the marketplace, 1966 sales were down slightly from 1965, but 1967 was a disaster. After back-to-back Mustang sales years of over 580,000 units, 1967 sales dropped to 394,482 as part of Ford's 48 percent downturn, even while supporting racing worldwide. Chevrolet sales were down just 14.7 percent, though the factory spent nothing on racing. After the new Camaro was introduced in late 1966, buyers took home 23,600 per month. Camaro sales fell off in '67 to average 18,000 per month. Plymouth (down 5 percent) and Dodge (down 7 percent) faired better than their rivals, largely because of their fleets of Hemi drag cars. Pontiac, no longer in racing, maintained sales totals with a Camaro clone, the new-for-1967 Firebird.

If stock-car racing actually supported the "Buy on Monday" rule, it was not clear by looking at the 1967 sales figures. The kids, however, bought increasing numbers of personal-size cars – Mustangs, Camaros, and Firebirds – the types of cars seen in Trans-Am racing. The big-engine full-size and intermediate cars sold in small numbers to qualify for NASCAR began to pose a new problem: they were simply too fast for the street, as shown by the increasing carnage on highways. Lawmakers were taking notice, and 1968 brought mandated safety legislation that began putting the brakes on high-powered engines and fast cars. NASCAR had already turned the corner allowing race teams increasing latitude in building cars for racing, and strictly stock withered away.

CHAPTER TEN

Above and facing page: Dan Gurney raced his 427 Torino Ford into the record books at the Motor Trend 500 at Riverside in 1968 by setting a new track record of 100.598 mph to better his own track record set in 1966. Answering the power of the Chrysler Hemi with lighter weight and improved aerodynamics, the new Torino proved highly competitive with 20 wins in NASCAR's 49-race schedule. (Ford photos)

1968: Power and Aerodynamics

The 1968 NASCAR season opened with a flourish as new-car sales took off. Ford moved ahead of 1967 model year sales (a boost of 38.8 percent), averaging 44,500 more units sold per month. Chevrolet sales rose almost 12 percent, registering the biggest increase in the midsize Nova and Chevelle lines. Plymouth was up 12 percent and Dodge had its best year, racking up a 25-percent increase, selling 621,136 units across all models. Overall sales showed more models resonating with buyer interests, and muscle cars with big-inch mills cranking out lots of power topped the list. Engines with over 400 ci were everywhere by then, fulfilling America's thirst for speed. With Carroll Shelby's said: "Too much is just right." With aftermarket equipment for any desire, traditional hot rods were out of favor and factory-built HP ruled.

Racing had an increasing influence on the engines and styling of showroom models, because NASCAR rules required at least 500 of the model raced to be offered to the public. Among intermediates in NASCAR, the Plymouth GTX, with its 116-in wheelbase, was smoother and cleaner, and was expected to take over where the Petty-blue cars left off in 1967, trouncing everything.

Meanwhile, over at Chrysler, inter-make rivalry was stirring as stylists shaped the new Dodge Charger with sleeker lines in an effort to solve the previous fastback's high-speed handling problems. The Charger was fitted with the same Hemi that went into the GTX, and since there was no improvement in his Plymouths, Richard Petty wanted to switch to Dodge. His request was denied. Petty was Chrysler's No. 1 driver and Petty-blue Plymouths had helped sell many cars. This refusal proved a point; the factory men were dictating which teams got what, and they had little interest in promoting individual interests or established loyalties. Richard saw it very clearly, and it led to a very different season in 1968.

The Chrysler factory men set to the task of making the GTX and the Charger as good as they could be, and they produced very trick cars. However, the Charger's better aerodynamics benefited even more from repositioning the body shell on the wheelbase and lowering the body around the pan. The nose-to-front-wheel centerline was shortened on some cars, as the body was shifted rearward. Further improvements were made in suspension geometry with repositioned mount points and by moving the engine for better weight distribution and handling. Body panels not subject to NASCAR templates were reshaped to improve aerodynamics, and underbody panels were smoothed toward a belly pan over the rear axle, common in other forms of racing, but not in NASCAR. The front fender shape permitted lower front ends with sufficient internal tire clearance and produced a noticeable rake. Whether on Goodyear or Firestone tires, the need for more speed put designs and rubber compounds to the test of near-200-mph laps for the first time.

The Charger's lines were good, better than Plymouth's, but the season proved two things: the inset grill and headlights created turbulence in the front, and the inset rear glass with pillar-sails (that looked so stylish) created turbulence in the rear. Although they looked like stock cars from a distance, there was nothing strictly stock about NASCAR entries, other

CHAPTER TEN

Because Mario Andretti won the Daytona 500 in 1967, Smokey Yunick contracted him to drive his updated 427 Chevelle, in '68 the car that Curtis Turner put on the pole the year before. During practice, Andretti wrecked the car, and it never turned another race lap afterward. (Smokey Yunick photo)

than template fitting. Preparing racing cars had matured as an art. NASCAR eliminated weight handicaps, specifying a minimum weight of 3,650 lbs. Engine displacement was capped at 430 ci for any type of engine, and induction was limited to a single 4-bbl carburetor. By midseason, NASCAR relented to driver and team pressure and allowed dual 4-bbl carbs on any engine. Although engines were not significantly different from the previous year, sleeker cars went faster with the same power as a result of attention to aerodynamics. Modest gains in HP were achieved in 1968, but better aerodynamics was the focus of the season.

Coming off a spectacular year of victories in 1967, A. J. Foyt was one of Ford's top drivers in '68, but the Southern drivers took stock-car racing up a notch that year. Foyt entered only four races, taking no wins. (Ford photo)

1968: POWER AND AERODYNAMICS

Richard Petty won 16 races in 49 starts in Plymouths and was in the hunt for the Grand National title right up to the end of the season. David Pearson and Ford won 16 races in 48 starts, but Bobby Isaac in his K&K Dodge squeaked out a few more points from his three wins to finish second overall in the points. These three drivers raced a ferocious season, leaving only a few races to other drivers, with Pearson, Isaac, and Petty finishing one-two-three. (Ford photos)

CHAPTER TEN

NASCAR was still recovering from the previous two years of bickering, so it scheduled just 49 races that year. As the year progressed from the opening round at Daytona, Chrysler's engineers and race teams learned two more things: the Ford men had their act together, and the 427 Tunnel Port was tough to beat. The new midsize fastback Fairlane Torino and Mercury Cyclone came on strong right from the beginning. Ford had top drivers like Cale Yarborough driving for the Wood Brothers and LeeRoy Yarbrough driving for Junior Johnson and a host of Holman Moody drivers led by David Pearson. Unlike the Dodge Charger, with its history of high-speed instability, the fastback Fords and Mercurys proved both stable and fast.

At Daytona, Cale set the pole at just over 189 mph, 9 mph faster than Turner in Yunick's Chevelle the previous year. During the race, he had to overcome early ignition problems, resulting in lightning-quick pit stops by the Wood Brothers crew, and then had to pit to remove debris blocking the radiator. At one point, Cale was three laps down, and to get back into it, he ran successive record laps (the fastest race lap of 184.80 mph). Unfortunately, the race was marred with wrecks, and only 21 of the 50 entrants finished. The duel in the final laps was Mercury against Mercury as Cale and LeeRoy put the field behind them. Yarborough, Yarbrough, and Bobby Allison finished in that order, one-two-three, Mercury-Mercury-Ford.

The normally impeccably prepared Petty Plymouths came apart at Daytona speeds. The top above the windshield peeled up, the result of a lack of attention to detail, and pit stops to duct tape it didn't help much. When Richard hit the wall and ended his day, he was two laps down and finished in eighth place. The highest-

The hard-fought Daytona 500 went to Cale Yarborough (No. 21) in a Wood Brothers Mercury with full factory backing for the first time in 1968. Yarborough came back from two laps down and made the final laps a duel with Junior Johnson's Mercury, driven by LeeRoy Yarbrough (No. 26). Yarborough won only six races that year, but they were big wins that netted $138,000 in winnings, more than David Pearson's championship-season total. (Ford photos)

154   NASCAR'S WILD YEARS

1968: POWER AND AERODYNAMICS

finishing Hemi was Cotton Owens' Dodge Charger driven to fourth place by Indy 500 driver and USAC star Al Unser. These four were the only cars to complete 200 laps.

All of GM was still officially out of racing, but the Chevelle was a threat in the lower weight class, as Smokey Yunick proved the year before. The new Chevelle set the tone for future stock-car racing with a tube frame.

Smokey said: "…Examinin' the rulebook, I went by what they said, and anything they didn't say, I assumed I could do, the way I always handled it. Built my own frame…The '67 race just shocked everybody. We stuck her on the pole so easy. Chrysler and Ford were spendin' money ass over head and General Motors ain't spendin' a dime.

"We get over there the last day (1968), and I'd underestimated the shit they were gonna put me through. Well, that was the last day you could practice and qualify. I was plannin' on bein' on the racetrack by 'bout 'leven or 'leven-thirty, give (Gordon) Johncock some practice and then qualify right at the end of the day at four o'clock. We finally get through inspection and push it to Union to get fueled up to go out and practice and qualify. Then the guys come back and say they won't give me any gas 'cause the chief inspector hadn't signed off. So, I go roarin' up to him, he's sittin' in there readin' *Superman* or *Spider Man* or somethin', he was a comic book nut, I said, 'Sign this thing. We ain't got but a few minutes left here, and I ain't been on the track yet. We got to qualify today.'

"He laid his comic book down and said, 'I got to inspect that car myself.' So, he went and inspected it and made a list of ten or twelve things. Number one on the list was 'Remove

LeeRoy Yarbrough proved Junior Johnson's judgment of his driving talent correct when he won two races, the Dixie 500 at Atlanta being his biggest. Fifteen top-five finishes in 26 races were good for $88,000, a third more than Bobby Isaac won in his second-place finish in the points from 49 races. (Ford photos)

Pearson takes Foyt with the low groove at Daytona while both drivers had to take back seat to the show put on by Yarborough and Yarbrough up front. (Ford photo)

homemade frame and replace with stock.' Well, that would take two months. The car was a throw-away car. I wanted to win the race, and I didn't give a damn about what happened at the next race.

"'You got to do what's on that list.'

"'Fine.' I was goin' to drive it out o' there, and I went back to break the seal on the empty gas tank. I went down to Union and told them I needed three or four gallons of gas. I went back to the car and put the gas can up there and everybody seen me. Now, I could'a prob'ly cranked it up and drove it home without puttin' any gas in it 'cause I had about a inch and half fuel line, held five gallons."

Then came the final huff with Bill France. Smokey drove his Chevelle back to his shop, and France arrived a little later. The words that flew cannot be repeated, and the feud resulted in France banning the car from the track forever; it never turned a lap in the 20 years that Smokey kept it, not even for off-season tire testing.

The schedule went on, and David Pearson took the next two races in Holman Moody Fords. When the cars rolled to start the Atlanta 500 in the seventh round, the Torinos and Cyclones put the season in perspective. Late in the race, Yarbrough was leading but was black flagged for jumping the green-flag restart after a caution, and Cale put his Wood Brothers Mercury into the lead to win again – two superspeedway victories in a row. Yarbrough finished second, instead of likely getting his first win of the season.

In both races at Bristol, Pearson kept Petty behind him to take the wins. Their season-long duels produced memorable racing at new levels of speed and durability – Ford 427 wedge against Plymouth 426 Hemi. (Ford photo)

1968: POWER AND AERODYNAMICS

Tiny Lund rose to the championship of NASCAR's first season of the Baby Grand series driving Bud Moore's Mercury Cougars, but his entry in 17 Grand National races netted only five top-five finishes. (Ford photo)

Chrysler's iron-fisted racing boss, Ronney Householder, was a force to be reckoned with. His continual challenges of NASCAR's waffling rules throughout the 1960s made him a legend. He was a hard-liner who demanded rules that he regarded as fair (favoring Chrysler entries). (DaimlerChrysler Historical Collection photo)

Petty won two short-track rounds. The first major Dodge win came in the World 600 when Buddy Baker took the checkered flag. In the second Charlotte race that year, Charlie Glotzbach won in another Dodge, the second of the make's only major wins that year.

Meanwhile, in mid-July, Yarbrough put Junior's Cyclone on the pole in a 300-mile race in Trenton, New Jersey, and led almost the entire race to capture his second win of the season. Then four races later at the Dixie 500 at Atlanta, he won again, sweet revenge for the first-round denial, and icing on the rivalry that had developed with Cale Yarborough. Mercurys tallied more major wins than Ford (7 to 6) when the season ended. By then, Pearson and Petty had notched 16 wins apiece. Pearson's point total led all drivers to win the Grand National Championship. Bobby Isaac made it a tough points race, winning just three races

NASCAR'S WILD YEARS

CHAPTER TEN

but finishing consistently high. That bumped Petty to third. The manufacturer's points went Ford-Dodge-Plymouth, but Cale was far and away the biggest money winner. By leading many laps and winning major races in his Wood Brothers Mercurys, he set a new season record for winnings, $136,786.

During the season, Pearson twice won four races in a row in his Fords. After dominating the previous season, the Petty team was a disappointment, even with the Hemi.

The 600-plus-hp big-block engines had to work hard to push the big, flat-front cars to superspeedway speeds. Despite the advances, the cars were aerodynamic bricks, with the high frontal area pushing into the wind. By 1968, aerodynamic streamlining was the last variable left to exploit for significant gains in speed. Of course, there was always more power from newer, more modern powerplants, which was one branch of Ford's dual-pronged approach for the coming season of stock-car racing. The Tunnel Port 427 was the end of racing wedge-shaped combustion chambers at Ford. The Total Performance men produced the "Blue Crescent" Boss 429, the second Ford Hemi. Chrysler's Hemi had a lot of development in it, so 1969 was certain to be a tough year for Ford. The Chrysler Hemi and the Boss 429 were both single-cam-in-block V-8 production engines. Back in Dearborn, the Ford men produced the "Calliope," a dual cam-in-block 427 that was raced a little in the Can-Am series, but it became just another mystery engine on the shelf.

The 1968 season was not the spectacular year expected of Petty, even though the Petty team had Chrysler's best showing with 16 wins. Richard was not happy about having to drive the Plymouth, which he considered inferior to the Dodge Charger. The Dodge boys turned out a new super-slick Charger 500 with aero-refinements including a forward-mounted grill that was sealed along the edges, and rear glass that was even with the aerodynamic skin of the car, both areas that produced instability in the 1968 cars. Needless to say, Petty saw no possibility of being competi-

In Donnie Allison's first year on the Ford factory team, he won the Carolina 500 at Rockingham and received Rookie of the Year honors. (Ford photo)

1968: POWER AND AERODYNAMICS

Inset: In winning the Rebel 400 at Darlington and setting a new track record of 132.70 mph, Pearson showed the potential of John Holman's experiments with the 427 engine. With a 390 crank, displacement was reduced to 396 ci, permitting the weight of the car to be reduced according to NASCAR's ci-per-lb rules. Quicker in the turns, Pearson was able to set a new track record of 132.70 mph to better Petty's 1966 Hemi Plymouth record. (Ford photo)

Pearson raced to victory in the Richmond 400, one of his 16 wins while running the full season during 1968. The tight championship points race was exhausting and began tilting his interests toward selected races with big purses rather than a race almost every weekend of the season. (Ford photo)

tive in Plymouths the next year. Plymouth had nothing similar to the Charger 500, and Richard was denied his request to race a Dodge. The longest-running and most productive factory-team relationship ended in a huff. Petty stunned everyone; he signed on with Ford late in the year, and Chrysler lost its best team.

For the 1969 NASCAR season, more power and smoother aerodynamics were the goals, as cars were expected to run 200 mph for the first time. A new longer track, Bill France's widely proclaimed Alabama International Motor Speedway, Talladega, was to debut. It featured 2.66 miles of high banks scaled up in layout from Daytona. The longer track promised higher speeds, and no one was confident of tires holding up. Safety issues were hot topics, so drivers and team owners organized to have a say in how racing was conducted. France called it "unionizing" and refused to recognize anything about or from the organization. France had ejected Curtis Turner some years earlier for trying to give the drivers a greater voice, and it finally came to fruition.

The Ford men knew the Dodge boys were pulling out the stops with the sleek Charger 500 and would stuff it with a powerful Hemi, so they paid further attention to aerodynamics. From

Ford's new for 1968 fastback Torino was both a marketing success and a racing champion. Fairlane/Torino sales that year skyrocketed 245 percent, contributing to a banner year for Ford, up 39 percent compared to Plymouth, up 12 percent, and Dodge, up 25 percent. Chevrolet, with no involvement in stock-car racing at all, was up almost 12 percent. The styling was carried over to the next year, resulting in a decline in Fairlane/Torino sales of 40 percent, but it was still Ford's midsize leader.

an engineering standpoint, the three major components draining speed were wind resistance – or drag, rolling resistance between tires and asphalt, and mechanical losses in the drivetrain. Mechanical losses consumed about 10 percent of engine power. Engineers were able to lower friction and add torsional rigidity, but the gains were small at best.

Reduction in car-to-pavement resistance did offer some gains. Rolling resistance per 1,000 lbs continually changes during a race. It varied due to differences in surface quality and condition, vehicle bounce direction, compound adhesion, and tire air pressure, which is a function of tire temperature. A rule of thumb was that a 3,650-lb car rolling on smooth, dry concrete required about 120 hp at 200 mph, up from 91 hp for 180 mph (it's a nonlinear function, but not quite a square function, as with drag versus speed, explained below). Racing bumpy high banks required somewhat more power, but teams had little influence on tires other than the selection of compounds. Tire engineers were hard pressed to produce tires that held together at the sustained levels of stress and temperatures produced at 200 mph. Stronger tires with new compounds, which were now tubeless for the first time, met the challenges.

Aerodynamics was more tricky and depended more on factory designers than anything race teams could do. Decades earlier, the coefficient of drag, or penetration coefficient, known as Cd, was invented to quantify drag. Multiplying Cd by frontal area produced the actual drag. The typical Cd for a boxy 1960s production car was about 0.45, which meant it required about 65 hp at 90 mph to push the 25-sq-ft cross-section through still air at sea level. The square-of-velocity rule said that doubling speed to 180 mph required 260 hp under the same conditions. But adding rolling resistance and mechanical losses, the predicted power requirement was at least 418 hp to reach 180 mph. Adding another 10 mph required about 100 more hp, but making such a prediction was a highly complex analysis, involving a host of constantly changing variables: varying handling characteristics, wind conditions, tire wear, track temperature, and more. Since NASCAR engines had more than 600 hp on tap, actual power requirements proved to be much greater than aerodynamics predicted. Since reaching maximum speed in the shortest time was a critical factor, engine output had to be far more than aerodynamic requirements, a further complication of the scientific analysis of stock cars at the time.

Although the submarine shape approaches the hydrodynamic ideal, that shape does not fit automobiles, which tend toward rectangular cross-sections. Land speed-record cars of the time exploited the submarine shape, but stock cars could not. To achieve the highest speeds from available HP, air must flow as smoothly around and over the skin of the stock car as possible, rather than under the car, and fastback tops were the best available choice. But being too slippery presented problems, too.

Skin friction, how air sticks to the surface as it flows over it, and surface condition, the smoothness of the surface, also influences top speed. Just as water slows near stream banks, air slows near the surface of cars. This boundary layer begins at the front of the car and grows in thickness toward the rear and forms rolling turbulence along the way. The smoother the surface, the lower the turbulence, and the faster a car can go with available power. This is interference drag. Any imperfection in the surface produces drag, such as holes in the body (windows), abrupt changes in body contour (hood to windshield angle), and ends of bumpers sticking out. Because air must flow faster over a car than under it, lift is produced, and typical stock cars of the time produced about 300 lbs of lift at 100 mph. A balanced car divided this 300 lbs evenly front and rear, while unbalanced cars tended to have more lift in the rear. This condition causes reduced adhesion and lower-speed breakaway. Cars with "light" front ends had less steering control.

The primary aerodynamic goal is always to disturb the air the least, but getting a car to stick to the pavement at high speeds requires sufficient downforce and tire adhesion. The goal

The frontal area of the vehicle – the product of width and height – is a linear function; doubling the area doubles the wind resistance. However, the shape of the outline has a far greater influence on drag than the total area. Car designers learned from hydrodynamics: the drag of fish-like submarines was about 50 times less than a square box of the same cross-sectional area at the same speed. Corners are aerodynamic disasters that create intense turbulence, so rounding and smoothing corners significantly improves laminar flow of a fluid over a skin layer. Unfortunately, the typical stock car was closer to a brick than a submarine in terms of frontal area. Things like door handles, bumper ends, chrome strips, water channels, and any other protrusions into the slipstream siphoned off speed.

is to hold the weight of the car perpendicular to the track stronger than in the lateral direction, parallel to the track surface. When the ratio of lateral/perpendicular nears 1:1, a puff of crosswind may be sufficient to send the vehicle into uncontrolled flight. By 1969, with racing speeds near 200 mph for the first time, drivers were in the uncomfortable territory. Imagine driving on the edge of breakaway, skating along on the fringes of physics where any turbulence on the track, track surface imperfection, or any combination of small perturbations in air movement, were potentially disastrous. High-speed driving required instantaneous correction to maintain control. Racing was more a flirtation with disaster than ever before, requiring constant driver attention and quick but subtle action.

CHAPTER TEN

Left, below and facing page: Plymouth's Hemi Satellite sales were few, making them exceptionally rare, but overall Belvedere/Satellite sales were up big-time in 1968, almost 68,700 more than were sold in '67. The Beach Boys' hit single "Little Ol' Lady From Pasadena" rolled from jukeboxes across America and told of the "Super Stock Dodge." The drag strip was the place to be.

162   NASCAR'S WILD YEARS

1968: POWER AND AERODYNAMICS

Chrysler stylists had penned the previous Charger's lines into a handsome showroom model, but when engineers studied the flow of air over its fastback top, they learned that its slope fell away from the aerodynamic ideal contour. The air couldn't bend to the shape, and instead created lift, the very effect that the Wright brothers searched for to enable flight. Consequently, drivers of the previous Chargers had already been skating on the big tracks. A partial solution was to install a spoiler on the rear lip of the trunk to create turbulence and hold the car to the track. This Kamm-effect was so named for the German scientist, Dr. W. I. E. Kamm, who had showed in the 1930s that air management around the tail of a car did not require long bodies, as with world land speed record cars. When cropped at the critical point of balance between lift and downforce, the resulting bobbed tail has no more drag than a long tail. Since all stock cars were bobbed by design, a small spoiler angled properly across the trailing edge of the trunk improved stick, and a bigger spoiler angled at a greater angle produced much more stick, but reduced the car's balance and top speed. So, finding the right combination of spoiler dimensions and angle became another trick that NASCAR would later address in detail using templates.

In the late 1960s, finding the aerodynamic ideal proved to be highly involved and elusive. Factory engineers were constrained by tight model-year production schedules, and racing teams did not yet include aerodynamicists. Racing engineers provided wind-tunnel studies and refined shapes for high speed. Their research and development was a new influence on showroom models, but the design outrageous was yet to come.

Ford's designers didn't make the instability mistake with their fastback shape. The Ford Torino and the Mercury Cyclone had much more stable aerodynamic envelopes than the Charger. Chrysler's engineers tried to correct the mistakes with the Charger 500, but the was a quick fix that still needed refinement to be competitive. So, Ford won 20 of the 49 races during the 1968 season.

CHAPTER ELEVEN

The aerodynamic Ford Talladega, the powerful Boss 429 engine, and the finest set of drivers made Ford's 1969 NASCAR team a formidable combination. (From left rear, counter-clockwise: Richard Petty, Cale Yarborough, David Pearson, Donnie Allison, and LeeRoy Yarbrough.) (Ford photo)

1969 and Beyond: The Aero-War

Factory one-upmanship between Ford and Chrysler became an all-out war, resulting in the wildest cars yet seen on American highways and racetracks. The time was permeated with continual development, and people couldn't wait to see what was coming next. The most powerful engines got the most attention. Ford's 427 Cammer (capable of 810 hp in normally aspirated form by 1969) never went racing on the high banks. Meanwhile Chrysler dropped its DOHC 426 Hemi project after the Ford's Cammer was banned by NASCAR. Chrysler built only one DOHC Hemi engine, but canned it based on NASCAR's rulings, then turned to refining the Hemi's induction for more power.

Back in '65, Ford had a thoroughly developed engine without a production car, so they offered the Cammer complete in the crate for $1,963. Chrysler's Hemi cost only $900 and attracted a lot more buyers. Unlike Ford's Cammer, the Hemi was installed in a variety of production cars and was sure to be a threat on the NASCAR circuit in 1969. With the Ford men working on the new 429-ci Blue Crescent hemi, designers also dug deep into aerodynamics to pick up more speed. At the time, almost 17 hp was needed to gain 1 mph in top speed, but smoothing airflow enabled 17 hp to increase top speeds around 5 mph.

For 1969, NASCAR upped minimum weight requirements to 3,900 lbs but permitted dry-sump engines. Without oil pans, engines could be positioned lower in the car for better handling. The engines were still held to 430 ci and a single 4-bbl carburetor, though they were capable of 600-plus-hp. The three new paved tracks – Dover Downs in Delaware, Michigan International Speedway, and Talladega in Alabama – added up to a 54-race season. NASCAR moved further from its dirt-racing heritage onto more asphalt and higher speeds and attracted a huge number of spectators, making 1969 the best attendance year up to that time.

In late 1968, John Holman fit longer Mercury front fenders to a Torino and mounted the grill flush (as on the Dodge Charger 500). He created the new aero-Ford, a droopy-nose Torino that became the Torino Cobra (with 427 power) and the Torino Talladega (with the Boss 429). He also rolled the rocker panels to give an additional inch of ground clearance so that stock-car builders could drop the entire body an inch and still maintain NASCAR ground-clearance requirements. The Cyclone Spoiler II was the aero-Mercury. These limited-edition Ford products were oddballs and slow sellers in the showroom, but they were faster than ever on the ovals. These cars were built in the Atlanta assembly plant and fitted with production engines, not the Boss 429, which may account for their lack of sales popularity.

Ford Motor Co. celebrated Dan Gurney's contributions to Ford's "Total Performance" era in Indy 500 racing, sports-car racing, and stock-car racing with release of the blue-and-white Dan Gurney Special Mercury Cyclone Spoiler in 1969. (Ford photo)

In response to the re-rolled rocker-panel trick, Chrysler engineers "channeled" the bodies of three stock cars. Removing a 2-inch belt in the body achieved similar results, making a lower profile with reduced frontal area. This trick got by NASCAR inspectors initially, but was banned later. Bobby Isaac drove one of these cars, which became a transition vehicle to the wild new Dodge Charger Daytona.

With the Hemi, the 1968 Dodge stock cars proved capable of 184 mph, some 3 to 4 mph faster than the year before. This gain fell short of the new Fords, that gained 5 to 6 mph to around 187 mph, while the Mercurys topped 189. With no similar car, Plymouth was sure to be uncompetitive, so 1969 promised to be a Ford-versus-Dodge shootout. Try as he did, Bill France could not find a niche for Chevrolet. Smokey Yunick's Chevelle was

NASCAR'S WILD YEARS 165

CHAPTER ELEVEN

Left, below and facing page: Petty stunned the Plymouth camp when he signed on to race Fords in 1969. He went to Ford because Plymouth did not have a competitive car that year and he was not allowed to switch to Dodge. It was a fateful decision that sealed Chrysler's fate in stock-car racing. Petty won 10 races for Ford, almost half the number Dodge won that year, 22. Had he been driving for Dodge, a different chapter in NASCAR racing might have been written. Note the spoiler on the back of Petty's Torino Cobra, finally permitted by NASCAR. (Ford photos)

166 NASCAR'S WILD YEARS

1969 AND BEYOND: THE AERO-WAR

LeeRoy Yarbrough crashed Junior Johnson's main car in practice, then raced the back-up Ford to a tight finish. He closed on Charlie Glotzbach's Ray Nichels Dodge in the final 10 laps, storming back from an 11-second deficit to pass Glotzbach on the final lap in the Daytona 500. (Ford photo)

1969 AND BEYOND: THE AERO-WAR

the newly built Lockheed-Martin wind tunnel, the first project of the just-completed facility. Testing the new Dodge stock car served as the wind tunnel's checkout for automobile-based studies, and served to improve the Dodge design. In late December 1968, the nose shape emerged. It was a molded fiberglass fairing that could be mounted to the existing bumper and front-end sheetmetal mount points. It extended about 18 inches forward with a low, penetrating nose. The new nose also included a chin spoiler that worked best when mounted 13 inches back from the leading edge of the fairing. With the new design in hand, Plymouth, certain of their Petty Enterprises exposure, turned it down, while Dodge bought in, but only for PR and advertising

Pearson started 51 of NASCAR's races in 1969 and scored 42 top-five finishes with 11 wins, a formidable season that showed Ford's one-two sweep was the result of aerodynamics, power, and driver talent. Pearson led Petty in the final points and dollars won by a considerable margin, the first over-$200,000 season. (Ford photo)

outlawed, and no one else was capable of making a Chevrolet run fast enough to compete with the fastbacks and Hemis. Chevrolet was back to no wins in 1969, a repeat of the winless 1965 season.

Against the sleek Fords and Mercs in '68, the Dodge Charger teams had a tough year on the big tracks, winning only 5 races that year, verses 27 for the aero-Fords and Mercurys. Not only were their cars slower than the Ford products, they were unstable at top speeds, largely because the shape of the Charger created high front-end lift and the rear-window-to-rear-deck shape created high drag. To get more speed required a different shape.

With engines locked in by the rules, Dodge Division General Manager Bob McCurry authorized advanced designs for more speed. Chrysler's engineers at its design studio and proving grounds in Chelsea, Michigan (the Special Vehicles Group led by Larry Rathgeb), turned to aerodynamics. They smoothed the Dodge design into the '68-1/2 special-edition Charger 500, penned initially by test engineer John Pointer in December 1967. Since the Charger 500 was a limited-production vehicle, its construction was contracted to Creative Industries in Detroit, rather than an internal assembly as was done by Ford in producing its stock cars.

The wizards at Chelsea were sure they had a winner in the Charger 500, but the Fords and Mercs went aero as well and proved embarrassingly fast. First approached by Chrysler Corporation personnel associated with the Apollo Space Program at Chrysler's facility in Huntsville, Alabama, aerodynamicist John Vaughn was later tapped to lead Charger testing in

To the victor goes the spoils, and a couple of Union-76 beauties to help spend Daytona 500 winnings. What a great day, the beginning of Pearson's second NASCAR championship in a row, his third championship season. (Ford photo)

NASCAR'S WILD YEARS 169

CHAPTER ELEVEN

LeeRoy Yarbrough's 1969 NASCAR season was spectacular by all measures. He won by courageous last-ditch efforts, and by sailing to long leads to win seven superspeedway victories in one of the greatest driving years on record. (Ford photo)

purposes, with a wink given to beating the Ford teams. When Petty opted for Ford shortly afterward, Plymouth management saw the error of its complacency, and had to play catch up to Dodge. Plymouth had lost its role as Chrysler's lead racing make.

The long-nose Dodge Charger Daytona, named for the Daytona 500, began to emerge in early 1969 after the Ford teams trounced the Charger 500 on the Florida high banks. Dodge boss McCurry gave approval for the new aero-Dodge, and within weeks, the new fairing was fitted to the Bobby Isaac car used for testing at the Chelsea Proving Grounds. More problems showed up; one was the channeled body. Wind-tunnel testing showed the advantage of a slight rake on the front end, so the production

The Dodge Charger 500 and Ford Talladega were the best efforts of their respective factory engineers, but with high-speed instability, the Charger 500 proved to be less than hoped for against the faster and more stable Fords and Mercurys. (Ford photo)

1969 AND BEYOND: THE AERO-WAR

When the top teams boycotted the debut of the 2.66-mile Talladega superspeedway, unknown drivers got the chance of their lifetimes. Richard Brickhouse raced the new Dodge Charger Daytona to victory in its first race, but against little competition. (Ford photo)

body profile was lowered to the point where it contacted the tires. The car needed more front-tire clearance on the underside of the fenders to clear maximum upward tire movement. So, rectangular holes were cut in the tops of the fenders and covered with rearward-facing scoops. There was much debate about whether the scoops were front brake cooling ducts and/or underbody pressure relief vents.

The new nose cut into the wind beautifully, but it so upset high-speed balance that the car was dangerous at top speed. Attention to rear airflow, an afterthought considering the amount of time put into the nose, resulted in a variety of cobbled-up spoilers that became a giant slab across the trailing edge of the car that could not be easily integrated into a production car.

Something had to be done to balance the car aerodynamically, and the trunk lid had to be functional. The aerodynamicists had forgotten that detail. The trunk lid had to be able to move up and down on its hinges, so any spoiler had to be mounted high enough to clear the arc of its movement. The resulting wing was an inverted aerofoil on vertical stabilizers 23.5 in high. The wing was over 7 inches wide, and extended across the entire back end of the car. Once this combination was tested and proved to be stable and fast, the engineers ran into trouble with engine overheating.

Making a smooth and balanced aero package was only part of the winning combination; the engine also had to survive. Tests were conducted on the heavily instrumented development vehicle to determine what opening in the nose and what shape produced sufficient cooling. Testing showed that at least 40 square inches were needed to provide adequate cooling, and that took a big chunk out of the nose with a decrease in top speed. Additional aerodynamic drag points along the body were discovered and resolved to produce the wildest stock car ever seen. It was originally planned as a 1970 model, but Ford's dominance of the early 1969 NASCAR season changed the plan. Word came down from

CHAPTER ELEVEN

1969 AND BEYOND: THE AERO-WAR

McCurry in mid-March to hasten release of the Charger Daytona for the inaugural 500-mile race at Talladega in September. So, the new car had the wrong name, but Charger Talladega wasn't possible because Ford already had the Torino Talladega.

Over at Ford, the new Boss 429 engine was the product of Dearborn's own little-known skunk works, the Race Experimental Department of the Engine & Foundry Division. With Holman Moody and the factory's warehouse of can-do racing craftsmen, the Ford steamroller was well built to win in '69, and Total Performance ruled. The aero-Fords and Mercs with their new Boss 429 engines didn't come together until midseason, but in the Daytona 500, LeeRoy Yarbrough rolled into the winner's circle with the '68 427, averaging 157.950 mph, 14.7 mph faster than Cale Yarborough's victory in a similarly powered Mercury the previous year. Rumors of Ford's new and more powerful engine forecast more big wins to come. The Chrysler teams saw a tough year ahead.

The Talladegas and Cyclone Spoiler IIs began rolling out of Ford's Atlanta assembly plant in January 1969, just in time to be homologated for NASCAR racing at Daytona, but Bill France didn't allow them to race. Final production that year totaled 754 Talladegas and 519 Spoiler IIs, but they didn't get on the track until later in the season, first with 427 power, and then with the Boss 429 when enough had been built. These aero-cars were half of Ford President Bunkie Knudsen's strategy to retain the NASCAR crown.

Knudsen had been hired away from General Motors in a corporate raid in the spring of 1968 that caused high-level consternation at Ford. Why bring in a GM guy when plenty of Ford men knew the ropes? The answer was, apparently, that Knudsen knew what GM was doing and planning, and Henry Ford II thought he was worth lots of bucks.

To meet NASCAR's engine rules, Kar-Kraft, Inc. in Dearborn was contracted to stuff Mustangs with the new engine, and to have the first one out by December 1968. So, the 1969-1/2 Boss 429 Mustang was born. Kar-Kraft set up a new facility in Brighton, Michigan, to build at least 500 cars. Ford announced the car on January 16, 1969, and production ended in July with 859 built. Ford met NASCAR production requirements in March, and the Talladega and Boss 429 engine went into battle on March 30, 1969, at Atlanta. Cale Yarborough (Mercury) led David Pearson (Ford) across the line in an aero-Boss Ford one-two romp.

Ford now had cars, engines, and drivers (Yarborough, Pearson, Richard Petty, LeeRoy Yarbrough, and Donnie Allison), making the best team yet – and the Chrysler teams screamed foul. Dodge built and marketed the cars it raced fitted with the engine it raced, while the Talladegas and Cyclone Spoiler IIs came with regular production engines that had no chance against the Hemi. Bill France was in another quandary; if he changed the rules again, in midseason, saying that engines raced had to be offered to the public in the cars raced, the new Fords and Mercurys would simply leave, and NASCAR would collapse into another single-make go-round. His rules didn't specifically state that cars had to race with engines sold in them, so any production engine could be installed in any production car that fit wheelbase and minimum weight requirements. The Mustang didn't fit. Such fine points in the rules resulted in continual grumbling about who was given the unfair advantage. Prior to the Atlanta debut, Ford teams raced plain-front Torino Cobra and Mercury Cyclone entries with 427 engines, then the droopy-nose cars with 427s while the Boss 429 was undergoing homologation. When the Boss 429 engine was unleashed in the aero-nose cars, the bar was instantly raised.

When the Talladegas showed up in dealerships, they were very strange cars that came only in three colors – Wimbledon White, Royal Maroon, and Presidential Blue – each with a

Above and facing page: The fastest of the fast, David Pearson and his Holman Moody-prepared, factory-backed aero-nose Torino Cobra, so named because it ran the Tunnel Port 427 early in the 1969 season. When fitted with the Boss 429, the fast Fords and Mercurys proved to be the terror of the ovals. (Ford photos)

CHAPTER ELEVEN

Ford's Boss 429 Mustang of 1969 had one purpose – to homologate the Boss 429 engine for stock-car racing. When the engines were not ready as the Ford Talladega and Mercury Cyclone Spoiler II were geared up for production in Ford's Atlanta assembly plant, plans were laid for stuffing the new Blue Crescent 429 hemi into Mustangs.

matte-black hood. The stark black interior came with a bench seat up front, a column-shifted automatic behind a 428 Cobra Jet engine, and no options beyond a radio. There was little incentive to buyers. However, everything was super heavy-duty, and on the driver's door an identification plate told that the car was a Special Performance Vehicle – and they were cheap! The list price was only $3,680.10 for a 145-mph turnpike cruiser! The Cyclone Spoiler IIs with similar bodies, but fitted with a rear wing. They came with much more dramatic color combinations: red-and-white as the Cale Yarborough Special, and blue-and-white was the Dan Gurney Special. However, the Mercs were fitted with a 351 Windsor and an automatic, making them even less inviting to buyers than the Fords. The cars made no impact in the marketplace, however unusual and NASCAR-related they were.

Richard Petty was right; Plymouth had nothing to compete with Ford's formidable arsenal. Plymouth won just two races in the 1969 season, and one of those came from Petty before his new Ford ride was finished. The only real competition came from Dodge with 22 wins, while Ford took 26, Petty with 10, and Mercury taking 4.

The season was another Richard Petty-David Pearson slugfest. It began with older-styled Hemi Plymouths against Torinos and Cyclones running Tunnel Port 427 engines until the aero-Fords and Mercs and their new engines were homologated. Once the new cars were on the big tracks, they stumped the confident Chrysler teams, giving up few top wins.

With his new ride still in development, Petty opened the 1969 season by winning the first round in the fall of 1968 in his very trick Plymouth. So, even though Petty Enterprises was not racing for Chrysler, Plymouth led in the early points race. Then Richard finished second to Bobby Allison's Dodge in the second round, so Chrysler was still dominating. The Petty team arrived at Riverside for round three ready to begin the new year in a new Ford, but the nine-turn road course was a handful because of the Ford's very different handling characteristics. Once he had the car dialed in (after a couple of off-course excursions in his Torino Cobra), Richard drove to the point and led 103 of the 186 laps to win his first race in a Ford. A.J. Foyt, having qualified on the pole at 110.366 mph, finished second in a Jack Bowsher Torino Cobra, giving Ford a one-two victory. The sleek new Dodge Charger 500 couldn't catch the fast Fords. Petty now had a healthy lead in points in what looked to be the start of another sensational season.

Prior to the Daytona 500 in February 1969, the Petty team built up new Ford shells received from Holman Moody, rather than building their own cars as had been the team's practice for 10 years. Holman Moody supplied engines as well. The Petty team was looking really tough coming into Daytona, especially after the trouncing Richard gave the field at Riverside. But action at the giant oval proved less satisfying than anticipated. Barbs flew that Holman Moody's engine men were not providing the power that Ford regulars got. The Petty team raced as Ford independents rather than a Holman Moody team, but they were dependent on Holman Moody-supplied engines. A rivalry emerged when Richard was only able to qualify 12th with an eighth overall finish in the 500, four laps down to Junior Johnson's Torino Cobra in the hands of LeeRoy Yarbrough, who was beginning a spectacular season. Soon, Richard's brother Maurice learned how to get power from the new Ford 429, and the Petty cars no longer had to rely on Holman Moody engines.

It wasn't until mid-April at the 16th race of the season that Richard returned to the winner's circle, taking the Virginia 500 at Martinsville. The nine races following Daytona proved to be a Dodge-fest, with Bobby Isaac winning three in a row and Bobby Allison taking two wins to Ford's three. The Dodge Charger was holding its own on the shorter tracks. Finishing high in those races, Petty maintained his point lead while the "Bobbys" tore up Ford's steamroller on the short tracks. Meanwhile, Pearson, Yarborough, and Yarbrough ruled the big tracks, where most of the publicity was focused, and Chrysler's stock-car racing boss Ronney Householder, didn't like it one bit. Yarbrough took the spring Darlington race, the Rebel 400, and the World 600 at Charlotte in Junior Johnson cars, with a two-lap victory margin at Charlotte. Householder's suspicions were confirmed; the Chrysler team knew they had to do something quickly or Ford was going to run away with the season. The aero-Fords and Mercs had taken all five major wins.

The 1969-1/2 Dodge Charger Daytona was the answer. Production began on June 10, with the inaugural 500-mile race at Talladega in September just three months away. When the NASCAR series rolled around to Daytona again for the Firecracker 400 on July 4, Petty's three wins and high finishes still gave him a slim lead in the points race. But Yarbrough in Junior's cars put on another show of domination, beating Buddy Baker in Cotton Owens' Dodge for the victory.

High-speed testing of the new aero-Daytona took place in late July, and longtime Chrysler racer Ray Nichels was contracted to bring driver Charlie Glotzbach and a Charger 500 to serve as a benchmark. Glotzbach's first efforts in the Daytona were impressive, 194 mph, but engine problems limited further testing until the next week. A few days later, he stuck his foot into it and powered around the nearly 5-mile Chelsea Proving Grounds track to tag 204 mph. Grins spread across every face. Then Yarbrough won again, this time in the August running of the Dixie 500 at Atlanta, and media focus fell on the Ford-Johnson-Yarbrough prospects of winning NASCAR's Triple Crown (the Daytona 500, the World 600, and the Southern 500) with a victory in the upcoming Southern 500 at Darlington. Everything the Dodge boys did seemed to be upstaged by Ford's on-track achievements.

David Pearson was the reigning NASCAR champion when the 1969 season opened, and he returned to drive for Holman

CHAPTER ELEVEN

Production Talladegas reached Ford showrooms among the most austere, least-optioned vehicles available. Fitted with 428 Cobra Jet engines, a much lower performer than the Boss 429, the cars were still capable of 145 mph. The new Boss 429 engine in stock-car racing form delivered around 660 hp and propelled the cars to near 200 mph.

NASCAR'S WILD YEARS

Moody. Petty told the media that he thought he had better prospects of winning the NASCAR championship in a Ford than a Plymouth. His move alone is said to have resulted in Plymouth building the 1970 Superbird in an effort to attract him back to Plymouth. Cale Yarborough was behind the wheel of the Wood Brothers Cyclones, providing stiff competition, and LeeRoy Yarbrough was on a roll in Junior's Fords.

NASCAR rules required a minimum of 500 examples of a car to qualify for racing, and Ford met the requirements with the aero-Fords and Mercurys and Boss 429 Mustangs. The earlier Dodge Charger 500 was planned to be built in that quantity, but only 382 were actually built. Strictly speaking, they were not NASCAR legal, but France bent his own rules to have the factory team cars race. A total of 503 Charger Daytonas were built in 1969, with only 70 of the showroom Daytonas fitted with 426 Hemi engines. During 1970, 1,920 Plymouth Superbirds were built, also with a similarly low number of Hemi engine models. During August, Richard Petty earned a NASCAR milestone with his 100th victory and continued his roll to the Grand National Championship. Unlike the Wood Brothers Mercury team with Yarborough, the Petty team was regarded with suspicion by the other Ford teams – if they found something, would they share it? Not likely. As the season progressed, the likelihood that Richard would steal the spotlight of what was sure to be a Ford season and make off with the championship loomed large. If he did, it would serve as a moral victory for Plymouth, proving that Richard Petty could drive anything better than anyone else. He handled his Talladegas to three more wins and a succession of high finishes by midseason, and the Southern 500 was seen as a showdown among the Ford teams.

Like the Pettys, the Wood Brothers team was a longtime Ford regular that operated independently of Holman Moody. Already with a formidable reputation for fulfilling Ford's ambition of having competing factory teams, the Virginia-based Wood Brothers team was always a threat.

At the Southern 500, heavy rain forced a red-flag delay, and then blown engines and crashes produced the lowest race average speed in years. When the track dried, officials recognized that 500 miles couldn't be completed before dark, and the decision was made to call the race after 230 laps (316 miles). Team strategies suddenly changed, and everyone pitted around the 200-lap mark for a showdown to the finish. Pearson's Holman Moody crew opted for soft compound tires, while Junior thought a harder compound would work best. Pearson roared to the lead until the final laps, then had to slow to maintain traction. Yarbrough drove hard and low to take Pearson in turn three on the final lap, then roared to victory as the first Triple Crown winner in NASCAR history. It would be five more years before Pearson accomplished the same feat, only the second driver to do so.

Two weeks later, one of the few major Dodge wins of the year was taken in the first Talladega 500. This race was the grand opening of the Alabama International Motor Speedway, hyped for weeks as the fastest track in the world. Richard Brickhouse took the checkered flag in a winged Dodge Daytona, partly as a result of a walkout by the top drivers. There was some concern about the bumpiness of the new track and the speeds its longer length – 2.66 miles versus Daytona's 2.5 miles – allowed. Both of the top Dodge drivers, Glotzbach and Buddy Baker, exhibited blurred vision and slurred speech, medically diagnosed as the "pogo effect" experienced by astronauts in high-vibration takeoffs. The effect was due to the rhythmic frequency of the bumpy track above 185 mph, and both tires and drivers were predicted to come apart at Talladega speeds. The new Professional Drivers Association petitioned France to postpone the race until the tire manufacturers could develop compounds and structures to handle the problem of shredding tires.

Meanwhile, drivers saw themselves as human guinea pigs in France's spectacle of speed, racing at the highest speeds in stock-car racing with unpredictable tire performance and physiological effects that they'd never encountered before. Bill France maintained his stance of ignoring the drivers "union" and held the race anyway. His ultimatum to get the cars on the track to qualify forced team owners and drivers to boycott. Glotzbach and Baker refused to drive. Petty and Pearson refused to drive their Fords. Bobby and Donnie Allison joined them, as did Cale Yarborough and LeeRoy Yarbrough. Lesser known drivers got the chances of their lifetimes, and the next day, France began waiving rule after rule to get enough cars to make a race of it. He got his first race at Talladega, although it was less than auspicious because the top teams were not on the track. Brickhouse took the only win of his NASCAR career.

A couple of weeks later, Junior and Yarbrough were back at Talladega testing tires for Goodyear, and once again the treaded tires shredded. Among the tires on hand were slicks, tires without the normal stock-car racing tread required by NASCAR. Junior had them mounted and they worked. He knew at once that France would approve them because he had to have tires that would safely last at Talladega speeds. He was right, and the era of slicks in NASCAR began.

After Talladega, the season returned to normal, and David Pearson and his Holman Moody rides stopped in the winner's circle in 11 races out of 51 starts. He finished in the top five 42 times to win his second consecutive Grand National driver's crown. Richard Petty held his own throughout the season, but was edged out by 357 points.

As the 1969 season came to a close, the NASCAR Boss 429 had proven superior to Chrysler's Hemi and the aero-Fords proved superior to the wild Charger 500 from Chelsea. During the season, Yarbrough produced NASCAR's first "Grand Slam" by winning on all five major Southern tracks, including the Daytona 500 (averaging 157.95 mph), the World 600 at Charlotte (134.361 mph), and Darlington's Southern 500 shortened to 230

CHAPTER ELEVEN

Dodge put its wild Charger Daytona into production mid-1969 and built a few with the 426 Hemi. Most showroom models came with lower-performance engines, and were slow to sell.

178 NASCAR'S WILD YEARS

In more sedate form, the Dodge Hemi Super Bee of 1969 was a monster street performer and equally rare.

laps (105.612 mph). For such a spectacular season, he was voted American Driver of the Year, the first stock-car driver to be awarded that distinction. He also received Ford's Man of the Year award during festivities in Dearborn.

A total of 26 Ford wins in 1969 led all makes and earned another Manufacturers Championship for Ford. Mercury added four more, mostly on major tracks. Dodge drivers took 22 wins, Bobby Allison with five in 27 starts, and Bobby Isaac with 17 in 50 starts. Isaac scored the most wins of the season, but had only enough points for sixth in the final Grand National points tally. As the season came to a close, events quickly unfolded in favor of the bullet-shaped Daytonas and Plymouth Superbirds the next year.

The 1970 stock-car racing season was filled with changes that shaped the sport for years to come. Although Dodge engineers had led the way with their Daytona, Plymouth soon had its own aero-warrior, though it was a near copy of the Dodge. The Superbird was a slightly different version of the superspeedway warrior. With renewed prospects, Petty returned to drive No. 43 Petty-blue Plymouths in 1970, and the aero-Dodges and Plymouths combined for 38 victories (21 Plymouth and 17 Dodge). Ford and Mercury took six and four, respectively, in year-old cars with little factory support. Bobby Isaac was the Dodge hotshoe again. He won 17 races and set 20 poles in Dodge Daytonas entered in 47 of NASCAR's schedule of 48 races that year. Pete Hamilton took the first victory for Plymouth with the Superbird's debut in the 1970 Daytona 500. Drivers proclaimed the Daytonas and Superbirds the fastest, most stable machines they had ever raced. But there was little competition.

What happened to the Fords that dominated in '69? As the 1969 season wound down, changes were made in Dearborn's

CHAPTER ELEVEN

Aerodynamics Over Thirty Years

1940 Ford as raced into the early 1950s.

1956 Ford with the "Forward Look."

1956 Chrysler, the NASCAR champion that year with Hemi power.

1969 Ford Talladega made from using longer Mercury front-end sheetmetal.

1969 Dodge Daytona, the ultimate in aerodynamics applied to automobiles.

180 NASCAR'S WILD YEARS

1969 AND BEYOND: THE AERO-WAR

Cotton Owens Garage press release:
"A happy, smiling Buddy Baker chalked up an official closed-course world record of 200.447 mph on March 24 at Alabama International Motor Speedway. Baker, driving a Dodge Charger Daytona, also turned laps of 200.096 and 200.330 mph in becoming the first man to break the 200 mph barrier." To reduce speeds, NASCAR required carburetor restrictor plates on all cars as of mid-August 1970.

racing plans; there were no wild and exotic developments of the aero-Fords, so the '69s were raced in 1970 with no external changes. The Boss 429 was only slightly improved to solve some internal parts-failure problems. The brightest spots for Dearborn that year were the Donnie Allison victories in the World 600 at Charlotte and the Firecracker 400 at Daytona. LeeRoy Yarbrough added another superspeedway win for the aero-Fords with his National 500 victory in the fall feature at

Bobby Allison ran his #22 '69 Dodge to wins and 13 top-5 finishes in the 1969 season. Of course, this was relatively early in his long and successful career. (Photo courtesy International Motorsports Hall of Fame)

Charlotte, and David Pearson's Southern 500 win showed that the old Fords could still beat the latest from Chelsea, but the wins were few that year.

Along the way, Buddy Baker became the first man over 200 mph on a closed course when he set the speed record at Talladega in a Dodge Daytona at 200.447 mph on September 10, 1969. Later in the year, Bobby Isaac, 1970 NASCAR champion, topped that mark when he sailed around Talladega to set a new mark of 201.104 mph. By then, Goodyear slicks proved capable.

Wins, speed records, and factory rivalries no longer mattered at Ford. All the special race-derived cars of the preceding decade had been sales busts (by some judgments), and cost lots of money, even if they contributed to superb history-making years and promoted overall sales because of Ford's Total Performance reputation. All that decade, factories had to dance to Bill France's tune if they wanted to race, but Henry Ford II stopped the music.

FACTORY PULLOUT

While Chrysler fans reveled in blowing the Fords into the weeds during 1970, it was Henry who pulled the rug from under the fast Fords. He announced in December 1969 that a $7.5 million research facility aimed at reducing exhaust emissions was under construction in response to federally mandated clean-air rules, and the funding came from the racing program. First, $3.5 million was cut from Ford's racing budget. Within 60 days, another $3.5 million was cut. That left only $3.5 million where there had been $10.5 million, and the remainder was further whittled away. Within months, Ford was completely out of racing.

The cuts left Ford's teams holding the bag. Factory engineers were reassigned to other jobs, and racing died at Ford; the era of Total Performance was over just that quickly. Only the diehards with enough money and spares kept competitive Fords on the track.

Then Chrysler got out, continuing to support only the Petty team, much to the consternation of Nord Krauskopf, who owned

1969 AND BEYOND: THE AERO-WAR

Qualifying races for the Daytona 500 increased in length to 125 miles in 1969. The 1970 qualifiers saw Cale Yarborough in a Wood Brothers Mercury scorch Daytona in the first round, setting a new record of 183.295 mph, which was not surpassed until 1998 (Terry Labonte, Ford, 189.554 mph). The only new 1970 stock-car model was the Plymouth Superbird built to bring Richard Petty back to the make. With a two-car Petty team that year, Pete Hamilton was signed on to drive the second car. He dueled David Pearson to win the Daytona 500, then won both the Talladega 500 and the Alabama 500 races. New NASCAR rules required 1,000 cars produced for public sale, to inhibit special editions like the Ford Talladega and Dodge Charger Daytona. (Ford photos)

This is Petty in his short-track Plymouth winning at North Wilkesboro. At Atlanta for the Dixie 500, Petty set a blazing new track record of 142.712 mph in his Superbird. He won 18 races in 40 starts to finish the season fourth in points. Petty cars scored all 21 Plymouth wins on NASCAR's schedule that year, while Bobby Isaac (Dodge) became Grand National Champion with 11 wins in 47 starts. New to NASCAR were non-automotive corporate sponsors such as Coca-Cola (Bobby Allison, Dodge) and Dow Chemical (Charlie Glotzbach, Dodge). Without the factories, stock-car teams faced hard times beginning in 1970, and the sport began radical changes. At the end of the year, Junior Johnson's request for a few thousand dollars from R. J. Reynolds Tobacco Company resulted in millions going into the season-long sponsorship and the Winston Cup. (Ford photo)

NASCAR'S WILD YEARS   183

CHAPTER ELEVEN

Donnie Allison started ninth to win the 1970 World 600 in a year-old Ford. LeeRoy Yarbrough, driving a year-old Mercury, won Charlotte's second race, the National 500. With A. J. Foyt's opening win in the Western 500 at Riverside, Ford and Mercury went on to combine for 10 wins in 1970, while Plymouth won 21 and Dodge took 17. Ford Motor Company's withdrawal from stock-car racing at the end of the season a severe drought for Ford teams. (Ford photo)

Allison also won again at the Firecracker 400 at Daytona. Ford's final win of the 1970 season was Cale Yarborough, who took the American 500 at Rockingham with a new track record of 119.81 mph. Four days later, Ford Motor Company announced that the $3.5 million in motorsports funding remaining in the $10 million from the previous year would be eliminated. Ford's longtime motorsports manager Jacques Passino was so upset that he resigned rather than switch to a factory job. (Ford photo)

NASCAR'S WILD YEARS

1969 AND BEYOND: THE AERO-WAR

On a blustery day, November 24, 1970, Bobby Isaac wheeled the K&K Insurance Dodge Daytona onto Talladega's high banks and set a new closed-course speed record of 201.104 mph, breaking Buddy Baker's record set earlier in the year. When Chrysler cut the K&K team for 1971, little effort was made to repeat the team's 1970 NASCAR championship. Late in '71, Isaac was on the salt flats of Utah setting 28 new world speed records, 216.946 mph in the flying mile and 217.368 mph in the flying kilometer among them. (DaimlerChrysler Historical Collection photo)

the K&K Insurance Daytona driven by Bobby Isaac to the 1970 Grand National Championship. During the next two years, leftover hardware from both manufacturers was gradually used up. Petty scored back-to-back Grand National Championships in 1971 and '72. From 1972 through 1974, Fords won no races at all, although Mercury tallied 27, largely due to the efforts of the Wood Brothers and David Pearson, who won 11 of 18 races he entered in 1973 and was named American Driver of the Year. Benny Parsons won the Grand National Championship that year driving a Chevrolet! Dodge and Plymouth combined for 21 wins between them during those years, and Chevrolet notched 27.

The bowtie boys had watched the HP and aero-wars of the 1960s from the sidelines, but in 1972 and '73, Junior Johnson showed that the ancient Chevrolet Mk IV 427 truck engine in a

CHAPTER ELEVEN

Chevrolet was back with a competitive car in 1971. A new team run by Junior Johnson, with Charlie Glotzbach driving, heralded a new era for NASCAR. Engine displacement was initially ruled to a maximum of 366 ci, but was then waived, and Junior dug into Chevrolet's truck engine displacing 427 ci to find the power. He was helped by NASCAR's restrictor plates, which were more restrictive on the Chrysler and Ford hemi engines than on the wedge engines. Chevrolet won three races that year. (Ford photo)

Chevrolet's hot new Mk IV 396 of 1965 had gone on to fame as the 427 and 454, but all of them went by the way of economy in the austere days of the 1970s. Winding up as a high-torque big-block for heavy-duty service, it was retrieved by Junior Johnson and made into a stock-car winner. (Chevrolet photo)

Left and above: Bobby Allison brought his Coca-Cola sponsorship over to the Richard Howard/Junior Johnson team in 1972. He continued his streak of leading race laps, eventually reaching a record of leading in 39 races, winning 10 of 31 entered that year. The season-long feud with Richard Petty gave their points chase some of the sport's most memorable races. By 1972, NASCAR was back to "strictly stock" – sort of. (Ford photo)

186   NASCAR'S WILD YEARS

1969 AND BEYOND: THE AERO-WAR

Glen Wood, winner of four Grand National races in the early days, and the Wood Brothers team signed on A. J. Foyt and produced the first Winston Cup Daytona 500 champion. Foyt led 167 laps and finished two laps ahead of the second-place car. With no factory backing for any team in 1972, the Wood Brothers fielded the fastest car in NASCAR that year, and when Foyt left to return to USAC racing, David Pearson stepped to win six races in 12 starts. (Ford photos and Glen Wood collection photo)

Monte Carlo could be a winner. Chevrolet's star began rising. With no racing program for a decade, Chevrolet emerged from the year-to-year factory shootouts as the winner. The Monte Carlo was an aerodynamic brick, but it has since won more races than any other model in NASCAR's history. And Chevrolet didn't spend a dime to reach the top.

During America's golden age of world-class racing, Ford led all makes to win everything worth winning. Record books were

CHAPTER ELEVEN

Bill France finally got what he searched for throughout the previous 10 years – Chevrolet's return to NASCAR. The 1973 Winston Cup champion, Benny Parsons, was a surprise winner who took only one race in 28 starts to clinch the title with high finishes in the L.G. DeWitt Chevrolet Monte Carlo with 427 "big block" power.

Below and facing page: Plymouth produced about 2,500 Superbirds in 1970, and was the only make to field new cars in NASCAR that year. Once in showrooms, the cars were so wild that they attracted few buyers, even with the formidable 426 Hemi. They were among the most sought after of American cars a decade later.

1969 AND BEYOND: THE AERO-WAR

stuffed with Ford victories while Chevrolet factory achievements were little more than footnotes, although Chevrolet engines were widely used in winning cars of many types. Powerful engines from both Ford and Chrysler were legends during the era of thundering big-inch V-8s. The battles among these radical round trackers would, in just a few years, be looked back on nostalgically as some of the best racing ever seen.

The sensational 1960s passed into the somber 1970s, a decade of doldrums when diehard racers with little funding turned to whatever was available. The Mk IV 427 had remained in production as a truck engine, while Ford and Chrysler big-blocks were dropped early in the 1970s. Once again, just as the 348 and 409 produced Chevrolet's flourish in the early 1960s in the hands of Rex White and Ned Jarrett, Bobby Allison and Benny Parsons ran Junior Johnson-built 427 truck engines. Junior's race shop in Ingle Hollow near North Wilkesboro, North Carolina, trained a generation of 427 bowtie engine builders, allowing Chevrolet to roar onto the center stage of NASCAR racing.

INDEX

A

Aerodynamic, 159-161, 163, 28, 49, 72, 123, 131, 164, 173
Alabama 500, 183
Alabama Gang, 126
Alabama International Motor Speedway, 160, 179, 181
Allentown, 82
Allison, Bobby, 136, 155, 120, 126, 175, 177, 182-183, 186
Allison, Donnie, 158, 164, 175, 179, 184, 189
Allman, Bud, 41
AMA, 3, 17, 22, 28, 30, 39, 51
AMC, 33
American 500, 136, 2, 112, 184
American Hot Rod Association (AHRA), 113
Amick, Bill, 21, 28, 84, 87
Andretti, Mario, 143, 152, 2
Ardun, 17, 30
Arkus-Duntov, Zora, 3, 17, 23, 30, 65, 70, 84, 119, 126, 131
Atlanta 500, 144-146, 155, 157-158, 51, 104, 177
Atlanta's Lakewood Speedway, 41

B

Baker, Buck, 15, 23, 43, 51, 70, 83, 95
Baker, Buddy, 158, 2, 177, 179, 181, 185, 189
Beach Boys, 162, 69
Beam, Herman, 115
Beauchamp, Johnny, 21, 49, 83
Belvedere, 149, 162, 87, 135
Best Damn Garage, 11, 19, 31
Black, Keith, 115
Blackburn, Bunkie, 57
Blair, Bill, 64
Bonneville, 19, 21, 37, 60
Boss 429, 146, 159, 2, 119, 164-165, 173-177, 182, 189
Bowsher, Jack, 175
Boycott, 112, 179
Brickhouse, Richard, 171, 179
Bristol 500, 57, 80
Byron, Red, 5, 13

C

Cammer, 95, 101, 109, 117-118, 128, 130, 165
Campbell, Malcolm, 101
Canada, 148, 115
Carolina 500, 145, 158
Charger 500, 160-161, 2, 165, 169-171, 175, 177, 182
Charlotte Motor Speedway, 47, 72
Chelsea Proving Grounds, 171, 177
Chevelle, 140-144, 151-152, 154-155, 157, 2-3, 106, 109, 120, 125-126, 129, 132, 169
Chrysler 300, 38, 65
Clark, Barney, 31
Clements, Crawford, 48, 84
Clements, Louie, 36, 48, 70, 85
Cobra Jet, 175-176
Coca-Cola, 183, 186
Cole, Ed, 11, 17, 30-31, 83
Convertible Division 20-23, 35, 39, 41, 54, 58
Coon, Frank, 21
Corvair, 33, 70, 101, 104
Corvette, 17, 23, 30-31, 55, 70, 84, 126
Cowley, John, 43
Crash, 137, 41, 49, 57, 79, 87, 95, 125
Cross-Ram, 34, 93
Cunningham, Briggs, 31
Cyclone, 154, 158, 2, 165, 173-175

D

Darlington, 137, 144-145, 159, 15, 20, 22, 30, 35, 38, 41, 56-58, 90, 99, 102, 113, 177, 182
Dart, 34, 66
Davis, Denny, 119, 131
Daytona 500, 137, 140, 142-144, 152, 154, 2, 35, 41-43, 48-49, 56-57, 69, 71, 77-79, 89, 95, 103-104, 112-113, 125, 168-169, 171, 173, 175, 177, 182-183, 187
Daytona Beach, 10, 13, 15, 17, 21-22, 31, 57, 64, 101, 104, 126
Daytona Kennel Club entry, 74
Daytona Speed Week, 21
Delroy, Frankie, 83
Dieringer, Darel, 141, 69, 85, 89, 99, 103, 110, 112, 120
Dixie 400, 139, 59, 81, 85
Dixie 500, 144, 155, 158, 177, 183
Dodge Daytona, 2, 7, 171, 177, 179-181, 183, 185, 189
Drafting, 57, 103
Dyno, 147, 71, 85, 89, 119, 128

E

Eckstrand, Al, 75
Edwards Air Force Base, 13
Elliot, John, 148
Engle, Elwood, 72
Evans, Dave, 43
Exner, Virgil, 10, 72

F

Fairlane, 138, 143-144, 146, 149, 154, 160, 2, 33, 95, 109, 120
Falcon, 33, 39, 109, 123
Firecracker 400, 141, 145, 80, 100, 104, 113, 177, 184, 189
Firestone, 151, 31, 95, 123, 126
Flat Rock Speedway, 82
Flock, Tim, 21, 91
Fogt, Red, 5
Ford, Edsel, 8
Ford, Henry, 8, 55,
Ford, Henry II, 51, 95, 173
Fox, Ray, 136, 3, 57, 74, 86, 89, 93, 98, 100
France, Bill, 157, 160, 13, 48, 54, 72, 77, 91, 95, 100, 107, 112, 118, 125-126, 169, 173, 175, 179, 188
Frank, Larry, 57-58, 75
Frey, Don, 43
Frincke, Fred, 119, 131
Funk, Vernon, 57

G

Galaxies, 53, 94
Glen, Watkins, 114
Glotzbach, Charlie, 158, 168, 177, 183, 186
Golden State 400, 81
Goldsmith, Paul, 22, 49, 74, 79, 89, 95
Grand National Championship, 139, 146, 158, 59, 63, 70, 74, 84, 177
Greenville-Pickens Speedway, 41
Gurney, Dan, 150, 55, 75, 109, 123, 126, 165, 175

H

Hall, Jim, 70
Hall, Robert, 83
Hamilton, Pete, 183, 185
Hawkins, Alvin, 82
Hemi, 136, 140, 143, 145-146, 150-151, 155-156, 158-159, 161-162, 2-3, 21, 87-93, 95, 97, 99-101, 103-105, 107, 109, 114, 117-124, 126, 128, 131, 133, 135, 165, 169, 174-175, 177-180, 182, 186, 188
Hernandez, Fran, 51, 103
Hickory Speedway, 41
Holly Farms, 137, 139, 48-49, 56-57
Holman Moody, 139, 141, 143-144, 146, 154, 157, 2, 7, 18, 20-22, 28, 39, 41-43, 50-51, 55, 57-58, 68, 72, 75, 79-81, 85, 87, 95, 99, 107-108, 111, 115-117, 120, 123, 130, 173, 175, 177, 182
Holman, John, 139, 159, 21, 39, 51, 72, 107, 165
Howard, Richard, 186
Howell, Bill, 71, 85
Hudson, 6, 10-11, 15, 19, 118
Hurtubise, Jim, 77
Hutcherson, Dick, 137, 141, 144, 112, 114, 123, 129
Hylton, James, 131, 135

I

Iacocca, Lee, 54, 72
Indianapolis 500, 9, 31, 143, 155, 74, 100, 165, 192
Innes, Bill, 43
Isaac, Bobby, 139, 141, 153, 155, 158, 2, 95, 165, 171, 177, 182-183, 185, 189

J

Jarrett, Ned, 137, 43, 48, 50-51, 70, 75, 85, 87, 90, 97, 113
Johns, Bobby, 43, 51, 79, 82, 103
Johnson, Fred, 48
Johnson, Joe Lee, 47
Johnson, Junior, 136-137, 154-155, 14-15, 35, 41, 43, 47-48, 51, 56, 74, 77, 81, 89-90, 93, 95, 97, 103-104, 110, 113, 121, 132, 168, 175, 177, 183, 186
Jones, Bobby, 42
Jones, Parnelli, 138, 143, 146, 75, 87, 91, 110
Jones, Possum, 82-83

K

K&K Dodge, 153, 2, 185
Kar-Kraft, 173
Keating, Thomas H., 10
Keinath, Dick, 70, 79, 85, 106
Keinath, R. L., 70
Keller, Al, 82
Kiekhaefer, Carl, 6, 15, 21
Kirkland, Tom, 35, 58
Knudsen, Bunkie, 60, 70, 74, 173
Kolbe, Al, 31

L

Labonte, Terry, 183
Lanham, West, 81-82
Lawton, Bill, 117, 130
Lincoln, 18-19, 26, 28, 38
Lorenzen, Fred, 136-137, 141, 51, 57-58, 75, 90, 99, 103, 108, 110, 112, 121

INDEX

Lovette, Rex, 48-49
Lund, Tiny, 142, 157, 2, 78-79
Lyall, Dave, 123

M

Mahoney, John, 119
Mainline, 18-19, 21
Mantz, Johnny, 15
Martin, Dode, 45-46
Martinsville, 250, 57
Mathews, Banjo, 51, 74
McKeller, Malcolm, 65
McNamara, Robert, 22, 33, 39
McQuagg, Sam, 146
Michigan International Speedway, 165
Midwest Auto Racing Circuit, 72
Monte Carlo, 188
Moody, Ralph, 21, 51, 72
Moore, Bud, 146, 157, 59, 63, 74, 85, 89, 91, 95, 129
Motor Trend 500, 138, 150, 109
Motorama, 30
Musser, Jim, 126
Mustang, 2, 55, 109, 115, 117, 130, 173-175
Myers, Billy, 21
Mystery Engine, 139, 159, 70, 74, 77, 79, 82, 85, 93, 95, 104, 106-107, 128

N

National 400, 57, 81
National 500, 184, 189
National Hot Rod Association (NHRA), 13, 147-148, 46, 60-61, 75, 113-114, 117, 123, 126, 130
Nichels, Ray, 168, 177
Nicholson, Don, 147, 46, 117
Nick, Slick, 123
North Wilkesboro 400, 57

O

Old Dominion 500, 131
Olds F-85, 33
Oldsmobile, 10-11, 21, 23, 38, 41, 46, 109
Olley, Maurice, 30
Owens, Cotton, 142, 144, 155, 21, 42-43, 51, 56, 79, 84, 131-132, 177, 181

P

Panch, Marvin, 137, 21, 49, 75, 79, 84, 87, 113-114, 131
Pardue, Jim, 95
Pardue, Jimmy, 95
Parks, Wally, 13
Parsons, Benny, 188
Paschal, Jim, 21, 51, 57, 74, 97
Passino, Jacques, 51, 184
Pearson, David, 136-137, 140, 144, 153-154, 157, 79, 81, 95, 99, 102-103, 118, 121, 129, 131, 133, 135, 164, 173, 175, 177, 182-183, 187, 189
Petty, Lee, 41-43, 49, 57, 87
Petty, Richard, 137, 143, 145, 149, 151, 153, 43, 45, 48-49, 51, 56-57, 72, 76, 81, 84, 87, 95, 97, 99-100, 102, 109, 121, 135, 164, 175, 177, 182-183, 186
Piggins, Vince, 146, 77, 85
Pointer, John, 169
Polara, 92, 128

Poole, Tom, 71
Prior, Paul, 146, 85
Proffitt, Hayden, 60

Q

Qualifying, 47, 74-75, 77, 95, 106, 123, 183

R

R. J. Reynolds Tobacco, 183
Radtke, Jack, 31
Ramcharger, 46, 65, 75, 93, 97, 109, 123
Rathgeb, Larry, 169
Rathmann, Jim, 24, 41, 83
Rebel 300, 137, 22, 30, 56, 58, 102, 113
Rebel 400, 159, 177
Reed, Jim, 21, 23, 82, 84
Riverside 500, 138, 150, 75, 109, 123, 184
Roberts, Fireball, 137, 21-22, 30, 35, 41-42, 48, 51, 56, 63, 80-82, 85, 87, 97, 99, 101
Robinson, Pete, 45, 118, 123
Rochester fuel-injection, 18, 23
Roe, Mike, 126
Root, Alan, 115
Rose, Mauri, 31, 83
Roth, Ed, 192
Rutherford, Johnny, 74, 77

S

Satellite, 162, 135
Schneider, Frankie, 81, 83
Scott, Wendell, 81, 87
Shelby, Carroll, 151, 38
Skelton, Betty, 101
Skylark, 33, 109
Smith, Bruton, 47
Smith, Jack, 42
Sneden, Tom, 123
Society of Automotive Engineeers (SAE), 36-37, 89-90
Sosbee, Gober, 10, 13, 15
Southeastern 500, 57
Southern 500, 137, 11, 15, 17, 20-21, 23, 31, 41, 56-58, 80, 85, 120, 129, 177, 182, 189
Speed Week, 21
Stacy, Nelson, 58, 75
Staley 400, 76
Stevenson, Robert, 28
Strickler, Dave, 46, 60
Stroppe, Bill, 138, 21, 26, 28, 75, 87, 89, 91, 99
Studebaker, 10, 33, 39, 50
Sullivan, Don, 43
Sullivan, Jack, 57
Superbird, 7, 177, 183, 185, 187

T

Talladega, 160, 2, 164-165, 170-171, 173-174, 177, 179-183, 185, 189
Talladega 500, 179, 183
Tar Heel Speedway, 75
Teague, Marshall, 101
Thomas, Herb, 11, 15, 17, 31
Thompson, Mickey, 46, 60
Thompson, Speed, 83
Thunderbird, 17-19, 28, 31, 35, 38, 41-42, 69, 118
Torino, 149-150, 154, 160, 165-166, 173, 175

Townsend, Lynn, 95
Trans-am, 145
Travers, Jim, 21
Tri-Power, 39, 50, 53, 61
Turner, Curtis, 137, 140, 142, 152, 160, 2, 20-21, 26, 30, 43, 47, 72, 82, 91, 112, 126-127, 131

U

United States Auto Club (USAC), 143, 155, 2, 19, 51, 55, 72, 77, 87, 187
Unser, Al, 155

V

Vaughn, John, 170
Vogt, Ken, 123

W

Wade, Billy, 89, 91, 95
Wade, Cal, 119, 131
Ward, Rodger, 75
Weatherly, Joe, 20-21, 30, 35, 48-49, 56, 59, 63, 74, 76, 81, 84-85, 87
Welborn, Bob, 23, 82-83
Wells, Frank, 30
West Lanham Speedway, 82
Western 500, 184
White, Rex, 136, 3, 36, 43, 48, 50-51, 59, 70, 74, 81, 89
Williams, Robert, 192
Wilson, Ace, 46
Winchell, Frank, 126
Winston Cup, 187-188
Wood Brothers, 145-146, 154, 158, 43, 75, 78-79, 87, 109, 115, 177, 183, 187
Wood, Glen, 138, 47, 187
World 600, 137, 144, 158, 47, 58, 81, 97, 103, 131, 177, 182, 184, 189

Y

Yankee 300, 143, 2
Yarborough, Cale, 137-138, 141, 145-146, 154, 158, 2, 68, 112, 115, 123, 164, 173, 175, 177, 179, 183-184
Yarbrough, LeeRoy, 141-143, 154-155, 2, 101, 164, 168, 170, 173, 175, 177, 179, 184, 189
Yunick, Smokey, 139, 142, 152, 155, 2, 11, 17, 19, 22, 31, 43, 51, 55, 57, 74, 77, 126, 129, 132, 169

Z

Zeder, James C., 90
Zervakis, Emanuel, 51

More GREAT Titles from CarTech® ...

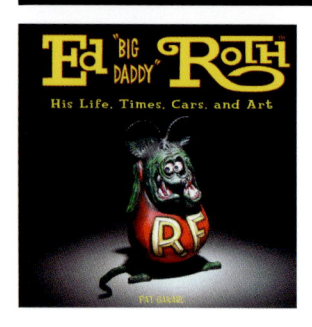

ED "BIG DADDY" ROTH: HIS LIFE, TIMES, CARS AND ART by Pat Ganahl. Foreword by artist Robert Williams. Who was Ed Roth? The answer depends on who you ask, and when they knew him. To some, he was a counter-culture, greasy-fingernailed, renaissance man of the mid 20th Century. To others, he's the creator of Rat Fink and builder of some of the most creative custom cars ever to get a coat of candy paint – cars like the *Beatnik Bandit*, the *Mysterion*, and the *Outlaw*. Ed's rise to fame began in the '50s, and peaked with the custom car boom of the early '60s – every kid in America knew who Rat Fink was, and many built models of his custom cars and wore his "monster" T-shirts. To say his life was interesting is an understatement – and this book covers it all, from art to custom cars, monster shirts to VW-powered trikes, and the wild life that brought it all together. Hardbound, 10 x 10 inches, 192 pages, 100 color photos, 150 B&W photos. *Item # CT968*

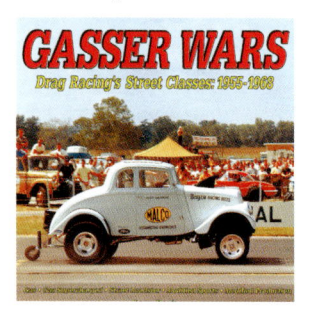

GASSER WARS: DRAG RACING'S STREET CLASSES: 1955-1968 by Larry Davis. In the late '50s, thousands of street legal hot rods participated in organized drag races across the country – they ran in three major categories: Gas, Modified Production & Modified Sports. As racers got more serious & car manufacturers began sponsoring cars & touting their accomplishments in ads, the "Gasser Wars" were born. This book covers the '60s most exciting classes of drag racing classes in detail, with vintage never-before-seen photos of VERY rare versions of the cars that raced during this era. This is the ONLY book on the subject currently in the marketplace! Hardbound, 10 x 10 inches, 192 pages, 100 color photos, 200 B&W photos. *Item # CT977*

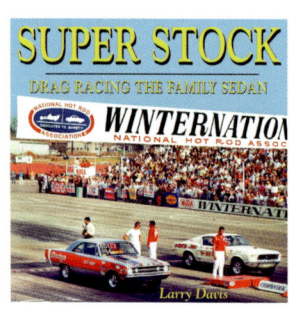

SUPER STOCK: DRAG RACING THE FAMILY SEDAN by Larry Davis. This book takes a look at what was, in the 1960s, the most popular class of drag racing – factory Super Stock. It traces the evolution of the cars, the engines, the rules, the personalities, and many of the teams, from its beginnings in the mid-1950s through to the 1960s. This was the period that saw emergence of the term "musclecar" and the production of a whole class of American automobiles. Includes first-person accounts of what drag racing was really like in the early 1960s: how the manufacturers controlled the competition and even race results, and how the sanctioning bodies attempted to control the manufacturers, who in turn simply sidestepped the rules. Appendices include the major event winners and the rules defining the classes as well as information detailing the engines and chassis in Top Stock categories. Hardbound, 10 x 10 inches, 216 pages, 33 color photos, 300 B&W photos. *Item # CT953*

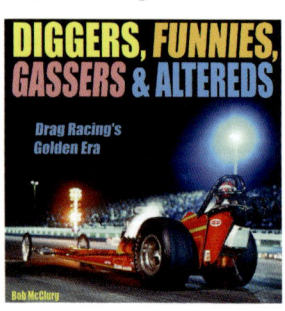

DIGGERS, FUNNIES, GASSERS & ALTEREDS: Drag Racing's Golden Age by Bob McClurg. During the '60s, drag racing evolved from a grass roots effort to a full-blown professional motorsport – along the way, it created some of the most exciting racing & race cars ever built. Bob McClurg, an accomplished magazine writer & photographer, is best known for his drag racing images of the '60s and '70s – his lens captured the Roadsters, Gassers, Altereds, Top Fuelers, Funny Cars, Pro/Stocks, & even the modern age of nostalgia drag racing. With more than 350 color and black-and-white photos, this book is an exciting visual history of the Golden Age of drag racing. Hardbound, 10 x 10 inches, 192 pages, 200 color photos, 150 B&W photos. *Item# CT990*

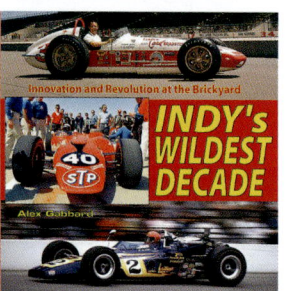

INDY'S WILDEST DECADE by Alex Gabbard From the start, Indy has been a hotbed of racing innovation. Then in the '60s, all hell broke loose, with one revolution after another racing around the 2.5-mile Brickyard. In this book, Alex Gabbard covers the history of innovation and racing experimentation at the Indy 500, from the Miller era through the Junk Formula and the Roadster era, then gives you a year-by-year account of Indy's wildest decade ever, the 1960s. The transition to rear-engine cars, followed by Ford's stock-block V-8 challengers, turbo versions of both Fords and Offys, STP's turbine cars, DOHC Fords, wider tires, engineers, aerodynamics — all combined to produce some incredible racing that changed the face of Indy forever. Profusely illustrated with more than 300 photos (over half of them in color), this book is sure to become a classic among Indy racing fans. Hardbound, 10 x 10 inches, 192 pages, 150+ color photos & 150 b/w photos. *Item # CT971*

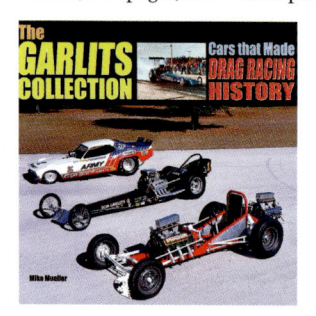

THE GARLITS COLLECTION by Mike Mueller It isn't just his racing accomplishments that set Don "Big Daddy" Garlits apart in drag racing history. This is a man who truly loves drag racing, and on his own he has constructed one of the best motorsports museums in the world – The Don Garlits Museum of Drag Racing, in Ocala, Florida. His museum contains hundreds of cars, but in this book, author Mike Mueller takes an in-depth look at the cream of the crop – the most significant cars in Big Daddy's museum, and probably the most significant cars in all of drag racing. Funny cars, Pro/Stocks, Fuel Coupes, roadsters, streamliners, Super Stocks, Gassers and more – this book covers them all, with spectacular color photos of the restored machines, right alongside vintage black-and-white images from Garlits' own collection. Hardbound, 10 x 10 inches, 192 pages, close to 300 color & b/w photos. *Item # CT981*

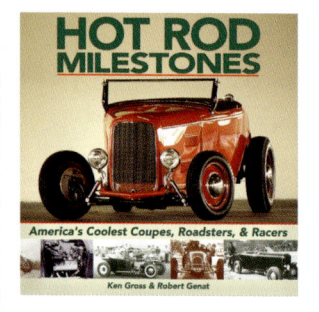

HOT ROD MILESTONES by Ken Gross & Robert Genat You've seen these cars before. They're some of the best-known, coolest hot rods ever built. Each represents a clear vision, usually from one talented person. These hot rods set the standards; they were imitated, and when they made show appearances, they were coveted and revered. Hot Rod Milestones covers 25 of the most influential, innovative hot rods ever built from the late 1940s to the mid '60s. Each car's history, technical background, and influence is discussed, along with information on the builders and owners. Photos include contemporary pictures of the cars as they exist now, along with vintage photos of the cars when they were first built and shown. Hardbound, 10 x 10 inches, 150 color & 100 b/w photos. *Item # CT980*

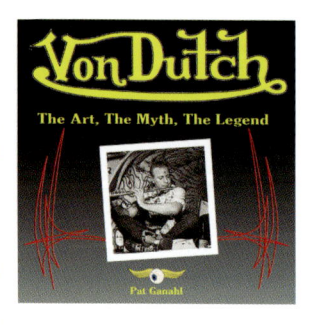

VON DUTCH by Pat Ganahl Von Dutch is one of the most interesting characters in hot rod and popular culture history. Considered the founder of "modern" pin-striping, he was a prominent character in many of the rodding magazines of the late '50s, and his fame endured long after he apparently tired of it. Besides being a striper, he was a gifted artist, machinist, and gun- and knife-smith. Using stories and quotes culled from interviews, vintage photos, and images of the art and other works he left behind, this book chronicles Kenneth Howard's life from pinstriping beatnik to bus-dwelling hermit. Where it can, this book sets the record straight on Von Dutch the man, but in many cases conflicting stories will serve to illustrate the contrary, colorful, and sometimes difficult nature of Von Dutch the legend. This book is a must-have for fans of hot rodding and hot rod culture! Hardbound, 10 x 10 inches, 192 pages, 100 color & 200 b/w photos. *Item # CT998*

CarTech®, Inc., 39966 Grand Avenue, North Branch, MN 55056
Telephone: (651) 277-1200 or (800) 551-4754 Fax: (651) 277-1203, www.cartechbooks.com

More great titles available from CarTech®...

S-A DESIGN

Ford Performance — Practical building tips, for all Ford V-8 engines. (SA05)

Smokey Yunick's Power Secrets — Smokey explains race-engine prep from carbs to shop tools. (SA06)

Small-Block Chevy Performance, Vol 1: 1955-81 — Block, head selection & prep., ignition, carb & more! (SA07)

Super Tuning & Modifying Holley Carburetors — Perf, street and off-road applications. (SA08)

Custom Painting —The Do-It-Yourself Guide to – Advice on choosing paint, prep and touch-up. (SA10)

Super Tuning and Modifying Carter Carburetors — Tuning and modifying for power or economy. (SA11)

Street Supercharging, The Complete Guide to — Bolt-on buying, installing and tuning blowers. (SA17)

Engine Blueprinting — Using tools, block selection & prep, crank mods, pistons, heads, cams & more! (SA21)

How to Build Horsepower, Vol. 1 — Building horsepower in any engine. (SA24)

Super '60s Fords — The inside story of the most powerful Fords ever built from 1957-1973. (SA25)

How To Rebuild the Small-Block Chevrolet — How to build a street or racing small-block Chevy. (SA26)

Holley Rebuilding and Modifying — Tuning, modifying, and rebuilding all Holley modular carbs. (SA27)

Chevrolet Big-Block Parts Interchange Manual — Selecting & swapping high-perf. big-block parts. (SA31)

High-Perf Crate Motor Buyer's Guide — Complete guide to all factory & aftermarket high-perf engines. (SA32)

How To Design & Install High Performance Car Stereo — A beginner's guide to high-tech sound systems. (SA45)

How To Build Max Performance Chevy Rat Motors — Hot rodding big-block Chevys '90s style. (SA48)

High Performance Honda Builder's Handbook Vol. 1 — How to build & tune high-performance Honda cars and engines. (SA49)

How To Install & Use Nitrous Oxide — How to make max power with nitrous oxide injection. (SA50)

Desktop Dynos — Using computers to build & test engines. (SA51)

How To Build Horsepower, V.2 — Carbs & intake manifolds. (SA52)

Chevrolet TPI Fuel Injection Swappers Guide — Interchanging & modifying TPI systems. (SA53)

The 5.0L Mustang Bolt-On Performance Guide — Covers Mustangs from 1973-1995. (SA54)

Chevrolet Small-Block Parts Interchange Manual — Selecting & swapping high-perf. small-block parts. (SA55)

High-Performance Ford Engine Parts Interchange — Selecting & swapping big- and small-block Ford parts. (SA56)

How To Build Max Perf Chevy Small-Blocks on a Budget — Would you believe 600 hp for $3000? (SA57)

High-Performance Honda Builder's Handbook Vol. 2 — Suspensions, body mods, brake tech, nitrous. (SA58)

Chrysler Performance Upgrades — Performance improvement on Chrysler muscle cars of the '60s & '70s. (SA60)

5.0L Ford Dyno Tests — Data from over 2000 dyno pulls on aftermarket bolt-on performance parts. (SA61)

Building Ford Short-Track Power, Official Factory Guide to — Written by Ford Racing engineers. (SA63)

Sport Compact Bolt-On Perf Guide, Vol 1: Import Cars — A catalog of aftermarket components for imports. (SA65)

How To Build High-Performance Chrysler Engines — Parts interchanges, factory crate motors, cylinder heads, etc. (SA67)

How To Tune and Win With Demon Carburetors — Selecting and tuning for high-perf race, street, & off-road applications. (SA68)

How To Build Max Performance Ford V-8s on a Budget — Dyno-tested engine builds for big- & small-block Fords. (SA69)

How To Build Honda Horsepower — Data from 1000s of dyno pulls on aftermarket perf parts and mods for Hondas. (SA71)

Builder's Guide to Bolt-Together Street Rods — Advice and how-to info on building bolt-together street rods. (SA72)

Sport Compact Nitrous Injection — Imports on nitrous! Expert tuning tips for installing and tuning NOS systems on tuners. (SA73)

Building High-Perf Fox-body Mustangs on a Budget — Building the complete package. Covers 1979-95 5.0L Mustangs. (SA75)

How To Build Max-Perf Pontiac V8s — Mild perf apps to all-out performance build-ups. (SA78)

How To Build High-Performance Ignition Systems — Complete guide to understanding auto ignition systems. (SA79)

How To Build & Modify GM Pro Touring Street Machines — Classic looks with modern performance. (SA81)

How To Build Max Perf 4.6 Liter Ford Engines — Building & modifying Ford's 2- and 4-valve 4.6/5.4 liter engines. (SA82)

Building & Tuning High-Perf Electronic Fuel Injection — Custom engine management systems for domestics & imports. (SA83)

How To Build Big-Inch Ford Small-Blocks — Add cubic inches without the hassle of switching to a big-block. (SA85)

How To Build High-Perf Chevy LS1/LS6 Engines — Modifying and tuning Gen-III engines for GM cars and trucks. (SA86)

How To Build Big-Inch Chevy Small-Blocks — Get the additional torque & horsepower of a big-block. (SA87)

Harley-Davidson Bolt-On Performance — Max performance for Big-Twins and Sportsters motorcycles. (SA88)

Sport Compact Turbos & Blowers — Guide to understanding, installing, & using sport compact turbos & superchargers. (SA89)

Ford Focus Builder's Handbook — Data from 100s of dyno runs on aftermarket perf parts and modifications. (SA90)

Six-Pack: Mopar Street Muscle in the '60s — Development history, turning & modifying, tech information. (SA92)

Honda Engine Swaps — Step-by-step instructions for all major tasks involved in engine swapping. (SA93)

How to Build Supercharged & Turbocharged Small-Block Fords — Everything you need to know about supercharging & turbocharging your small-block Ford. (SA95)

High-Performance Pontiacs 1955-1974 — Covers the best years of Pontiac, including GTO & Firebird as well as Wide Track, Trans-Am, Bonneville, Tri-Power, & Grand Prix. (SA96)

Quarter-Mile Muscle: Detroit Goes to the Drags — Covers the development & success of muscle cars at the drags in all classes in the '60s. (SA98)

How to Build Ford Restomod Street Machines — Modify your vintage Ford to accelerate, stop, corner & ride like a new high-performance car. (SA101)

How to Rebuild the Small-Block Ford — Covers a small-block Ford rebuild step by step, including planning, disassembly & inspection, choosing parts, machine work, assembly, first firing & break-in. (SA102)

How to Build Big-Inch Mopar Small Blocks — How to get big-block power out of your Mopar small block. (SA104)

How to Build High-Performance Chevy Small — Block Cams/Valvetrains — Camshaft & valvetrain function, selection, performance, and design. (SA105)

Rebuilding the Small-Block Chevy: Step-by-Step Videobook — 160-pg book plus 2-hour DVD show you how to build a street or racing small-block Chevy. (SA116)

HISTORIES AND PERSONALITIES

Total Performers: Ford Drag Racing in the 1960s — Covers Ford Motor Company's "Total Performance Years" in 1960s drag racing. See the cars & the drivers that made them famous. 10 x 10, hdbd. 192 pages. (CT407)

NASCAR's Wild Years — Covers stock-car racing in the 1960s, including the intense behind-the-scenes battles between factories, rule-makers, track owners, promoters, & racing teams. 10 x 10, hdbd. 192 pages. (CT409)

Super Stock: Drag Racing the Family Sedan — Takes a look at the '60s most popular class of drag racing — factory Super Stock. 10 x 10, hdbd. 210 pages. (CT953)

Ed "Big Daddy" Roth: His Life, Times, Cars and Art — The creator of Rat Fink had a profound influence on hot rodders and popular culture. 10 x 10, hdbd. 192 pages. (CT968)

Gasser Wars — Drag Racing's Street Classes: 1955-1968 — An entertaining look into the most exciting drag racing action of the '50s and '60s. 10 x 10, hdbd. 192 pages. (CT977)

Diggers, Funnies, Gassers & Altereds — An exciting visual history of the Golden Age of drag racing. 10 x 10, hdbd. 192 pages. (CT990)

Indy's Wildest Decade: Innovation and Revolution at the Brickyard — Year-by-year account of Indy's wildest decade, the 1960s. 10 x 10, hdbd. 192 pages. (CT971)

The Garlits Collection: Cars that Made Drag Racing History — Coverage of the most significant cars in Big Daddy's museum. 10 x 10, hdbd. 192 pages. (CT981)

Hot Rod Milestones: America's Coolest Coupes, Roadsters, & Racers — Covers 25 of the most influential, innovative hot rods ever built from the late '40s to the mid '60s. 10 X 10, hdbd. 192 pages (CT980)

Von Dutch: The Art, The Myth, The Legend — Chronicles the life & art of pinstriper Von Dutch, from his days as a pinstriping beatnik to bus-dwelling hermit. 10 X 10, hdbd. 192 pages. (CT998)

CarTech®, Inc. 39966 Grand Ave, North Branch, MN 55056. Ph: 800-551-4754 or 651-277-1200 • Fax: 651-277-1203
Brooklands Books Ltd., PO Box 146 Cobham, Surrey KT11 1LG, England. Ph: 01932 865051, Fax 01932 868803
Brooklands Books Aus., 3/37-39 Green Street, Banksmeadow, NSW 2109, Australia. Ph: 2 9695 7055 Fax 2 9695 7355

Visit us online at www.cartechbooks.com for more info!